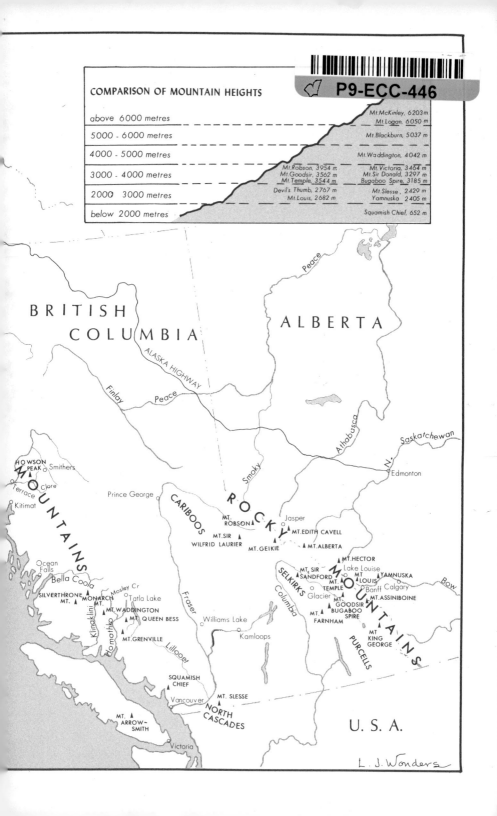

The Mountaineers

The Mountaineers
Famous Climbers in Canada

Phil Dowling

Hurtig Publishers
Edmonton

Hurtig Publishers
10560 105 Street
Edmonton, Alberta

Canadian Cataloguing in Publication Data

Dowling, Phil.
    The mountaineers

    Includes index.
    ISBN 0-88830-170-7

    1. Mountaineers — Canada — Biography.
I. Title.
GV199.44.C2D6   796.5′22′0922   C79-091143-4

Printed and bound in Canada

Contents

Acknowledgement

An author's first book is seldom completed without good professional direction and supportive friends. Fortunately, I have had both.

The government of Alberta gave me a grant which was authorized by the Honorable Horst Schmid, minister for Alberta Culture. I was subsequently well served by the advice and encouragement of John Patrick Gillese and Grant Kennedy, both writers who know the trials of working alone on a manuscript. Another author and climber, Randy Morse, discussed content and style with me. These men never failed to listen and advise when I needed it most.

The bulk of my research was carried out in Banff at the Peter Whyte Foundation, which is directed by Ted Hart. He and his staff, Karin MacAulay, Mary Andrews, and Margie McDougall assisted my search for written and photographic material in both the Archives of the Canadian Rockies and the Alpine Club of Canada Archives. They were pleasant working companions.

When the material was written, Carol Takyi typed and retyped the changing manuscript until I could refine it no longer. To Mel Hurtig, my publisher, I owe my sincere thanks for accepting me as one of his authors and for assigning me a gentle and forgiving editor, Eva Radford.

Lastly, I want to acknowledge my climbing friends, both great and near great, who scoured their photographic collections for pictures and who filled my interviews with anecdotes. It was not all work; we had a good time too.

Introduction

Much is said about mountains but little about mountaineers. Few outside the mountaineering fraternity know about them, their adventures, or the perils they have faced. This book invites the reader to share in some personal adventures of nine men and one woman who have achieved fame for their climbing activities in Canada.

As with other recreational activities, mountaineering is broadly based and includes a multitude of practitioners, many of whom are skilled and proficient. But the personalities whose biographical sketches appear in this book are above the common ilk. They possess in real measure greater imagination, perseverance, and dedication than the main body of climbers. They, and some few others, are exceptional.

Firstly, their careers have weight both in length and achievement. Secondly, all have dared to penetrate the existing barriers to climbing, setting new standards for others to follow. Thirdly, they are tougher than most, possessing physical strength, emotional calm in the face of danger, tolerance for pain, and a willingness to bivouac, however uncomfortable. No big mountain route, especially if new, can be safely assured without preparedness for a night on the rocks.

In an age when it is easier to spectate than to participate, mountaineering seems to carry personal involvement to unreasonable limits. Why do they do it?

There is no simple answer, just as there is no simple

explanation for the human personality. Adventure, physical enjoyment, the view, comradeship, ego building, a substitute for war, and "it feels so good when I stop doing it," are some answers. A combination of these reasons is likely closer to the truth. One thing is certain: there is no other human activity quite like it.

"It's so dangerous!" some say. To deny mountaineering is dangerous would be to lie in the face of evidence. Men and women die every year from falls, avalanches, and other causes. The older climber says, "Better that way than crumbling in a geriatric chair." But for the young a life is too much to pay.

No one goes to the mountains to die. Guido Rey, the Italian mountaineer, put it plainly:

> It is important to affirm and prove that we go to the mountains to live and not to die; that we are not fanatics but firm believers; and that the few accidents which occur are hard but not useless lessons. There is something more than a vain ambition; there is a soul.

And perhaps therein is the answer. Somewhere deep inside of man there may lie a vision of himself not bound by earthly limitations but rising triumphant, free of his bonds, not master over the earth but master over himself.

*To
my beloved
Regan*

In this book, elevations and other measurements are given in metric units.

Chapter One

Charles Fay
1846 – 1931

*Great things are done when men and
mountains meet.*

William Blake

During their ascent, towering storm clouds had been
gathering, and now thunder rolled in the hot, heavy air. Just
as Fay and Edmands reached the mountain top, a black,
menacing cloud formation came to bear against it, and the
temperature dropped noticeably. Lightning was highly
probable. Quickly the two men retreated in search of safer
ground.

Not far below, hail began, slowly at first and then increased to a fury, stinging the climbers with a thousand tiny
stabs. They sought cover in the lee of some rocks, but in
twenty minutes both were coated with ice, soaked and
chilled to the bone; they would have to keep moving.

No sooner had the two renewed their descent when
Edmands suddenly snatched at his hat and peered into it,
puzzled. At the same instant, it seemed, his hair began to
buzz. In rubber-soled tennis shoes, Fay did not feel the same
sensation, but when all around him the rocks began to hiss,
he knew it was a prelude to a lightning strike. Frightened,
the two climbers hurried back to their insecure shelter.

In a little while, however, the storm diminished, and they
descended the ridge again, surrounded by playful electric
currents which danced and sang on the rocks. When they
reached the aspen groves, the discharges ceased. That evening Fay recounted to his hostess the events of the day, his

first personal ascent of a high mountain, Shavano Peak (4337 metres) in the Colorado Rockies. The date was 23 July 1888.

Charles Ernest Fay was born on 10 March 1846 in Roxbury, Massachusetts. His father was the Reverend Cyrus H. Fay, pastor of the local Universalist Church. His mother, Anne Hyne Fay, came from Devon. When Charles was only four years old, his mother died.

The boy's early life was filled with self-discipline, religious devotion, and scholarship. He was educated in New York and at various schools in New England and after graduation taught grammar school for a brief period. Returning for further education, he entered Tufts College in Massachusetts and received a bachelor of arts degree in 1868, after which he taught mathematics during the week at a local school and preached on Sundays at the Unitarian Church in North Cambridge.

However his principal academic interest lay in language and literature, and in 1869 he was appointed instructor of French and German at Tufts and given one year's leave to study in France, Germany, and Italy. In Florence he met another Bostonian, Mary W. Lincoln, whom he married after their return to the United States in 1870. Eventually they parented five children, one of whom was a deaf mute.

Later Fay was appointed a full professor earning his master's degree in 1877 and an honorary Doctor of Letters degree in 1900. Throughout his professional life, he was prominent among American educators, and he ended his academic career in 1923 after eleven years as dean of the School of Graduate Studies at Tufts.

Fay's earliest climbing adventures were among the White Mountains[1] of New Hampshire, where he recorded his first personal ascent in August 1874 on Tripyramid Mountain

[1] The White Mountains, part of the Appalachian Chain, are modest in terms of elevation. However, their highest peak, Mount Washington (1917), has recorded the highest wind velocities on world record, with winds reaching speeds up to 372 kilometres per hour (231 miles per hour).

(1250), locally known as the Waterville Haystacks. With a few others, he formed the nucleus of a group of persons interested in mountaineering and so it was not surprising when, on New Year's Day 1876, he received an invitation to attend a meeting at the Institute of Technology in Boston for those interested in mountain exploration. One week later, Fay sat as chairman of the meeting which founded the first mountaineering club in North America, the Appalachian Mountain Club. Fay became the editor of the club's official journal *Appalachia* and served more than forty years in this position, as well as four terms as president.

During the next ten years, Fay was content with climbs in the mountains of New England, ascending, among others, Black Mountain, Northern Kearsage, Mount Corrigain, Baldface, Mount Lincoln, the Eastman Range, and King's Ravine. None of this climbing was comparable in severity to that which he would encounter later in Canada: only once, in a gorge on Mount Lincoln, did he consider a rope was needed, something he had never before used.

During the same period, he wrote articles for *Appalachia* on a variety of topics, especially concerning himself with the translation into English of foreign papers on mountaineering, particularly those written in German.

It was not until 1888, when Fay was forty-two years old, that he climbed his first "big" mountains, those of Colorado and California. Without a rope or other equipment, he ascended Shavano Peak (4337), Long's Peak (4345), and Ypsilon Peak (4117). These were long climbs but largely uneventful ones due to their simplicity.

That same summer, Fay and a companion attempted to climb Blanca Peak (4372) in the Sierra Blanca of California. This expedition ended in failure. Once again shod in tennis shoes, Fay reached what he thought was the summit and discovered to his chagrin that the main peak lay some kilometres distant. To make matters worse, he could clearly see another party successfully scaling the summit's final slopes. The hour was late, the peak too far, and a bivouac without shelter over forty-two hundred metres was out of the question. Disappointed, he and his companion began the descent towards two shepherd campfires, which could be seen far below. To descend the steeper places, they clasped each other's hands for protection and proceeded downwards in this ropelike fashion. After a night by a campfire in the valley, they returned to their starting point and met a member of the successful party. Fay's feelings can be imagined when he discovered that one of the climbers was a journalist from *Harpers Weekly* who had been on assignment for his magazine.

In 1889 Fay made the first of twenty-five visits to Canada with a canoe trip to the headwaters of the Saguenay River in Quebec. Risking all, he shot the foaming Saguenay Rapids without mishap and on his return to Boston was filled with excitement from his Canadian adventure.

In the following year, Fay and his friend Edmands travelled to the Sierra Madre in California in search of an ideal site for an astronomical observatory for Harvard University.[2] There they climbed San Antonio Mountain (3048) in a driving rainstorm. After the climb, they left California by steamer for Vancouver and the Canadian Pacific took them to a new hotel in the heart of the Selkirks. It was called Glacier House.

Fay's first trip to the Canadian ranges came at an opportune time. Only three years earlier, in 1887, the railway had opened its services through the mountains. Mountain exploration began the following summer with the ascent of Mount Bonney (3107), but little more had taken place in the interval. Opportunities for first ascents abounded. But with little time remaining in his schedule, Fay stayed only two days and caught the train homewards. He knew he would return as soon as he could.

In 1894 he made another roundabout tour of North America via California with Rest Curtis, a member of the Appalachian Mountain Club. They arrived at Glacier House in August. After successfully ascending Mounts Afton (2554)

[2]At that time, the Harvard College Observatory was located on Mount Wilson (1740), near Pasadena. A state-owned observatory is still located there.

and Abbott (2466), Fay and Curtis directed their attention to Eagle Peak (2854) in the same area. In this case, success did not follow success.

About five o'clock one morning they made their way up the "lofty fir-draped valley" of the Illecillewaet River to the sound of glacial torrents racing through the woods. Carrying a rubber pouch containing corned meat, pilotbread, prunes, and chocolate, they had ample food for a long excursion; otherwise they were poorly, if not inadequately, equipped for the task at hand.

When difficulties were encountered about one hundred and fifty metres below the summit, they moved onto the west side of the southwest ridge, traversing flat rocks overhung by a bulging section that forced them backwards and out of balance. Finding no easier route beyond, and quite insecure in their present position, they decided to retreat.

The day was now spent and the night was coming quickly. They descended as fast as possible, until darkness finally rendered further descent dangerous. Unprepared, they were forced to bivouac, Fay having only his "sweater," a long woolen garment which he regarded with attachment. Above the tree line without a fire, survival meant sharing body warmth. Thus Fay, with his back against a rock wall, had Curtis sit before him and "held him in a fast embrace" throughout the night. In the morning light, they had no trouble finding their way home.

From Glacier House the two men took the train to Field, where Fay enquired as to how to ascend Mount Stephen (3199). It had been the first peak over 3050 metres (10,000 feet) to be climbed in the Rockies. What little information Fay received was of no use to him, but not deterred, he and his party took to the bush, whacking through the trees until they reached a shale slope which contained many fossils. The fine, broken material offered a "wretched foothold," and the "climbing became toilsome." After seven hours, sometimes charging in "short bursts," Fay's party reached an escarpment some two hundred metres below the summit. Skirting the bottom of the wall, Fay found a gully, but its entrance was blocked with granular ice. He estimated it could be climbed by a party equipped with rope and ice axes, however his party was without them. Having climbed more than eighteen hundred metres, they turned back, rushing to reach the station in time for the next train. This they succeeded in doing without difficulty: the train was held at the station for an extra five hours while passengers completed their evening meal at the local hotel!

Up to that point the success of Fay's mountain expeditions had been hampered by lack of adequate equipment and alpine experience, but this changed in his climbs of 1895. His AMC party included a young lawyer from Milwaukee, a graduate of Harvard Law School and an experienced mountaineer, Philip Stanley Abbot. Although only twenty-seven, Abbot had travelled widely and had climbed in Mexico, Norway, and the Yosemite Valley of California. Fresh from two seasons in the Swiss Alps, he was ready to attempt the first ascent of Mount Hector (3394), a castellated peak standing high and alone at the confluence of the Bow and Pipestone Rivers. Only one higher mountain, Mount Temple (3547), had been climbed in the Rockies up to that time.

The party set out northwards from the CPR station at Laggan (Lake Louise) on 29 July.[3] The group consisted of Fay, Abbot, Charles Thompson, Tom Wilson who was a Rocky Mountain outfitter, and one of Wilson's men, a fellow called Hiland. Mount Hector was about twenty-five kilometres from Laggan. The first section of the journey followed the CPR railroad tracks, and the rest was over burnt timber and bog. Each man carried his own blankets and a camera. They packed four ice axes and a climbing rope between them.

The party started up the track "with a swinging gait that was much too good to last," and, after three hours in the deadfall and swamp, they had worked off their "boyishness." The ice axes were found useful for clawing, balancing,

[3]Philip Abbot described the approach march in an article published later in *Appalachia*.

18

blazing, and chopping in the bush. Everyone thought them to be very adaptable tools, falling short only of killing the hordes of mosquitoes which plagued them. And the mosquitoes were a damned nuisance.

That night after sunset, the party camped on a grassy platform below the north ridge of Mount Hector. Sweltering in their blankets with only their noses peering out, the men defied "the multitudinous hosts of hell outside," while "whole orchestras, shrill with rage, hovered above . . . and all around." Sleep had been all too little when Fay woke them at three in the morning. The early start was accompanied by its usual aggravations,

> the search for water in the darkness; the depressing chill of the dying night; the half-warmed and wholly unappetizing breakfast; the silence, not to say crustiness, of the other members of the party; the unconfessed half-wish for some decent excuse for not starting at all; and the interminable delays.

The three climbers got away just before five, leaving Wilson and Hiland to take care of the camp.

The party had come too far north on the preceding day, and the climbers had to turn southwards again, thereby increasing the distance travelled in the bush. But soon the going improved; the timber gave way to grass; and the grass yielded to broken shale. Fighting lassitude, drenched in sweat, and lost in their own silent thoughts, the three mountaineers finally broke the crest of Hector's north ridge. There they beheld a dazzling new world.

Before them lay the Hector Glacier, a broad expanse of snow-covered ice, brilliant in the morning sun. Virtually unbroken by crevasses and with only one set of prominent cliffs, the ancient icefield rose gently towards the south, ending in the final rock pile of the summit. The climbers were enthralled.

In joyful expectation of success, Fay for the first time in his life roped himself to others, and with Abbot leading they started southwards along the ridge, skirting the valley wall.

Finally they came to a last, steep fifty-metre section, and Abbot kicked steps "as large as coal scuttles" up the slopes to the summit. Shortly after noon, Fay, Abbot, and Thompson were relishing the rewards of their labour.

In three-quarters circumference, their view from Hector's summit was unobstructed for a very great distance. Fay was elated, more than ever before, as he looked down the mountain's steep west and south faces and into the valley below. Far off, thousands of unclimbed peaks appeared, each beckoning as if it were some mysterious enchantress.

The group built a rock cairn. In its base, Thompson placed an empty, but unwashed, jam bottle containing a paper with their names.[4] Then the climbers went to sleep in the afternoon sun. When their descent began an hour later, they hurried down the slopes, joyous at their success. The final pleasure of the day came when they arrived in camp. Hiland had cooked a dinner of fresh fried trout.

Five days later, 4 August, Fay made the third ascent of Mount Stephen with Abbot and Thompson and later, in the Selkirks, traversed Asulkan Ridge (2847), which resulted in the first ascents of Castor Peak (2779) and the Rampart (2586). With this final achievement, Fay went home well satisfied; even then, he was mulling over plans for new ascents in 1896. One would result in tragedy.

The ill-fated climb began when four climbers from the Appalachian Mountain Club made plans to make the first ascent of Mount Lefroy (3423) at Lake Louise. Lefroy is in close proximity to Mount Victoria. The two peaks form the main backdrop for the lake as seen today from Chateau Lake Louise. In 1896 these mountains were approached by rowing a boat the length of the lake, then following the moraine to the toe of the Victoria Glacier, and, finally, climbing its Death Trap eight hundred metres between the steep walls formed by Victoria on one side and Lefroy on the other. Above the pass between the two mountains, Lefroy's sweep-

[4]Edward Feuz, Jr. and Joseph Hickson made the second ascent of Mount Hector in 1923 and found the record in almost perfect condition.

ing west face soars upwards, a continuous, ice-covered rock wall.

Just past six o'clock on Monday morning, 3 August 1896, Fay, Abbot, Charles Thompson, and George Little gathered at the small boat landing in front of the chalet. They rowed across smooth water to the end of the lake and beached the boat. Making their way first through the trees and then over the moraine, the four men eventually reached the toe of the glacier and chose to ascend it close to the wall of Mount Victoria, where the crevasses were smallest. At the first crevasse, they roped up.

The passage through the Death Trap was uneventful yet tense because of the danger of avalanche from the upper glacier. Shortly before noon, the climbers reached the pass, relieved to escape the avalanche threat and to have the tedium of the long snow climb behind them. For a short while they paused, awed by the unobstructed view of Lefroy's great west face.

The party ate a noon meal and then, leaving some unneeded rucksacks behind, began to cut steps up the ice, each climber enlarging them as he passed. On the rock sections the footholds were treacherous, and as they rose higher the consequences of a slip became obvious. Moving one man at a time, it took four and a half hours to reach the rock cliffs which begin about sixty metres below the summit.

The first terrace of cliffs presented no obvious route, and Abbot, who was still leading, set out to scout the bottom of the bastion-like walls. Advancing to the end of the rope, he found a vertical cleft and asked Fay and Thompson to unrope and take cover from possible falling rock while he climbed. Some ten metres up Abbot took a belay stance and signalled Little to follow him.

Just as Little was preparing to climb, the rope dislodged a small stone and then a much larger one. The first struck Little, and the second half-severed the rope with its impact. Little tied a knot in the rope to regain some of its usefulness, but, as the likelihood of further stonefall was probable, Abbot advised him to unrope also and to climb without it.

When Little reached the stance, Abbot followed a shelf to the left, discovered a gully, and climbed its lowest pitch. Little looked in the other direction and questioned Abbot's route, but Abbot called back, "I have a good lead here." These were his last words.

Little was still scanning other portions of the crag when he became aware that something had fallen swiftly past him, while Fay and Thompson, standing at the base of the cliffs, saw their "dear friend falling backward and head foremost." Abbot struck the upper margin of the ice slope less than five metres away, turned completely over, and then tumbled down the steep face.

Fay and Thompson, horrified by the reality of what was happening, watched helplessly as the rope, attached only to Abbot, spooled around his body as he spun and bounced down the slope. There was no stopping until he caught on a ledge about three hundred metres below, just short of a cliff.

By that time the full impact of the disaster was upon the others. Aghast at the terrible consequences of the fall, the fateful moments raced through their minds again and again. Fay was uncertain, but he thought he had seen Abbot falling backwards with a large piece of rock clasped in his arms. Meanwhile, Little was still on the cliff urging his companions to help the victim. But they knew it would take several hours to reach Abbot, so instead they directed Little down from his perch.

It was now 6:30 P.M., and, without the rope, Fay made the survivors make "a mutual promise of self-command and unremitting caution" as they began their individual descents. Three hours later they reached their fallen companion. Fay thought Abbot murmured faintly as if in recognition of their presence. On examination, his comrades saw he had suffered a severe blow to the back of his head, where a bleeding depression was evident; but otherwise only his face and hands seemed to be bruised and scratched. As they looked sadly upon their friend Fay said, "His spirit is passing," and the three bared their heads in respect for their dying comrade. But miraculously Abbot's breathing resumed, and they quickly set about freeing him from the rope. Lifting him, they started down to the pass. To their sorrow they did not go far before he died in their arms.

To continue moving the body was a great risk for the survivors. They left their dead companion and went down the mountain in search of the rucksacks which they had cached earlier. The three men were further distressed when they could not find them and were forced to bivouac without additional food and clothing.

All night the mountaineers huddled miserably together against the cairn which marked the top of the pass, intermittently hugging one another, pounding themselves to keep warm, and filling in chinks in the cairn to provide a meagre windbreak. At daylight they found their sacks, and by 9:30 A.M. they were back at the chalet seeking help.

On 5 August, aided by Tom Wilson and Willoughby Astley, a former manager at the chalet, they returned to Mount Lefroy for Abbot's body. When they found it, it was partially buried by a small snowslide. A sleeping bag was drawn over Abbot's head to below the knees, and the feet were left projecting. A rope was tied above the ankles, and the body was alternately lowered and pulled down the slope, always keeping to the snow to reduce friction. This process was a terrible risk to the party, especially as Wilson and Astley had no alpine experience. It was also laborious; barely a hundred metres were covered in an hour. But the going became better when the group reached the head of the Victoria Glacier, and by 8:30 that night they were down to the foot of the ice. On Thursday 6 August, Little and Astley led six strong CPR bridge builders to where the body had been left at the head of the lake, and together they transported it by boat back to the chalet.

Abbot's death was the first climbing fatality in Canada, and it shocked the mountaineering community. Solace went to the victim's family and commendation went to his companions. Abbot's father, who strongly supported his son's dedication to mountaineering, summoned his son's guide from Switzerland, Peter Sarbach, and commissioned him to prove that an ascent of Mount Lefroy was feasible.

A very experienced party of nine men, including Fay, was assembled. After practice climbs at Glacier, the party regrouped at Lake Louise in August of the following year. The climbing group consisted of some of the mountaineering elite of the day, among them Norman Collie, the distinguished British mountaineer and scientist; Herschel Parker, to be remembered for his three attempts on Mount McKinley in Alaska; and Charles Thompson, Fay's long-time friend. On the anniversary of Philip Abbot's death, 3 August 1897, this strong party safely completed the first ascent of Mount Lefroy in his memory. The pass below Lefroy's west face was subsequently named Abbot Pass.

Subject to this sad victory, Fay had planned another landmark first ascent and two days later sat down with Collie, Sarbach, and another climber to a predawn breakfast of beefsteak, hot rolls, and coffee. Their intended destination that day was the unclimbed snow queen of Lake Louise, Mount Victoria (3464).[5]

At an early hour, the boat carrying the climbers moved quietly away from the landing; no sound was heard but that of the oarlocks and the paddles working in the water. Beneath a clear, starlit sky the boat glided to the end of the lake.

By the light of candle lanterns, the men approached the walls of Mounts Victoria and Lefroy, which rose like spectres in the predawn darkness. By the time the climbers reached the Victoria Glacier, the peaks were rose-tinted, reflecting the first rays of the sun; it promised to be a fine, warm day.

The climb through the canyonlike Death Trap to Abbot Pass was debilitating. The snow had failed to harden during the night, and every step, deep on the calf, had to be won. But above the pass the four mountaineers were rewarded by clear, bright sunlight and stopped to cook a second breakfast of tinned, boned turkey, which they heated over an ether stove.

[5]A most majestic peak, Mount Victoria was formally named on the occasion of the Queen's Jubilee in 1897. Prior to this it was known as Mount Green, after an early mountaineer in the Rockies.

Collie led the way up the narrow, crested southeast ridge. While he kicked steps, the rest of the party examined Victoria's long, steep northeast face, which is scored with stonefall and avalanche runnels. At fifty degrees, the face is fraught with danger, and Fay concluded these conditions would "always defend any approach . . . to [Victoria's] icy citadel from this side."[6] The final snow pyramid of Victoria's south summit gave the party a view, for the first time, of the jagged and rotten rock crest which falls away to the north "into a deep depression filled with gendarmes." This route, too, Fay thought, would be improbable.[7]

The climbers identified the important summits within sight — Goodsir to the southwest, Temple to the southeast, and Hungabee close at hand. All of the peaks were in brilliant sunshine. And on Lefroy, their steps of two days earlier could be clearly seen dotting the west face. Being mindful of time, the mountaineers turned and retraced their steps. In two days Fay would commence an exploration of the Waputik Icefield.

Fay hoped to be the first to set foot on Mount Balfour (3272), the highest peak on the icefield. Unfortunately, the prize escaped him. Starting from Bow Lake, his party never reached the mountain, because of the great distance to their objective. Instead they settled for the first ascent of Mount Gordon (3147). In 1898 Fay approached Balfour again, this time from Sherbrooke Lake in the south and failed to reach it a second time. In consolation, he took Mount Niles (2972), an easy rock peak lying to the southeast of his goal. The first ascent of Balfour escaped him forever when it was climbed later that same summer by his friend, Charles Thompson, and others.

During the following winter of 1898 − 1899, the CPR completed negotiations to bring two Swiss guides to

[6]The first ascent of the northeast face of Mount Victoria was made by Val Fynn and Rudolf Aemmer, 15 July 1922.

[7]The first traverse of the north and south peaks of Mount Victoria was made by George Culver, Rudolf Aemmer, and Edward Feuz, Jr. on 4 September 1909.

Canada. Both came from Interlaken. They were Christian Hasler, Sr., and Edward Feuz, Sr. When Fay's train pulled into Glacier in the summer of 1899, Hasler and Feuz were pacing the station platform. Fay was glad to see them, because, with their expert guidance he hoped to achieve another ambitious first ascent, that of Mount Dawson (3390).

At the age of fifty-three, Fay thought he should prove to the guides that his "hinges and lungs were not yet worn out" and climbed Eagle Peak over the same route which had defeated him five years earlier. Then on 12 August, with Herschel Parker and the two guides, Fay set out for the twin peaks of Mount Dawson, some distance south of Glacier House.

Fay had not been sleeping well due to an ulcerated tooth, and at the bivouac camp that night he again slept fitfully. When they left early next morning, it was apparent to the others he was having trouble. Unaware of their client's linguistic abilities, Hasler and Feuz exchanged opinions in Swiss German as to the outcome of the climb and agreed that Mount Dawson was in no danger from them that day. But they pressed on, and as time passed Fay improved. They reached the greater of Dawson's summits before noon, to record the highest ascent in the Selkirks up to that date.[8] That afternoon they battled their way through the bush back to the hotel in a driving rainstorm, deafened by the roar of flooded cataracts.

Fay returned to Canada two years later, in 1901. With him were two "athletes of the intellectual type," one twenty and the other thirty years his junior. Their guide was Christian Hasler, who was now stationed at Field, British Columbia.

Seated on the cowcatcher of CP No. 1, surrounded by climbing "impedimenta," they rode to Ottertail Bridge, southwest of Field. The train made a special stop between stations to let them off. The party's objectives were all unclimbed mountains: Mount Vaux (3320), Chancellor Peak

[8]The twin summits of Mount Dawson were later named Hasler Peak (3390) and Feuz Peak (3350).

(3280), and the south tower of giant Mount Goodsir (3562). They succeeded on Mount Vaux only.

Chancellor defeated them near the summit with unexpected technical difficulties. On the south ridge of Goodsir, thirty metres below the south peak, they faced a reversed or double cornice which Fay felt could not be negotiated in safety. While contemplating the cornice, it broke away near Hasler's feet, and the avalanche hissed its way down the flanking slope. Fay thought it to be a "suggestive and persuasive sight," and the climbers all agreed to break off the ascent.

Back home in New England Fay became deeply involved in the creation of a national alpine club. His experience and prestige lent immense credibility to the enterprise, and when the American Alpine Club was founded in 1902 he was elected its first president, an office he retained for the next six years. In the meantime, he had undergone a knee operation, which put him out of climbing action temporarily. Although he visited Glacier in 1902, he did not climb. But the next year, when he was invited by Herschel Parker to join another attempt on Mount Goodsir, he quickly accepted. Hasler and a new guide, Christian Kaufmann, were engaged.

This time the party left the railway at Leanchoil, farther south from Ottertail Bridge, and followed a new mining road along the Beaverfoot River. In slightly more than a day, they had made a high camp on the southwest flanks of Goodsir, in Zinc Gulch. On 16 July, after waiting two days for new snow to melt, the men began the climb in the moonlight. High on the mountainside, they came to some steep cliffs which they climbed to gain the narrow, south ridge. Conditions there were found to be close to ideal, with firm snow all the way; the reversed cornice of two years earlier was no longer present. The knife-edge crest, greatly exposed on both sides, rose gently to the peak, which was gained in time for an early lunch. Years later, Fay considered it to be his finest ascent.

He made a second trip to the Rockies that same year. His objective, was a first ascent on Mount Daly (3125), in the

Waputik Icefield. The outfitter at Field would not hire out his horses for a trip into Sherbrooke Valley, which meant that the party had to carry their own loads. After a week of toil, Fay took a "solemn oath, in the sweat of [his] brow, never again to degrade the human form to the level of a pack animal." While bivouacking in a cave one night, the mountaineers ate all the food "caution would allow" to reduce their loads. And the next day, 23 August 1903, they completed Daly's first ascent.

In July 1904, Fay climbed Mount Temple (3547), the highest peak in the Lake Louise area, but his recollection of this summer was always to be tinged with bitterness. He was gravely disappointed when an unusual set of circumstances precluded him from making a first ascent he dearly wanted.

By that time Fay was greatly respected for his mountaineering achievements and his efforts to organize the sport. Recognition of such achievement was normally demonstrated by naming a peak for a chosen mountaineer, and Fay was consulted by the Geographic Board of Canada as to which mountain he would like named for himself. His choice was Peak One (3235) in the Valley of the Ten Peaks at Moraine Lake.

His request was under consideration when, in midsummer of 1904, the Swiss brothers, Hans and Christian Kaufmann, accepted separate guiding commissions for an ascent of Peak One. Fay engaged Hans, aiming at a first ascent of what would most likely be Mount Fay, and Gertrude Benham, an English climber, engaged Christian with the same project in mind.

Hans Kaufmann led Fay up Consolation Valley to the foot of a wall on the east side of the mountain. It was said that once there, Hans refused to continue; it was likely the wall appeared too difficult. In the meantime, Christian had guided Benham by way of an approach from Moraine Lake, on the opposite side of the mountain. He and the tireless English woman made the first ascent of Peak One on 20 July. Fay was terribly disappointed when he heard this news, but he returned to make the second ascent on 5 August — without Hans Kaufmann.

That fall, Fay wrote a letter to his old friend Charles Thompson. In Fay's elegant and graceful handwriting, he described the circumstances surrounding this event and intimated his deep unhappiness over it.

> I should have probably made the first ascent of the new Mt. Fay which I missed by Hans Kaufmann's leading me, against my protest, up Consolation Valley, while Christian led Miss Benham around by the familiar "Hourglass" couloir to its virgin summit. Hans alleged that he supposed I had your Mt. Little in view! Why did he suppose I wanted to get to it by going around the head of Moraine Lake, as I insisted? It is a curious case, however viewed.

And later in the same letter Fay wrote,

> I have just heard from the Secretary of the Geographic Board of Canada that the mountain . . . has been confirmed as "Mt. Fay."

It was reported that Fay also expressed his displeasure of Hans Kaufmann to officials of the CPR. Kaufmann never guided in Canada again. Curiously, this outcome coincided with a virtual close to Fay's climbing career; he participated in no significant ascents thereafter.

The naming of Mount Fay, however, signalled the beginning of a period of personal honours for Fay. He was elected an honorary member of the Alpine Club of Canada, in company with Edward Whymper and Norman Collie, and in 1907 represented the Appalachian Mountain Club and the American Alpine Club at the golden anniversary of the Alpine Club in London.

Another four years as president of the American Alpine Club brought him to retirement from that office in 1920. He was appointed delegate to the International Congress of Alpine Clubs in Monaco that same year, during which he was knighted by the reigning prince and made an officer of the Order of St. Charles.

After a five-year absence from Canada, Fay returned for the Alpine Club of Canada camp at Mount Robson in 1913 and shared a tent with his long-time companion, Charles Thompson. At sixty-seven, too old to attempt Mount Robson, Fay was able to climb Mumm Peak (2962) and was present to herald the success of Robson's first ascent by Kain, MacCarthy, and Foster.

Still possessing an amazing constitution, Fay made his twenty-fifth and last visit to the Rockies in 1930. He was eighty-four. After the ACC camp at Maligne Lake, he made the road journey to Kootenay National Park to see the Fay Hut, which had been built in his honour in 1927. Despite fallen timber and many creek crossings, the aged mountaineer with flowing white beard made the six-hundred-metre climb through the bush at a "nimble gait" (see photo).

When he returned to New England, however, Fay underwent surgery for appendicitis. The surgery produced complications which left him ailing, and when the annual meeting of the AAC convened on 25 January 1931, Fay was too ill to attend. In his absence, the members telegraphed a message of greeting, wishing him swift recovery. But Fay was completing his life journey, and a few hours after receiving the telegram he died. His death marked the end of an era.

Chapter Two

Val Fynn
1870 – 1929

Taking him all round, fair weather and foul,
it is unlikely that Fynn, among amateurs,
has ever had a superior

John Percy Farrar,
noted British mountaineer

Fynn and Bruederlin had made a costly blunder and had wasted a lot of time. Their only alternative was to recross the mountain's most dangerous face.

The two mountaineers had left an insecure bivouac spot earlier that morning and had climbed a steep chimney which led away from it. The climb took far more time than expected, and on the big face it was imperative they move quickly. An easier route appeared to the left, and they followed it across, but in five hours, stopped by overhangs and threatened by stonefall, they had not got much higher. Now they were retracing their steps.

Their last alternative was to climb the northern flank of the rock rib from which they had started. Apprehensively, the two climbers edged carefully onto its exposed slabs and ice-filled ledges. By five o'clock in the afternoon, the men had managed to reach some grey pillars about three-quarters of the way up the face, but another four hours brought them little further progress.

By then it was night. They were at the foot of an ice slope, much too serious to be attempted in the dark; a second bivouac could not be avoided, but they were in a poor position for bivouacking. There was no ledge on which they could rest.

Fynn looked around for a means of anchorage, for if they were going to survive they would have to prevent themselves from sliding off the face. He found a projecting rock above their heads and fixed a spare rope to it. With the lower ends he and Bruederlin fashioned loops to fit their size and position and, half sitting and half standing in these slings, they spent the night jammed together inside a sloping chimney.[1]

At dawn the two men, stiff from cold and exposure, tackled the steep ice slope straight on. Time, the elements, and the uncertain route were working against them. The good weather was breaking, and the wind rose in a fury to tear at their clothes. Soon snow began to fall. The climbers were paralyzed with fright when a sudden cannonade of rock caught them causing both to suffer minor wounds. Now too high to turn back, they had to keep on despite the danger. About midmorning, to their great relief, they came to the crest of the ridge and were off the face.

Fynn and his friend had completed the first unguided ascent of the northeast face of the Finsteraarhorn (4274), the monarch of the Bernese Alps.[2] The date: 14 August 1906.

Valère Alfred Fynn was born thirty-six years earlier, 11 April 1870, in Krasno, Russia. His father was a civil engineer in railway construction, employed by the Russian Imperial Government. Both he and his wife were Irish-born.

Shortly after Val reached school age, his parents, concerned about his education, sent him to live with his grandmother in Geneva. He was nine years old. When he

[1]This is likely the first record in history of climbers spending the night in slings. Today it is more commonplace, especially on long, high-angle rock climbs.

[2]The first guided ascent of the northeast face of the Finsteraarhorn was accomplished two years earlier, 1904. It was one of the first of the classic north walls in the Alps to be climbed and was described by Farrar as "a hopeless face, scored by shallow gullies, unsafe to climb and very exposed." The face is 1070 metres high with an average inclination of fifty degrees, increasing to sixty-five degrees for the last three hundred metres.

matured, the young man decided to follow his father's example and enrolled in the Swiss Federal Polytechnic in Zurich. He graduated as an electrical engineer in 1891, and, after postgraduate studies in Zurich and Heidelberg, he accepted a post with the famous international engineering firm, Brown Boveri of Baden.

These early years in Switzerland introduced Fynn to the joys of alpine adventure. He started climbing at the age of fourteen. By the time he was twenty-five, he had become one of the most brilliant young climbers in Europe and had developed a preference for steep face routes. Climbing without a guide, Fynn accomplished more than fifty new ascents in the Alps. Among these were the Fynn Weg on the Mürtschenstock (Glarus Alps); the first ascent of the Bifertenstock (3426) direct from the Bifertenstock Glacier in the Tödi Range (Glarus Alps); the northeast face of the Finsteraarhorn (4274, Bernese Alps); the second ascent of the northeast face of the Lauteraarhorn (4042, Bernese Alps); and the north or Argentière face of the Aiquille Verte (Mont Blanc Range).

The latter ascent took place in August 1895, when Fynn was twenty-five. With a companion, he left the Saleina Hut near the Italian border and in a long dash reached the foot of the Argentière face at three thirty in the morning. Barely pausing for the next thirteen hours, he and his friend put a new route up the face and then descended the other side. So difficult and remote was this north wall route that it was not ascended again for more than fifty years.[3]

As Fynn's climbing developed, so did his engineering career. By 1898 he had become expert in the design of alternating current motors and accepted two successive posts with manufacturing companies in England. Four years later, he left manufacturing altogether and moved to

[3]This first ascent route followed a prominent rib later called the Grande Rocheuse. Fynn did not actually go to the summit, which was about one hundred and fifty metres higher over easy snow. Because of the late hour, he and his companion, P. Goudet, elected to descend immediately over the Talèfre Glacier on the other side of the mountain. The face route was not repeated and completed until July 1946.

London, where he set up his own consulting practice. In the meantime, his reputation had reached North America; he received an offer from the Wagner Electric Company of St. Louis, Missouri. It enticed him to move to St. Louis in 1909.

Fynn was then only thirty-nine and had no desire to retire from climbing. Far from the Alps, he decided to try his luck in the Canadian Rockies. In July 1909, he stayed at the new Alpine Club of Canada clubhouse in Banff and met the guides, including Conrad Kain, Edward Feuz, Jr., and Rudolf Aemmer. Speaking Swiss German, Fynn and the guides talked about climbs in the Alps.[4] It became obvious quite quickly that Fynn preferred their company over that of the amateurs.

After helping the guides set up at Lake O'Hara for the ACC Annual Camp, Fynn led several parties on Mount Huber (3369) and Mount Odaray (3160). But they were not the kind of climbs which had lured him to the Rockies; these mountains were neither unclimbed nor difficult. He identified the area's virgin peaks and soon began a series of first ascents. He made a solo first ascent of Park Mountain (2948), an easy peak climbed via its northeast face. Two weeks later he made the first ascent of Glacier Peak (3302), located on the Continental Divide. Again raising his sights, Fynn planned the second, and first unguided, ascent of Mount Hungabee (3493) with nineteen-year-old Oliver Wheeler, son of the president of the ACC, Arthur Wheeler.

The climb of Hungabee began before dawn. The two men crossed Schaffer meadow amid the scent of pines and, making no sound except for the click of their nailed boots on the rocks, reached Opabin Pass just as the sun lit the mountain tops. Light winds swept up the valley.

In the shade of the great peak, master and novice started up, crossed the southwest face on a series of narrowing ledges, climbed an easy couloir, traversed, and then fol-

[4]According to his contemporaries, Fynn could speak and write six languages.

lowed a rock rib to the foot of an ice chimney which required much step-cutting. Following interconnecting systems of cracks and ledges, couloirs and boundary ridges, they climbed until they reached the summit shortly before eleven o'clock. The climbers were pleased with their effort.

During the day much melting had taken place, and on descending to the top of the ice chimney again Fynn and Wheeler found that a waterfall was racing down its surface, washing out steps and dislodging stones. Carefully, Wheeler moved onto the ice. In seconds a stone struck him and knocked him out of his steps. As he started to slide, Fynn was ready; he quickly arrested the fall as the rope snapped taut. They descended the rest of the route in safety.

Two days later, Fynn and another partner set out for Ringrose Peak (3281), situated immediately north of Hungabee. The lower section of the climb from Opabin Pass posed few problems. The face was ascended via couloirs and dividing ribs, with occasional traverses across subsidiary gullies. An irregular vertical crack in an overhanging bulge presented the greatest difficulty. Finally, a buttress gave the climbers access to the main ridge, which was wide and easy. They scrambled along towards the summit.

To their surprise, they came to a deep notch in the ridge about three metres across; the gap was too wide to be jumped. Moreover, it was some eight metres deep with smooth opposing walls. It was an unexpected problem so close to the top. The steep faces on both sides of the ridge provided no feasible alternative.

With great care, Fynn climbed down into the notch on loose unstable holds, leaving a rope in place for their return. He walked across and climbed the other side which proved less difficult. The first ascent was completed at noon.

After a six-day trip to Sherbrooke Lake by horse, Fynn travelled to Glacier House in the Rogers Pass and climbed the triangular pyramid of Mount Sir Donald (3298), the most impressive peak in the southern Selkirks. He followed the northwest ridge, bypassing occasional short, difficult sections by moving onto the northeast face from time to time.

35

When the climb was over, Fynn believed he had made the second ascent by this ridge, but several years later discovered this was not true. The first climbers to ascend Sir Donald had climbed the lower two thirds of the mountain by its northwest ridge and the upper third by its southwest face. Fynn therefore had made the first ascent of the northwest ridge in its entirety.

Val Fynn was a big, self-confident man, impressive to all who met him. He stood about 190 centimetres in height and in later years weighed more than a hundred kilograms (6'2", 220 lbs.). His size, experience, and general composure made him appear the most stalwart of mountaineers, and the rimless spectacles which he wore in middle age, gave him the air of an aristocrat. Edward Feuz, Jr. described Fynn as "a big, jolly man." It was true he was known for his buoyant personality.

His dress was fastidious and very personal in taste. He wore a broad, flat-brimmed hat with a pointed crown and tied a knotted handkerchief around his neck. He liked Norfolk jackets lined with Jaeger wool, whipcord knickers, argyll knee socks, and well-nailed boots laced with porpoise leather. Beneath his outer clothing he wore woolen knee drawers and a woolen abdominal belt for warmth in bivouacs. His ice axe was a Joerg, preferred because it had balance and plenty of drive and a short shaft which made its handling easier, especially on steep ice.

After his first season in the Rockies, Fynn attended the ACC Annual Camps regularly, but he missed Switzerland. As he became more affluent he could afford trips to the Alps "to follow the sardine tin trail." In 1911 he traversed the Matterhorn (4477) from Zermatt to Breuil. "Just take your time and put your feet down as if the mountain belonged to you, my boys," he shouted as a storm approached while the party was still high on the Fiefenmatten face. Two years later on the north face of the Combin de Valsorey (4145) with the noted British mountaineer, Percy Farrar, and a local guide named Omer Balleys, he experienced one of those incidents which make climbs memorable.

The descent route was over a glacier covered with a thick layer of softening snow. As the climbers worked their way downwards they knew they were travelling among hidden crevasses, any of which could entrap them. Using a long rope, they moved cautiously. Balleys was leading when, with only a brief cry as a warning, he disappeared into a hole.

Farrar was next on the rope. Sitting down quickly he braced himself to stop the guide's fall, but to his astonishment the rope continued to cut through the snowbridge almost to where he was sitting. Shocked, they realized at once they had been travelling along the length of a crevasse and might easily have all gone in together.

After twenty minutes Fynn and Farrar had Balleys near the surface, but in the last short pitch he was unable to climb out. According to Farrar, Fynn then stepped to the lip and with his powerful arms hoisted the guide free to the surface.

Fynn's fame to this time was based on his audacious face climbs, in opposition to the accepted practice of keeping to the ridges. In addition, he generally climbed without a guide, confident his skills were as good as any he could hire. However, his risk-taking independence changed when he married in 1916.

To help safeguard his wife while climbing and to provide himself with a reliable and competent companion at all times, he chose to engage a guide. This decision resulted in a friendship which lasted the rest of his life. He hired Rudolf Aemmer.

In 1917, Fynn started the season by climbing Haddo Peak (3071) and Mount Aberdeen (3152) alone, in order to improve his conditioning. Three days later, he and Aemmer climbed Mount Victoria's north peak (3389) and its sister, Mount Collier (3201). After two easy climbs on Devil's Thumb (2459) and Mount Whyte (2984), Fynn engaged Aemmer to join him in a climb of Mounts Victoria and Lefroy.

This feat of endurance began shortly after midnight when the two left the hotel at Lake Louise, took the trail around the lake, climbed the Victoria Glacier, and reached Abbot Pass just after dawn. In three hours they cut steps up the west face of Mount Lefroy (3424) to its summit and then returned to the pass. Resting only briefly, Fynn and Aemmer set out again in the opposite direction along the south ridge for Mount Victoria's south peak (3465). The going was heavy in places because of new snow; nonetheless they made the peak in just over four hours. About 8:00 P.M. they had returned to Abbot Pass for the third time that day, and, barely pausing to pick up some belongings, they headed down the glacier. Twenty-two hours after their departure, Fynn and Aemmer returned to the hotel.

It was a day Aemmer never forgot. Forty-five years later, when he was seventy-eight, he could still remember the big push with Fynn.

In September 1917, when Aemmer was otherwise occupied, Fynn engaged Aemmer's partner, Edward Feuz, Jr., for a climb of Mount Louis (2682), near Banff. Louis had been scaled for the first time the previous year.

Under a cover of low, thick cloud the two rode on horseback to Edith Pass. When close to the mountain, they hobbled their horses and soon reached the foot of Louis's east face.

Fynn had reconnoitred the peak a year earlier and knew something about its possible routes, but that day the mountain was obscured by cloud. He would have to rely entirely on his memory. He and Feuz pushed up into a broad couloir.

In a short while they encountered a smooth three-metre-high wall which cut them off from easier ground above. For protection, Fynn passed the rope around a chockstone jammed in a crack and then, taking a good stance, prepared to have Feuz climb over his shoulders. The smaller man stepped up, first onto Fynn's shoulders and then into Fynn's open palm, which he held extended above his head. Searching quickly for a handhold, the guide found one and pulled himself up.

The ceiling had been lifting gradually, but still the climbers could not see all the way to the top of the mountain. In a quandary, they made one false start and then found a chimney which led down onto the south face. A short climb brought them to a grassy platform. Above, all they could see were soaring vertical pitches disappearing into grey cloud.

Changing to their lightweight climbing shoes, the two men systematically followed a series of cracks and chimneys, which were interconnected by short and sometimes awkward traverses. Once they rappelled to get to the bottom of the next pitch. Eventually a large platform was reached about one hundred and fifty metres below the summit.

A deep cut ran up the face from the platform. The first section of the cut was about four metres deep and lay back at an angle of seventy-five degrees. The men jammed themselves between the wet walls and wriggled upwards, chimneysweep fashion, but the passage was comparatively safe.[5] Near the top, the chimney was blocked by three wedged boulders which forced the climbers out onto the face. The chimney then widened into a couloir, and the climbing was easy. Moments later Fynn and Feuz were on the summit of Mount Louis.

The regimen of activity in 1918 was similar to that of the previous year — some initial practice climbs gradually building to greater efforts. Fynn's wife became the first woman to climb Pinnacle Mountain (3067), and he was "agreeably surprised" at her composure during the climb.[6]

He and Aemmer did the first traverse of Glacier Peak ascending from the Horseshoe Glacier in Paradise Valley and descending to Lake O'Hara. On arrival at Wiwaxy Lodge in the alpine meadow near the lake the men were met by a large grizzly that sat on its haunches observing them. While

[5]Today this steep, long chimney is sometimes referred to as Fat Man's Agony.

[6]The name of Fynn's wife is not recorded in mountaineering literature.

Fynn and Aemmer puzzled at what it, or they, would do next, the bear settled the matter by ambling off.

Wiwaxy Lodge was no more than a decaying cabin used by passing mountaineers, and it had long been in need of repair. Fynn had arranged for materials to be packed in at his expense, and he and Aemmer spent several days mending and refitting the building. Before they left, they drew up a set of simple rules for the hut's use and maintenance and placed them in a prominent place.

In July Fynn and Aemmer made the second traverse of Mount Victoria's formidable summit ridge, tackling it from north to south.[7] The ridge is a colossal nightmare of rotten rocks piled like building blocks arranged by some insane architect; the route demanded all their physical and emotional energy. In places the ridge is extremely narrow and broken by deep notches. Shattered walls and gendarmes blocked the climbers' way frequently and forced them onto the northeast face which overlooks Lake Louise; the opposing face is a sheer drop four or five hundred metres into the depths. Finally, after crossing the south summit, they descended by way of the Victoria Glacier and reached the hotel at Lake Louise at one thirty in the morning.

The mountains easily reached from Chateau Lake Louise offer an abundance of climbing challenges. Mount Temple (3547), the highest peak in the area, had a "tourist route" but it failed to interest Fynn. He wanted to try a more challenging line of attack from Paradise Valley via a long, prominent snow gully, towards the eastern limit of the north face. The gully led high onto Temple's main northeast ridge.

Confident the route would "go", Fynn and Aemmer climbed the gully but arrived at the crest two hours behind schedule. Turning, they followed the ridge upwards over a subsidiary peak and then, unexpectedly, encountered some black towers which directly blocked their path. The men decided the towers had to be bypassed because they were too rotten to climb.

[7] The first traverse of the Victoria ridge was accomplished by Aemmer, George Culver, and Edward Feuz, Jr. on 4 September 1909.

Fynn and Aemmer could see a wide ledge below which led to a snow crest beyond, but saw no easy way to gain the ledge. Thinking about the situation for some minutes, they decided to retreat by way of the unknown southeast face to Moraine Lake. There, by prearrangement, a car would be waiting for them. Despite some cliffs which slowed them, they arrived safely at the Moraine Lake Chalets only to find that the car had left before dark because it had no headlights!

Fynn did not give up on the ascent of Mount Temple. Several days of snowy weather intervened, but when it cleared he and Aemmer started out again via a new route on the southeast face. They climbed an ill-defined ridge south of Temple's main amphitheatre. The ridge eventually petered out on the face. A traverse upwards and across many ledges led the two men to the main ridge northeast of the summit where they discovered the solution to the black towers; there was, after all, an easy way down to the wide ledge. The summit was reached along the snow crest some hours later.

The next year, 1919, Fynn organized an expedition to the unclimbed Royal Group located sixty kilometres south of Banff.[8] Fynn engaged an outfitter, two wranglers, and sixteen horses to carry the party and its equipment. The party included Fynn's wife, another couple, and Rudolf Aemmer. They left the Banff Springs Hotel and headed south along the Spray River. After several days of inclement weather, a base camp was made on the shores of Belgium Lake just below Palliser pass.

Leaving the rest of the party at the camp, Fynn, Aemmer, and one wrangler took five horses and departed for an attempt on the unclimbed Mount King George (3422), monarch of all the Royals. They crossed the pass and descended to Palliser Lake, where the trail turned eastwards

[8] The Royals had been seen only from a distance by survey parties, but Arthur Wheeler, the surveyor of the Continental Divide, had named each peak in the group after a member of the Royal Family.

and steepened. At that point the trail disappeared in a tangle of charred deadfall. (In earlier years a fire had burned the valley.) The men had to cut trail. It was heavy work, which took its toll of men and animals.

After the horses were led around a difficult corner, one animal decided to pass another and vaulted over a fallen log. On the steep ground the horse lost its balance and fell, rolling and pitching down the slope until it came to a halt on its back, jammed against a log. Bedlam ensued. Thrashing, the frightened beast whinnied and neighed; the men shouted and stumbled amongst the deadfall. In a moment or two, after they had quieted the other animals, an element of calm returned. Tying the distressed animal's legs to trees to control its kicking, they removed its packsaddle. Then, pulling on the ropes, they helped the horse back onto its feet. It took all their skill to soothe the frightened creature and saddle it again.

By nightfall the party had covered only six kilometres. Quite exhausted, they lay on willow beds that evening listening to a porcupine clawing at their provisions.

The going was a little easier the following day. Their second camp was made at the mouth of a creek draining the Royals. However, Fynn and Aemmer, constantly aware of time and weather, decided to leave immediately to assure every possibility of success. Equipped with food, sweaters, and raincoats, the two climbers left the outfitter with the horses and headed up the ridge which guarded the entrance to Royal Valley. For a long way they walked on suspended tree trunks, intermittently jumping into the undergrowth and then pushing uphill through the fireweed that reached above their heads. Just before nightfall, close to the tree line, they traversed to a place where they could hear water running. The men lit a fire and made themselves as comfortable as conditions would allow.

By ten thirty the next morning the climbers had reached the large glacier which fills the valley at the foot of Mount King George. They crossed the ice to the bottom of the northeast face and looked up at the ramparts of the immense black fortress. In the centre of the face is a hanging glacier and, to the right, a steep but promising rock rib. A large bergschrund separates the glacier from the face, but a precarious snow bridge permitted them to cross. On the rib the climbing was steep, but the rock was firm and reliable. Gradually, with height, the rock gave way to a narrow snow crest leading to the north summit ridge. The rest of the way proved easy, and in the late afternoon, 10 August 1919, Fynn and Aemmer stood on top of the great peak, the first to be climbed in the Royal Group. Fynn took photographs from its quartzite summit.

At eight thirty in the evening, the pair were back on the glacier and decided, mistakenly as it would turn out, to avoid the wooded ridge over which they had entered the valley. Instead they chose to go around it on the ridge's southern flank. Although it required less climbing, this route was much longer. Despite a brilliant moon, all the difficult sections of the route were in shadow.

About one in the morning they regained their bivouac of the night before. They lit a fire, brewed coffee, and ate some food. There was little talk. Fynn wrapped himself in a mackintosh and immediately began to snore. Before dawn the cold awoke him; the campfire was almost out. He got stiffly to his feet to rekindle it. Then a look at Aemmer caused him to smile. His friend lay spread-eagled on his stomach, a fallen hero, arms flung wide, collapsed in the remains of their meal. For both of them, the mountain had taken a tremendous effort.

The relationship between client and guide by that time had grown beyond formal bounds. They were close friends. Aemmer invited Fynn to visit his home at Golden, British Columbia where, during a few days of relaxation the two men planned a hunt in the Clearwater Forest of Alberta. Fynn happily recalled this adventure in a later account, pointing to his own ineptitude as a rifleman.

He carried a Winchester Model 95 rifle, bored for a British Army .303 calibre bullet, but he had never fired the weapon.

It was fitted with a military as well as a Lyman sight and, like all rifles, required sight alignment before it could be used reliably on a hunt. The military rear sight could not be used for distances under a hundred metres, and the front sight was too low for the Lyman rear sight. The combination shot was about thirty centimetres too high. "This discovery was not pleasant," Fynn remarked later.

After hunting several days without luck, Fynn climbed a ridge and spotted a fine sheep down the valley, grazing near the tree line. He left Aemmer to block its escape and started stalking the animal. He made a wide detour to stay out of sight, travelled very fast, and after an hour was within striking distance of where he had last seen the sheep. A half hour of anxious work brought him close to a weird-looking tree stump, but there was no sign of the quarry.

In the meantime Aemmer joined him, reporting that for at least half an hour he had closely watched the "big head," and it had not moved. The two abashed hunters concluded they had been stalking the queer-looking stump. "To say we were disgusted is to put it mildly," said Fynn. To make matters worse, the pair did not make it back to camp that night and had to sleep in the open.

The evening of the next day, however, Fynn and Aemmer found a clearing from which they could view the slopes above them. Aemmer spotted three goats, and soon a fourth came into view. It moved about a great deal, working lower and lower on a ridge, as if going down to feed for the night. The wind was blowing down the mountain into the hunters' faces. There was a reasonable chance for a kill. They took to the chase.

Both lost sight of the goat for a while but reached the place where it was last seen and spotted it again about four hundred metres away. Aemmer urged Fynn to shoot, which he did, although he held little hope of hitting the animal because of the faulty sight on his rifle. With the binoculars Aemmer observed the goat looking straight at them. When the shot rang out the goat walked away slowly, as if nothing had happened.

As it had not bolted off, Fynn concluded the goat had been hit and chased after it. Every few metres he fired again, with what accuracy he did not know. Finally the goat stopped, turned around, looked at his pursuers, and collapsed. Then, surprisingly, the goat recovered, got up, and went on.

The hunters followed two different lines of pursuit. Aemmer saw the goat when it broke the skyline and fired his carbine. Fynn, whose spectacles had long been blurred with sweat, thought he should shoot also. He took aim at a prominent object silhouetted against the setting sun, fired, and was rewarded with a shower of splinters from a large boulder on which he had registered a direct hit.

Aemmer crossed the skyline and, finding the goat in distress, killed it with a shot in the shoulder. The goat tumbled down a ledge or two and came to rest. In the fading light the men gutted the beast and the next day returned to recover the meat.

Fynn celebrated his fiftieth birthday in 1920. He was no longer young for a mountaineer; his number of ascents declined, but their quality remained high.

That year he made three significant climbs: the second ascent of Mount Quadra (3173) from Consolation Valley; the third ascent of Mount Freshfield (3336) via the Freshfield Glacier; and a new north route on Mount Lefroy from the Plain of Six Glaciers.

The ascent on Mount Lefroy occurred late in July. Fynn and a friend from Zurich entered the dark couloir at the foot of Lefroy's north buttress. Broken, snow-covered rocks led to a chimney in the steep right-hand wall of the couloir. There, the many rounded holds worn smooth by water had to be climbed carefully. At the top of the chimney, a tunnel running with water led off to the upper snow slopes of the buttress. Fynn led the climb into the watery passage, and when he and his companion emerged they were both thoroughly soaked. But from there it was an easy scramble onto the north slopes which led to the ridge and the summit beyond.

Fynn made a hunting trip to Alaska in 1922 and combined it with a stop at Lake Louise. Above the lake there was a climb he and Aemmer had tried four times before, and this time he hoped to complete it — the northeast face of Mount Victoria.

The vast face soars eighteen hundred metres above its base and closes the end of the valley with a giant wall of rock continually plastered with snow and ice. It has only the sky beyond as a backdrop. The upper face, about five hundred metres high, inclines at fifty degrees and under normal conditions is peppered with stonefall. At the bottom of this slope is the upper Victoria Glacier, perched on a mantel of rock from which ice showers more than four hundred metres down precipitous cliffs to the lower glacier.

Fynn and Aemmer travelled fast and reached the foot of the final wall by five thirty in the morning. By tilting their heads back, they could clearly see the summit snow cornice which they hoped to gain.

The bergschrund was surprisingly easy to cross. Above it was a steep snow slope covered with a hard suncrust, which was also easily negotiated. In an hour and a half they had surmounted this section and climbed a band of brittle rock above it.

By midmorning they were only two hundred metres below the summit. Fynn was leading. He tackled the last ice bulge and held to a line directly below the peak, but, as he climbed, the bulge pushed him outwards and, as it became steeper, the loose snow under the overhanging cornice became deeper. Each step also resulted in a slight slide backwards. After more than an hour the climbers had advanced only twenty metres while overhead the cornice continued to menace them. If it broke, an avalanche would result; the risk was too great.

Without proper belays, the men retreated downwards in the loose snow and changed their line of attack. They headed for the ridge where the first rocks could be seen on the north side of the summit. The rest was easy. Fynn and

Aemmer reached the top of Mount Victoria at one thirty in the afternoon.[9]

In 1924, Fynn's plans took him only briefly to Lake Louise. He spent part of the summer in the Ramparts of Jasper National Park, southwest of Jasper. In this mountain group there was a host of unclimbed peaks, including the highest, Mount Geikie (3308), which was reputed to be more difficult than Mount Louis. With Fynn on the trip were Malcolm Geddes, F. Slark, and Edmontonian Cyril Wates.

The virgin ascent of Mount Barbican (3078) took place first and without much difficulty, even though Slark, who was inexperienced, might have held them up.[10] Two days later, Fynn, Wates, and Geddes left for the first ascent of Geikie.[11] Although Wates had been on the mountain several times before, he was unable to point out an appropriate route, and the choice was left to Fynn. The complexity of Geikie's southeast face and east ridge, combined with much rotten rock and difficult cracks, posed major route-finding problems, but Fynn never became lost. When the climb was over, twenty-six hours later, he rated it as less difficult than Mount Louis, but much longer.

At Glacier some weeks later, Fynn made the second ascent of Mount Sir Donald by its west face and descended by way of the northwest ridge, the route he had made fifteen years earlier. This was his last climb of Sir Donald. Only one more big peak awaited him — he hoped to return to Mount Hungabee and climb it again with Aemmer by a new north ridge route.

[9]This northeast face route was not repeated until 1952, when D. P. Graham and Edmund Petrig, a guide, took a direct line to the summit over the ground Fynn and Aemmer had avoided.

[10]F. Slark was killed on a nearby mountain, Redoubt Peak, after making its first ascent in 1927. His body and that of his companion were never found.

[11]Malcolm Geddes was killed in 1927 on Mount Lefroy. Unroped, he lost control of a glissade while descending the west face and fell to his death.

On 17 July 1925, the two friends climbed the west face of Hungabee's north ridge, taking to the rocks directly below the summit of Ringrose Peak. Gradually working south across the face, they reached the low point between the two peaks without much difficulty. Once on the ridge, they followed it over rotten rock and, in some places where width allowed, the two men scrambled up side by side until they reached the top. Stopping for a while to enjoy the view, they talked about the future, but mainly about the past, and then turned towards the valley. Their long association was drawing to a close.

Fynn was then fifty-five years old. His success as an engineer-inventor was bearing down on him. He held more than three hundred patents in nine countries, including those for the Fynn-Weichsel electric motor, manufactured by the Wagner company. Unquestionably, he was one of the world's most eminent electrical engineers, but his success was demanding much time and energy, as he was called on as a consultant, writer, and lecturer. Fynn had been comfortably well off for some time, but there were two things which his success could not replenish — time and strength to climb mountains.

Eventually, Fynn gave up his vacations to devote his efforts to new designs, new patents, and lengthy litigation over old ones. The unparalleled pressure to which he was subjected finally took its toll. His health began to fail. Carbuncles developed on his neck and became infected; he contracted blood poisoning.

When word of his illness reached Aemmer, he responded by telegraphing the message, "Get well old-timer and together we will climb mountains." But it was too late; Fynn would not recover. The great mountaineer died in his bed in St. Louis on 20 March 1929.

Chapter Three

Albert MacCarthy
1876 – 1956

Ye Gods, Mr. MacCarthy, just look at that;
they never will believe we climbed it.[1]

Conrad Kain

At Devil's Door, the ice trail had collapsed. The ice lay on a slant in a torrent of water which steadily eroded its submerged lower edge. Albert MacCarthy and the three dog team drivers looked on with apprehension. The ice slope was their only passage between the steep granite walls of the canyon. If it collapsed completely, nothing short of a boat could save them from a loss of supplies and possible drowning.

The dogs, too, sensed danger; they began to whimper. Usually scrappy and with their tails held high, they cringed while the teamsters encouraged them with shouts and whistles to cross the sloping ice. The younger dogs lay cowering on their bellies and had to be dragged ruthlessly by their harnesses. All the while the current tore away at the ice slab, and it pitched to a greater angle. The desperate attempt to move the supplies and the frightened animals across the tilting ice was successful — with not a moment to spare.

A few minutes after the loads were across, the slab cracked, settled a little, and then broke off into the rushing stream, destroying the passage between the walls. The four men shook their heads and laughed with relief over their good fortune.

[1]Kain's comment to MacCarthy after they had made the first ascent of Mount Louis.

This was to be the first of many hazards which awaited MacCarthy and his men before they succeeded in climbing Mount Logan, Canada's highest peak, the culminating expedition of MacCarthy's climbing career.[2]

MacCarthy was born at Ames, Iowa, in 1876, was educated there and at Des Moines. He later entered the U.S. Naval Academy at Annapolis. After graduating in 1897, he served ten years in the U.S. Navy and saw action in the Spanish American War. He was discharged in 1907 with the rank of lieutenant commander.

During his naval service MacCarthy met Elizabeth Larned of Summit, New Jersey. Elizabeth was a year younger than he and came from a prominent New England family. She was a talented tennis player and was attracted to MacCarthy, who, like herself, enjoyed outdoor athletic activities. On 30 May 1905, they were married. The union brought together money, brains, and ability.

In 1909 Elizabeth (Bess) MacCarthy discovered mountaineering and made her first ascent in the Canadian Rockies. Two years later, in 1911, her husband followed suit. In July of that year he made his first climb on Mount Daly (3152), in the Waputik Icefield. He was then thirty-five.

Mack MacCarthy fell in love with Canada immediately. That same August he and Bess made a pack train journey from Castle Mountain (Mount Eisenhower), in the Bow Valley, through "magnificent and unknown country" to the town of Windermere, British Columbia, in the Columbia Valley. There, in the foothills above the nearby village of Wilmer, the MacCarthys bought a ranch and named it Karmax. It became their summer headquarters for many years.

In 1912 MacCarthy climbed in the area around Vermilion Pass between Banff and Kootenay national parks and in Strathcona Provincial Park on Vancouver Island, where he made a first ascent of Elkhorn Mountain (2195) with Arthur

[2]Mount Logan (6050 metres, 19,850 feet) is also the second highest elevation in North America, exceeded only by Mount McKinley (6194 metres, 20,320 feet).

and Oliver Wheeler, and others. But it was the summer of 1913 that brought MacCarthy his first fame. On 31 July, from the Alpine Club's camp at Berg Lake, he made the first ascent of Robson (3954), in the company of Conrad Kain and Bill Foster. It was a remarkable accomplishment for the three men and especially for MacCarthy, whose alpine experience was limited but whose fitness and ability were great.[3] After the successful ascent of Robson, MacCarthy looked for other challenges. The next was a mountain considered by one climbing party as "absolutely unclimbable."

Such was the report on Mount Farnham (3457). Climbers had just returned from this mountain, the highest peak in the Purcell Range, which lies west of the Columbia River and southwest of Radium Hot Springs. After his return from Robson, MacCarthy and his wife took a democrat and three saddle ponies from Karmax to check the report on Farnham. On observing the mountain, it seemed to offer two interesting and serious climbs — the second being Farnham's imposing hornlike tower (3353). Before returning to the ranch, the MacCarthy's climbed Nelson Peak (3283).

After the ACC Upper Yoho Camp in 1914, MacCarthy returned to Karmax to find a telegram waiting for him from Conrad Kain, whose steamer for New Zealand had been delayed for a few days. Kain was offering his guiding services in the interim and MacCarthy quickly accepted. They made plans to climb Mount Farnham. Its first ascent was completed 10 August 1914. The peak offered no great difficulties, although the complex route was quite exposed in places and the rock very weathered and friable. In his usual fashion, Kain took another route for descent, which led them into some blind alleys, especially as the climbers had only moonlight to assist them. The descent took longer than the ascent.

With this ascent and that of Mount Robson the year before, MacCarthy and Kain had climbed the highest peaks

---

[3]A detailed account of the first ascent of Mount Robson can be found in Chapter 4 of this book.

in both the Purcells and the Rockies in two consecutive years. The 1913 and 1914 climbing seasons taught Mac-Carthy that the employment of an accomplished guide such as Kain was a definite asset in the pursuit of first ascents and the forging of challenging new routes. It was an era for guides, and Kain was considered by many to be the best. MacCarthy chose to hire him exclusively for 1915 after Kain's return from the winter season in New Zealand. In this way the two men cemented a relationship which, for a short period, greatly affected their lives.

With earnestness and determination, MacCarthy planned a 1915 climbing program which would see many first ascents in the Purcells immediately surrounding Karmax. The party which MacCarthy organized that year was congenial and able. In addition to Kain, it included Winthrop and Margaret Stone and Kain's New Zealand patron, Otto Frind. The first peak to fall to their efforts was Mount Ethelbert (3158), named for a nun who died aboard a Columbia River steamer.

Then, in the first part of August MacCarthy's party turned its attention to the Commander Group adjacent to the Farnham Group. Commander Mountain (3362) and Jumbo Mountain (3399) were climbed by them for the first time. These were followed by other firsts in the Farnhams: Mount Peter (3354), Mount McCoubrey (3208), and Spearhead Peak (3231). A second ascent was made of Delphine Mountain (3376), and, after the Stones left, the MacCarthys and Kain made the second ascent of Eyebrow Peak (3380). Birthday Peak (3207) was climbed on Kain's birthday and was so named by the party. To close the season, MacCarthy made a solo first to the summit of Mount Sally Serena (3048).

Part way through the First World War, several events occurred of personal consequence to Kain and MacCarthy. The MacCarthys bought a second ranch, K2, on the Rocky Mountain side of the Columbia River. In addition, Kain was refused permission to return to New Zealand after his third season there due to anti-German feeling in that country. MacCarthy needed more help with his expanded holdings, and Kain entered his employment on a full-time basis.

In the summer of 1916 MacCarthy took Kain to Banff as his personal guide. Staying at the Alpine Club of Canada clubhouse, while the annual camp was in progress at nearby Healy Creek, MacCarthy assembled a riding party, and on Wednesday, 19 July, the group rode to Edith Pass, which lies just outside of Banff between Mount Norquay and Mount Edith. The excursion was intended to be an early season reconnaissance of the great tower of Mount Louis (2682) which lies north of Edith, but after the party crossed the pass and rested beneath Louis's east face, Kain began to investigate its lower slopes. MacCarthy followed.

Each disputed the other's tentative line of approach, and to prove his point Kain continued to climb higher. Finally, the two could not give it up. On a ledge above the bottom couloir, they cached their axes and went at it in earnest. When routes northwards appeared to peter out, Kain un-laced his boots to climb a ten-metre-high, one-centimetre-wide crack in his socks. MacCarthy was not pleased with that prospect and issued a firm no; instead, they moved southwards, finding a couple of short chimneys which, once climbed, led them over a rib into a deep cut on the south face. The south face drops steeply to the Edith-Louis col.

The route upwards from that point was complex and required negotiating several chimneys and short faces. At one point their route petered out, and a short rappel was necessary. Eventually MacCarthy and Kain reached a terrace about a hundred and fifty metres below the summit, above which ran "a truly wonderful chimney to delight the most exacting climber." They cached their rucksacks and the rope and walked four metres into the back of the chimney. To climb its steep sides they wedged themselves in, placed their perspiring backs and hands on one wall and their rasping boots on the other. Over the chimney's entire length, its configuration varied somewhat and the climbers' technique changed accordingly. Meanwhile it drizzled a bit and then sleet began. MacCarthy and Kain hurried to the summit, arriving just before 4:00 P.M., where Kain yodelled their success to their friends far below. The two built a small rock cairn and left a record of the climb in a tobacco tin.

The descent followed a similar route; the rough, sharp rock, running with water, took a toll on their hands. When they reached their rappel point, they lost time trying to snare a loop of rope on a rock horn above them to aid in climbing out of the gully. Once past this point, the climbers traversed on a downwards angle to the cliffs on the east side of the mountain and found it to be the most dangerous section of the descent. Here they double-roped and hooked it over every possible nubbin to give protection as they passed over scanty holds, rib ends, and small cracks. It was the only place where MacCarthy and Kain roped during the entire climb.

Shortly before 8:00 P.M. they rejoined their friends at the foot of Mount Louis. When the party reached the trail and looked back, the two climbers were incredulous they had made the route on such a difficult-looking mountain.[4]

Before 1916 the Bugaboo-Vowell Groups in the northern Purcells of southeastern British Columbia were virtually unknown. Little exploration had been carried out;[5] the elevations of the peaks had yet to be clearly established, and none of them had been named. There was much work to be done. For MacCarthy, who had climbed most of the big peaks to the south, it was natural to enter this virgin area.

On 25 August, MacCarthy and Bess, Kain, Frind, Mrs. George Vincent, and her son John, made camp in the forested valley below what would later be called Bugaboo Glacier. The next day, starting early, they plunged through

[4]It was at this point that Conrad Kain made the remark to MacCarthy which is quoted at the beginning of this chapter.

[5]Edward Feuz, Jr. and Joseph Hickson had been in the Bugaboo group earlier that summer and had returned without success because of heavy snowfall.

the undergrowth of the valley, across the glacier, and onto the mossy slopes above the tree line. There they were impressed by the three granite monoliths which shot out of the surrounding ice. They numbered them One (Marmolata), Two (Snowpatch), and Three (Bugaboo). Because these peaks appeared to have about the same summit elevation, Kain suggested the party climb to the col between Two and Three to see if a higher mountain lay beyond.

Once there they saw a beautiful icefield bordered on its south by another granite spire on which was perched a natural stone formation resembling a pouter pigeon (Pigeon). To the southwest a semicircular rock ridge containing three peaks (Howser Spire), soared skywards to delineate the icefield in that direction. The central peak of this latter mountain was judged as being the highest point in this entire group. With Kain leading one rope and MacCarthy a second, the party set out across the glare and heat of the glacier toward the five peaks.

On the rock above the bergschrund, various jamming techniques were used to climb angled cracks, which provided strenuous amusement as each climber experimented with his own style. Once on the col between the second and third peak of Howser Spire, MacCarthy used his clinometer to check the elevation of Peak Three, whose southwest face pitched down steeply for a thousand metres in one long, sheer cliff to a flat glacier far below.[6] His sighting determined that they were already above its top elevation, and were thus assured their objective for that day was the highest peak in the group.

The climbers gained the summit of Howser late in the afternoon. While Kain built a cairn, MacCarthy discussed subsequent climbs, and Bess MacCarthy suggested they attempt Peak Three later in the week. Shortly before five o'clock, they turned homewards, descending via the north ridge and east face.

The return passage over the glacier was very quiet as

[6]This face was climbed in August 1959 by Fred Beckey, Ed Cooper, Pete Geiser, and Roman Sadowy.

each climber struggled against his own fatigue. When darkness fell, northern lights appeared, streaking the sky with shifting shapes and patterns. Eventually the exhausted group reached the tree line and stumbled and fell through the bush. On arrival at their camp at one o'clock in the morning, they were pleased to find their patient outfitter awaited them with a hot supper.

As time would prove, Howser Spire would not be the most important ascent in the region, despite its height. The MacCarthys, John Vincent, and Kain chose to attempt Peak Three on 29 August. At four-thirty in the morning they left camp full of expectation as to what the day would bring.

The south ridge was climbed easily from the Two-Three col under scattered clouds. But at an elevation of three thousand metres the crux of the climb was encountered. MacCarthy described the obstacle as a *bugaboo*, a term which later gave the peak its name. Here the climbers were challenged by a gendarme with a long, sheer face on the west, ominously rising to a sharp point. The way was even less passable to the east, where steep, broken cliffs fell six hundred metres directly to the foot of the mountain.

MacCarthy watched with the others as Kain worked up the edge of the gendarme, paused a little, and then pulled himself around a corner. At this point Kain disappeared from sight as he worked to the left onto the face of the gendarme. MacCarthy thought their difficulties were over, but as time passed and no rope movement took place he realized Kain was in trouble. Soon Kain's fingers and then his whole body reappeared. This recurred several times as Kain attempted different methods of crossing; MacCarthy merely paid out the rope and pulled in the slack each time Kain retreated. The guide's problem was two metres of blank wall and a vertical crack on the wall's opposite edge.

MacCarthy was never certain exactly how his guide made the move, but after an hour or more the rope started to run out again for a length of twenty metres.[7] MacCarthy and

[7]For a description as to how Kain overcame this difficulty, see Chapter 4.

his companions followed the line onto the face to discover Kain had let down a double rope from the top of the gendarme. With this assistance, each climber hauled himself or herself hand over hand to a safe stance beside the leader.

The first summit of Peak Three was attained a little farther up the ridge. A more northerly point was sighted as being higher, and, after a rest pause, they placed a rope and rappelled down onto a very narrow causeway which linked the two peaks. So narrow was this horizontal passageway that MacCarthy considered it safe to traverse only while straddling the edge; thus each member of the group worked their way over, their legs hanging above an abyss on either side. Once across, a short climb up again brought them to the higher summit.

MacCarthy's party was thrilled with their achievement but were well aware that a safe return had yet to be effected. They recrossed the gap and climbed the rappel rope to the first summit. Descending again, the climbers reached the top of the gendarme and looked for a more direct and safer route around the obstacle. An examination to the east of the gendarme disclosed that a twenty-five-metre rappel would bring them to a ledge below and behind their ascending route. Kain wrapped his coat around a projecting rock to protect the rope and, doubling it, dropped its ends down the face behind the gendarme.

Each climber in turn executed a standing rappel by wrapping the double rope around one leg and pinching it between the feet to reduce the strain on the arms.[8] All were protected by Kain, who had tied a rope to their waists. After the rappel, which took an hour, they climbed a little up broken rocks to the foot of the gendarme and then returned to camp by their morning route.

The next day the party left the area. It was the end of the season, and MacCarthy was well satisfied.

In 1917 MacCarthy attended the ACC Cataract Valley Camp with Kain as his personal guide. They made an ascent of

[8]This method of rappelling is no longer recommended.

Mount Hungabee with Bess MacCarthy, who became the first woman to climb this impressive black mountain. However MacCarthy's climbing career began to change with his growth in experience. His ascents with Kain had greatly enhanced his reputation and had taught him many of the master's tricks and skills, so much so that his remaining climbs with Kain would be few.

The following year, when the ACC camp was convened in Paradise Valley, Kain did not accompany his employers. Instead, the MacCarthys climbed alone. After the Victory Camp in 1919, MacCarthy led his wife to the summit on Mount Lefroy and together, later in the summer, they scaled Mount Sir Donald in the Selkirks via its northwest ridge.

In 1920, at Mount Assiniboine south of Banff National Park, MacCarthy established a route of his own making. Twice he led other climbers in a traverse of Terrapin Mountain (2944) and a descent by the west ridge of Mount Magog (3094). After climbing a steep ice couloir on Terrapin and traversing its summit slopes, MacCarthy took his party below the vertical and overhanging walls of Magog. The only breach in its grey walls was a section of horizontal strata stained a light colour which gave the impression of a stairway with narrow white treads and yellow risers. Because of the formation's colour and conformation, the climbers named it the Golden Stairs.

The yellow rock was of a different texture than the main mass of the cliff. For the first six metres the rock was devoid of any significant holds and stood at a very high angle. The next twenty metres, only slightly less perpendicular, contained one vertical wall with two or three footholds of sufficient size to grant some relief to the arms. At the top of the pitch was a ledge with excellent anchorage.

Despite the frequent need to take his body weight on his fingers, MacCarthy led this wall while holding his ice axe in one hand. "His steady progress and aggressive and confident attack were striking . . . evidence of his skill and strength. It was a perfect example of the art of cliff climbing in its most highly developed form," wrote Frank Waterman, who was with him.

Another decade was finished. Over the past ten years Mac-Carthy had entered the world of mountaineering and developed another facet of his varied character. He had also made new friends. No better example of mountain friendship existed than the one he and his wife enjoyed with Winthrop and Margaret Stone; they had spent seven seasons climbing together. In 1921 everything would change. Joy would turn to sorrow; accomplishment to tragedy.

Eon Mountain (3310) is located just south of Mount Assiniboine, about 40 kilometres south of Banff on the Alberta-British Columbia border. The Stones wished to make the first ascent of this peak, and in mid-July 1921 they set out alone from a camp near Assiniboine. For two days they reconnoitred routes to their objective. On 17 July, having found the key to the mountain, a tower on the east side of the south face, they climbed towards the summit.

At six o'clock in the evening they were at the foot of the summit rocks. Margaret Stone took shelter from rockfall while her husband climbed a twelve-metre chimney. She enquired if he could see the top, to which he answered he could "see nothing higher." Stone then disappeared above the chimney, and, without telling his wife, unroped. Margaret stayed where she was.

Without warning, a large slab of rock shot past, narrowly missing her. To her horror, the rock was followed by her husband, who clutched his ice axe in his hand; he fell without uttering a sound. She braced herself for the expected shock of the rope snapping taut. It did not occur. Instead, Stone crashed onto a narrow ledge not far below and then rolled and plunged from ledge to ledge until he disappeared from view.

Nauseated and swooning, Margaret became incapable of action. When she recovered, darkness had fallen. She spent the night without moving, filled with anguish and terror. The next day, under severe stress and without food, she tried to find her husband but failed. Again she spent a night on the mountain.

On the third day she endeavoured to reach the valley. Following what she thought was the line of ascent, she made the mistake of roping down a chimney and dropped to a ledge three metres lower than the end of the rope. Below she discovered there were steep walls which prevented further progress downwards. Glancing upwards she saw the smooth walls of the chimney would prevent her recovery of the rope which was now out of reach. She was trapped.

On this narrow, sloping ledge she spent another five days, clad only in a flannel shirt and knickers. Fortunately her position faced south permitting warmth during the day, and a trickle of water flowed down the back of the chimney providing a drink about every four hours. Eight days after the death of her husband, on 24 July, she was rescued by Rudolf Aemmer, Bill Peyto, and Constable Childs of the NWMP. By that time she was extremely weak, and Aemmer had to carry her on his back to a bivouac site near the tree line.

When news of the accident reached Arthur Wheeler, the director of the ACC, he put a team together to recover Stone's body. Those who would do the work were MacCarthy, Kain, Edward Feuz Jr., Aemmer, and Lennox Lindsay. On 5 August Stone's body was found at an elevation of three thousand metres. Leaving it in place, the party climbed to the summit, built a cairn, planted Stone's ice axe, and left a record of his last ascent.

Stone had fallen some two hundred and fifty metres and suffered a crushed skull. Despite nineteen days in the open, the body was in a good state of preservation. It was prepared for recovery using oiled silk, blankets, canvas, and lashings. On 6 August the rescuers carried the body downwards, slung between them on shoulder poles. That night it was left at the tree line while the men made camp. The next day Stone's remains were brought on a log skid to a waiting pack horse at Aurora Creek.[9]

This event had tremendous impact on the mountaineer-

[9]At the time of his death Dr. Winthrop Ellsworth Stone was the president of Purdue University. His wife, Margaret, was a beautiful young woman more than twenty years his junior.

ing community, especially on MacCarthy. In 1922 he did not climb. The death of his friend and the resulting anguish to his friend's family caused him to pause and reflect on the price sometimes paid for mountain adventure. He chose to spend the summer months of that year in New York and Annapolis, attending to his expanding business affairs.

Revival of his mountaineering interest came in 1923, when he took time to write a stinging article in *The Canadian Alpine Journal* about the use of fixed ropes as an aid to climbing. "Let us hope no more of our peaks will be subjected to such indignity," he wrote. His interest was further stimulated by an important vote of the ACC membership that same summer. At its annual meeting, the members decided to launch an expedition to Mount Logan (6050), Canada's highest peak. A ways and means committee was created "with full power" to plan the assault. The committee included MacCarthy, Bill Foster, Fred Lambart, Arthur Wheeler, and Fred Bell.

"The magnitude of the project soon became very apparent to all," wrote MacCarthy after the committee first met at Vancouver in November 1923. Until then MacCarthy knew only that Logan was the second highest peak in North America and that it was located somewhere in Canada.

Mount Logan, named after Sir William E. Logan, founder of the Geological Survey of Canada, is situated in the isolated southwest corner of the Yukon Territories, three hundred kilometres west of Whitehorse and one hundred kilometres east of the Gulf of Alaska. It rises majestically from a sea of ice, and is the principal peak of the Saint Elias Mountains. This range comprises one of the largest glaciated regions on earth, ranking third only to the Antarctic and Greenland. Amidst this vast, icy domain, Mount Logan crests prominently more than four thousand metres above its surrounding glacial approaches.

Lying at a north latitude of 60° 35', Logan has an arctic character complete with heavy snowfalls, low temperatures, and high winds. Its stupendous bulk ranks as the largest mountain massif in North America and possibly in the world. Its circumference exceeds one hundred and fifty kilometres; if truncated at the three-thousand-metre level, it would present an area measuring twenty-six kilometres long and thirteen kilometres wide. It was little known in 1923.

The only proven route to Logan at that time was from Cordova, Alaska, to the town of McCarthy[10] at the foot of the Wrangell Mountains and thence overland in an easterly direction up the Chitina Valley to the junction of the Chitina and Logan Glaciers. From this point the Logan Glacier was followed southeasterly to the outflow of the Ogilvie Glacier and thence southerly up this ice mass to the mountain.

In June and July 1924 MacCarthy, with Andy Taylor and Scotty Atkinson, both local men from McCarthy, reconnoitred this route. By pack train they travelled one hundred and forty kilometres up the Chitina River to the toe of its glacier and from there on foot another eighty-four kilometres to the Cascades, a six-hundred-metre-high ice-fall which joins the upper reaches of the Ogilvie to the lower reaches of the King Glacier. To reach this point was an ordeal. The backpacking relay of heavy equipment and food took thirty-three exhausting days, leaving the men only four days for actual exploration in the icefall. There they climbed to a maximum altitude of thirty-one hundred metres, slightly less than three thousand metres below and thirty kilometres away from the summit.

At the ACC camp at Mount Robson later that summer, MacCarthy reported his findings and recommended that every possible provision for the expedition be cached on route before the main force took to the field. He then returned to New Jersey, and in the fall he drove back 8336 kilometres across the continent to Karmax, accompanied by his wife and two "police puppies" (see photo).

The expeditionary preparations to ascend Logan began in earnest early the following year.

[10]The starting point of the route (McCarthy) and the name of the leader of the climb (MacCarthy) are coincidental and bear no relationship.

MacCarthy's plan to lay in provisions for the climb took shape and went into action on 4 February 1925. While he was travelling by steamer to Cordova, Andy Taylor and Austin Trim from McCarthy spent nine days breaking trail and relaying cargo. Seventy-two-kilometres up the Chitina Valley, the two men made a cache of two and a half tons of supplies which were hauled overland on a heavy bobsled drawn by five horses. The weather had been difficult; the lowest temperature they recorded was −47° C.

On his arrival in Alaska, MacCarthy finished his preparations for the two months of work ahead. In addition to Taylor and Atkinson, Henry Olsen would also take a dog team; Trim and his six horses would be joined by William Weyers, a teamster. On 17 February, in front of the Golden Hotel, the people of McCarthy were entertained by the sight and clamor of Trim's heavily loaded bobsled pulled by four horses and Weyers's slightly smaller sled with two horses. Three dog-sleds drawn by teams of seven dogs each added to the din. The total loads made close to ten tons, comprising 3050 kilograms of equipment, fuel, and supplies, 1000 kilograms of hay and oats for the expedition in May, and 4500 kilograms of provisions for their own immediate use. As the men and animals set off under overcast skies towards the Chitina Valley, the frenzied barking of the dogs echoed across the snow. The next morning one of the dogs tore the eye out of another in protest to the gruelling pace.

The route was fraught with unexpected difficulties right from the beginning — open water, ice jams, and a lack of snow on the rocks, which made the pulling very heavy. The cold, as usual, presented problems. The horse harnesses could not be removed for thirteen days because they were frozen in place on the animals. The dogs refused to eat their ration of cornmeal and tallow because they were used to domestic scraps. As a result they lost weight, and, when shortened rations of rice, lard, and fish were given them, they failed to recover their lost flesh. The supply teams were soon behind schedule, but each day they moved forward.

On 27 February the party reached Hubrick's camp located about three kilometres below the toe of the Chitina

Glacier.[11] As the new month began they worked their way along the south edge of the glacier to a portal made by steep granite walls fifty metres high. Through this narrow gap they entered the Gorge of Fate. Six kilometres beyond this entrance they were forced to construct a log bridge when a natural ice crossing was washed out by a rushing stream. The teamsters returned to McCarthy, and the dog teams and strong backs of the men took over. Ten kilometres farther up the gorge a camp was set, and they made haste to move the outfit safely to this point. Combining relays, it took nine days to transfer loads by dog-sled upstream of the bridge and to backpack them farther to the camp. Above the bridge was a narrow, three-metre-wide ice passage overhung by a menacing serac. MacCarthy called this the Devil's Door, a stretch of three kilometres in length threatened by shifting ice bridges and open water.

One morning, without warning, a giant avalanche of ice thundered into the gorge and dammed it. Quickly it impounded water, in a few hours to a level of three metres over the ice, and a lake had formed two hundred metres above the dam. The men found themselves above the lake and their equipment below it. Bypassing the gorge, in an effort to get food for the dogs, the men encountered the heaviest going they had found so far. By the time they were ready to return, the water had breached the dam and normal levels had returned.

The party put on speed to move the remaining outfit to the camp, using the dogs as far as possible, where MacCarthy, in turn, carried forty-five-kilogram loads a short distance to a safe cache. They had not moved too quickly. They evacuated the narrow gap just as the ice collapsed.[12]

Now firmly committed beyond the Devil's Door, the men worked out new routes and both men and dogs ferried the loads ever upwards. The weather was deplorable. Late one afternoon MacCarthy became lost in a storm, and, without a

[11]Hubrick's was an abandoned camping place left by a prospector of the same name.

[12]The opening paragraphs of this chapter refer to this incident.

compass or a trail marked by willow wands to aid him, he stumbled over the rough terrain, moving all the time to keep his blood in circulation. Only by chance did he find a land-mark close to camp which led him there that evening.

By the end of March the camp had been moved to the centre of the Logan Glacier. Now well past a source of wood, gas stoves had to be used for cooking and for drying clothes. The tent was set in an excavation a metre deep to hold it in place and to protect it from the piercing wind. Four days later they reached the International Boundary Line between Alaska and the Yukon Territory.

By 14 April they had transferred 2130 kilograms of gear to a point fifteen kilometres up the Ogilvie Glacier, their ad-vance base camp, and had carried a further 450 kilograms two kilometres past it. Meat and other articles which would attract animals were placed in the centre of the cache under tarpaulins, rocks, and tinned gasoline. Photos of the area were taken for easy relocation later that spring.

Well behind schedule, the men turned for home. On 26 April they reached McCarthy, their starting point, two months and three weeks after they had set out. MacCarthy's plan to provision the route had been carried out success-fully in spite of objective difficulties. They had travelled over fifteen hundred kilometres under arctic conditions, and "the job proved to be twice as hard as anyone had calcu-lated." It had been an expedition in itself.

It had long since been decided MacCarthy would lead the expedition. With only a short time remaining before the climb began, he stayed in Alaska and awaited the arrival of his companions. They had been carefully chosen: Bill Foster of Victoria, then the deputy minister of Public Works for the province of British Columbia, a Lt. Colonel, and a member of the Mount Robson team of 1913; Fred Lambart of Ottawa, the climb's deputy leader, and a member of the International Boundary Commission Alaska-Yukon Border 1913, who was at that time with the Canadian Department of the Interior;[13]

[13]Fred Lambart, as a member of the International Boundary Com-mission of 1913, had seen Mount Logan before and participated in determining its altitude.

and Allen Carpé, a representative of the American Alpine Club.[14] In addition, there was Hamilton Laing of Comox, British Columbia, who worked for the Canadian Department of Mines and was to be the naturalist for the expedition; and three volunteers from Boston who paid their own way, Henry Hall, Jr., Bob Morgan, and Norm Read. At McCarthy, Andy Taylor joined them.

When the climbers arrived at Cordova by steamer from Seattle, they found MacCarthy waiting for them at the dock. By Northwestern Railway, the party travelled together to their starting point, the town of McCarthy. The expedition officially began on 12 May 1925.

By the seventeenth their pack train had reached Hubrick's camp. From there they followed the north side of the Chitina Glacier and then crossed it in a southerly direction to the Logan Glacier. On the twenty-second they crossed the International Boundary Line, and on the twenty-fifth the expedition arrived at MacCarthy's advance base camp, where the bulk of their supplies were now in place. By the end of May these supplies had been moved to the foot of the Cascades Icefall where, at 2380 metres, they established their new advance base camp and called it Cascades Camp.

There was still a long way to go. From Cascades it would be a matter of relaying loads upwards, until sufficient provisions were in place to make a summit bid. The next day "jerk-necking" began,[15] and twenty-eight pack loads and one Yukon sled were wrestled through the icefall to a snow dome at thirty-one hundred metres. There the expedition pitched Observation Camp, so called because from that

[14]Allen Carpé was an electrical engineer and the great grandson of Ezra Cornell, founder of Cornell University. Carpé was killed with a companion on Mount McKinley in May 1932 when he fell through a snowbridge into a crevasse on the Muldrow Gracier. His body was never found, but that of his companion, Theodore Koven, was later discovered on the ice.

[15]The men used Indian tumplines on their packs to help relieve the load on their shoulders. A tumpline is a strap which extends from the sides of a pack and fits across the forehead. Any unbalanced motion jerks the neck.

point they could see the entire length of the King Trench for the first time.

The trench lies in an easterly direction and contains a long, broad, rising glacier whose ramplike surface is broken only by a moderate icefall several kilometres away. The glacier is bounded on its right and south side by a continuous rock ridge surmounted in the distance by King Peak (5173). On the north the glacier is delineated by the long west ridge of Logan itself.

The party was ready for the twenty-eight-day siege. On 8 June they left Observation Camp with a sled loaded with three hundred kilograms of provisions. In snowshoes, the men dragged the sled by means of shoulder harnesses. The sun beat down, and they perspired in their woolen clothing. To protect themselves from the sun's harmful rays, they wore mosquito netting under their hats and snow goggles. At intervals willow branches, which had been carried from the valley below, were planted as trail markers. The branches could save their lives if they became lost in a blinding storm. During the day they worked in dense fog which alternated with driving sleet. Above the King Glacier icefall, the conditions became so violent the men close to cache their loads and return to Observation Camp. Most of their tracks had been obliterated and the willow wands became immediately useful. On returning to camp they experienced brilliant, warm sunshine again.

The King Col Camp was chosen at the head of the glacier and close to the north side of the col. The elevation of the camp was about 4420 metres. Using long-handled shovels, tent platforms were dug into the snow to give a smooth, flat base and high, protective sides. The first night there Mac-Carthy suffered severe pain from an overstrained eye, and when he rose the next morning he was still exhausted.

Above the col the obvious route lay through a gigantic mass of jumbled ice blocks which extends across the south face of Logan. In brilliant sunlight the scene appeared as an outlandish meringue, crumpled and collapsing from its own weight. By 10 June, MacCarthy, with two others, had penetrated this icefall and descriptively named some of its passages: Diamond Serac, Dormer Window, Corkscrew, Avenue of Blocks. Higher, the route gave way to a broad slope, and at 5180 metres Windy Camp was cut into the snow. Higher still lay the long back of the mountain, the main ridge. Directly on their route ahead was a double peak.

Returning to King Col for more loads, the party was caught there for three days by a storm. Efforts to reach Windy Camp were frustrated. It was not until the sixteenth of June that the camp was consolidated about five kilometres below the double peak. That night the temperature dropped to −36° C (−33° F), and MacCarthy noted in his diary that the group was "in fair shape but not strong for the work to be done."

On the eighteenth MacCarthy, Foster, and Read climbed to the saddle between the double peak to see what lay on the north side of the mountain. Fog obscured the view. The next day, while others went down for provisions from King Col Camp, the three tried again. On reaching the saddle they were prevented from going farther by a gale blowing across the crest, but by lying prone and peering over the edge they caught intermittent glimpses of another double peak several kilometres away. With no idea as to which peak was the highest, they decided that, when the time came, they would ascend the two highest summits to make certain they set foot on the topmost point. As for difficulty, the going on the north side looked straightforward. The only remaining question was whether the new double peak was the top of Logan or whether a higher summit lay beyond. In any event, Windy Camp was too far away for a dash to the top; another camp would be needed on the northern plateau.

The next day blew wild, and snow lay deeply in their tracks as MacCarthy, Foster, and Read went down to meet the others, who were bringing up new loads from King Col. On regaining Windy Camp they immediately crawled into their heavy down sleeping robes to escape the intense cold.[16] But it had already taken its toll. Morgan's feet and

[16]The sleeping bags (robes) contained two eiderdown quilts, a

fingers were badly frostbitten. There was no alternative for him but to descend. On 21 June in a moderating storm, Morgan, disappointed but concerned for his own survival, started down in the mist towards the first willow wand. Hall went with him and thus gave up the climb to ensure his companion's safe descent. By 3:00 P.M. the same day the storm was on the mountain with such force that all hands turned in and waited. Then, without warning, the storm snuffed out. The men each donned four or five pairs of socks and dry-tanned Indian mocassins in place of their usual rubber-soled shoe packs and started for the crest. At 5640 metres they made a short-term fly camp.

At that altitude the cold, the physical effort, and the shortening oxygen supply visibly affected them all. Work was more easily contemplated than done. Individual actions were slow, inefficient, and frequently broken by short periods of rest. But, oddly, MacCarthy noted that he suffered less from the feeling of suffocation at that height than he had lower down.

The next morning the packing of gear was slowed further by heavy clothing and thick mitts. At eleven o'clock the expedition left behind a two-day bag of provisions for their return and descended what they now called Hurricane Hill, on the north side of the mountain. The going was easy at first but soon gave way to deep snow. Bent under their loads, they stared at each succeeding footprint and followed the leader like sheep. In the early afternoon, they pitched Plateau Camp at 5425 metres. A storm broke immediately, but they were in a good position to wait it out, with eight day's food and fuel. Yet MacCarthy questioned whether their physical strength would last that long. He noted in his diary, "[We] must push and push fast as possible and then some more."

The test came on Tuesday, 23 June. "It saw the end of our doubts and fears," wrote MacCarthy. During the preceding

camel's hair blanket, a waterproof cover, and a ground cloth with clasps. Two bags could be joined to make a double bag two metres in width. Each weighed 10.9 kilograms (24 pounds).

night a storm had raged, threatening to blow their tents apart. As it died out in the morning it left a thick blanket of snow and enveloped the site in a dense fog. About ten o'clock the fog lifted, and glaring sunshine was all about them.

MacCarthy was wearing two sets of dark glasses to protect his weakened eyes, but they were not enough to prevent the intense pain caused by the glare. Foster led as two ropes set out. Below the slopes of the new double peak they strapped on crampons, and insulated their feet from the chilled metal with felt insoles. MacCarthy took the lead now and over hard snow set a course up the west side of the peak. The slope steepened, and in late afternoon they reached the top of Double Peak. Although the altimeter registered the summit elevation, what they had feared before was now confirmed. There, more than three kilometres distant, rose a still higher summit. What was worse, they discovered an intervening drop of about three hundred metres. Determined to finish the summit climb that day, the men slung on their heavy packs again and descended into the notch.

They had seen that the final summit ridge also presented two peaks; MacCarthy led the first rope over packed, windblown snow to the saddle between them. He peered over the crest, and saw beyond a startling spectacle. There before him, in the blue tinge of altitude, was his own reflection, centred in a small, perfectly circular rainbow. He was unbelieving at first; his head seemed as light as a feather, yet his legs and feet were as heavy as lead. He made a platform on the crest, and the others climbed to his position. He was relieved to hear Carpé say, "That is a Brocken Spectre with a halo," and Foster confirmed it. As Lambart's rope joined them, they, too, saw the same apparition.[17]

From the crest the remainder of the ridge presented no difficulty. At eight in the evening they negotiated the final

[17]A Brocken Spectre takes its name from the Brocken, highest of the Harz Mountains in Saxony, and is a magnified shadow of the spectator thrown on a bank of cloud when the sun is low.

rise of the main peak and stood for the first time on the highest point in Canada. Among other sensations MacCarthy later noted, "[We] were foolishly happy." The top, as they found it, was about fifteen square metres in area. It dropped off precipitously all around, and to the south a sharp ridge declined steeply for more than four thousand metres to the Seward Glacier far, far below. Every other feature lay far beyond like pebbles on a beach: away to the southwest Mount Saint Elias and the Pacific Ocean; to the south stood Mount Augusta; to the east rose Logan's east peak; and to the north stretched the vast snow regions of the upper Logan Glacier. It took only twenty minutes for their elation to subside and the cold to penetrate their clothing. The long descent began.

Shortly after they started down, a new storm blew in, and, although there was more than twenty hours of daylight at that time of year, they were soon in a dim light. Earlier that day the last wands had been used and now the tracks had filled with snow. Without proper bearings they agreed to halt. At one-thirty in the morning on 24 June they bivouacked in a snowbank. A hole was dug, using ice axes and snowshoes as shovels. At fifty-eight hundred metres it was exhausting work.

Tired, cold, and hungry, the men sat the night through without hot food or proper rest. Their faces were plastered with snow; nose drippings froze in place. Their balaclavas were encrusted with ice formed from breath moisture. Their parkas, mitts, and mocassins were stiff as cardboard. The temperature fell to $-24°$ C ($-12°$ F) that night. By daylight the falling snow blinded them and restricted visibility to fifteen metres. In the whiteout no bearing whatever could be fixed. Ground and sky were fused into one featureless universe without horizon. But movement had to be effected, regardless of the direction they should take. The cold was sinking deeper into their flesh, and their strength was draining rapidly. With many more hours of these conditions, they would be rendered helpless.

At noon MacCarthy ordered a start, but reaction to his

directions was slow, and it was two hours before they moved off. Taylor led, and the others staggered along in his steps. Into a deep blanket of snow he wallowed and thrust his axe. The storm raged on. Without lateral or vertical bearings, he could not see what lay ahead or below him; he merely floundered forward. Then, in one horrifying instant, he disappeared from sight. Quickly MacCarthy caught up to Read, who was holding the rope taut in his hands. Taylor had fallen over a cliff and lay half buried in the snow ten metres beneath their feet. Breathless for a while he found the low point on the cliff and groped his way out, shaken but unhurt. Within minutes the same thing happened to MacCarthy.

The shock of these startling experiences was relieved when Read discovered a willow marker. Spirits rose as they began to follow the path of slender black beacons towards Plateau Camp. At each wand the group paused until the next was sighted ahead of them; every thirty metres or so the wands hailed them homewards. By eight thirty that night Lambart's rope reached the camp, but not MacCarthy's. While stopping to fix a pack his rope lost sight of the others and became disorientated. They backtracked toward the summit. It was only after an hour or more, when Carpé questioned the angle of the slope, that they realized their error and reversed directions.

All night they wandered in a nightmare world of half light and ghostly images. Ice cliffs appeared and seemed to block their passage; barns and sheds were perceived where no such refuges could exist. They stopped twice to rest in miserable little snow holes; their strength and endurance were ebbing, and they needed shelter badly.

At five in the morning on 25 June they found Plateau Camp, forty-three hours after they had left it. The primus stoves roared as Taylor heated boned chicken, granulated potatoes au gratin, and melted snow for Ovaltine. An hour later, exhausted, they lay back and slept.

On 26 June the expedition abandoned all nonessential supplies and equipment and headed down. As they approached the main crest below their fly camp, another hurricane struck. To add to the difficulties caused by the wind, the slope was crusted with hard snow. The conditions demanded a change from snowshoes to crampons and because the bindings were frozen this became a terrible ordeal. Fingers exposed to do the work became frostbitten. Some men were close to exhaustion, some were partially snow blind, and all had their feet and hands penetrated by frost. The situation was the most menacing they had encountered. By midafternoon they managed to reach the dividing crest, cross it, and find life-saving shelter in its lee. They rested briefly.

They staggered into Windy Camp with only sufficient strength to recover their shoe packs but abandoned all else to the mountain; then, they pursued their downwards path into a dense fog and heavy snowfall. In the evening light the men, spent and weary, floundered and fought their way through the ice fall, its passages heavy with snow. Four times they changed from snowshoes to crampons and back again. On the last slope above King Col Camp where avalanche conditions existed, they wallowed straight downwards, caring little for anything but to reach the tents.

For thirty-six hours the party rested while MacCarthy counted the cost of the expedition in human terms: "All first joints of my fingers and thumbs frostbitten and turning black, Lambart's toes frozen, Foster's big toe and two fingers, Carpé two toes and two fingers, Andy one finger."

It was difficult to start down again. Below the King Glacier icefall the men recovered their Yukon sled and transferred their packs to it. At nine that evening they stood above Cascades Icefall, dazed but with the advance base camp in full view. At midnight 28 June they reached its shelter. Thin, blistered, and worn out, MacCarthy wrote in his diary, "Tents in bad shape, but I [am] in worse condition."

Cascade Camp provided relief, rehabilitation, and relative security, but civilization and home were still a long way off. Two sleds were loaded with the remaining outfit neces-

73

sary for the return trip. On 1 July the retreat resumed, and that night, at Turn Camp, a bird was seen and water ran on the ice. They were beginning to feel human again. Travelling by night because the glacier was wet during the day, they discovered two food caches had been destroyed by bears. The resulting shortage drove them forwards despite severely injured feet. The first cache found intact was reached at seven-thirty in the evening of 5 July. The next day they arrived at Hubrick's camp to be met by Laing. Morgan and Hall had already gone out, he said. For the rest of them, it was a welcome stop. They revelled in hot baths, more food, and the sight of green vegetation, the first they had seen in more than six weeks. But the retreat was not over.

The town of McCarthy was still a hundred and thirty kilometres away. With damaged, frostbitten feet the prospect of walking this distance along the gravelly shores of the Chitina River was horrendous. The men elected to build rafts. Two were constructed, each suitable for carrying three men. Laing, for his part, decided to wait for a pack train to carry the specimens he had collected. As it turned out, it was a wise decision.

With steering poles in position, they pushed the rafts into the main stream of the Chitina. On 11 July, Taylor, Read, and Lambart made a successful eighty-kilometre run downstream to a point fifty kilometres from McCarthy. They walked the remaining distance the following day and announced their success to the world. But MacCarthy, Carpé, and Foster, on the other float, ran only thirty kilometres and then overturned in the rapids. The three fought a desperate and losing struggle to land the upturned raft and salvage their remaining baggage. There was nothing for them to do but walk, hungry, frostbitten, and weary, the remaining hundred kilometres to the railhead at McCarthy. At noon on 15 July they made it.

Fame followed success; articles, speeches, reports, and international acclaim became the aftermath of the great expedition. For Taylor, who had contributed so greatly throughout every phase, the Alpine Club of Canada voted life membership. For MacCarthy there was tremendous prestige. He had set new standards of physical endurance, willful determination, and capability under stress.

That summer, MacCarthy reported on the expedition at the ACC Lake O'Hara camp. His account was received with great interest, and he was showered with admiration by his fellow members. Little did they know, however, that he had given more to the ascent of the mountain than was evident. In 1928 he entered the Mayo Clinic at Rochester, Minnesota, complaining of persistent stomach pains. The doctors' treatment, he believed, effected "satisfactory repairs," but the ailment was a recurring condition which he would suffer for the rest of his life. His illness was thought to have resulted from the hardships of the Logan campaign.

When the depression struck in the thirties, MacCarthy found it necessary to make some major changes in his business affairs. He "took back" a property he once owned called Carvel Hall located in Annapolis, Maryland. He spent much of his time there during his remaining years because it kept him close to the sea.

In 1942 Bess MacCarthy suffered a stroke, and MacCarthy himself was rushed to the hospital on two different occasions to undergo transfusions for blood losses caused by stomach hemorrhages. Greatly concerned about his wife and about his own health, he wrote to Fred Lambart shortly after Christmas 1943, "My dear Fred: Yes I am still in the land of the living although both Bess and I have had a rather bad time of it since a year ago." That winter they went south to their cottage at Camden, South Carolina, where they could have air and light exercise and enjoy their dogs. It brought Bess little respite; later in the year she died.

MacCarthy tried to contribute in some way to the American war effort by serving on the Gasoline Rationing Board, but his health and business affairs prevented much involvement. He was, by that time a man of considerable property and wealth. Without heirs, he could afford to contribute to any cause he thought worthy, and, in 1946, when the American Alpine Club decided to buy a property in New York as their permanent headquarters, he and Henry Hall donated fifteen thousand dollars each to get a fund under way.

Among his other interests he supported the SPCA, the Navy football team, and wrote widely to his mountaineering friends encouraging them to visit him at the old sailing town of Annapolis, in which he took great pride. In his last years he kept as active as possible. Elements of his early physical endurance never left him. He continued to climb as late as 1944 and attended ACC camps until 1952 when he was seventy-six years old.

Eventually the journey across North America to the Rockies and his declining health forced him to give up that pleasurable annual holiday. He was left with the memories of his many accomplishments and past victories. On 11 October 1956, at the age of eighty, Albert MacCarthy died.

Chapter Four

Conrad Kain
1883 – 1934

*It is well that our sport should have at
least one outstanding figure upon whom
we can look back with admiration.
Conrad Kain will never be forgotten in
Canadian mountaineering, and a little
hero worship, one feels, will do no harm.*

J. Monroe Thorington,
noted American mountain historian

Kain's climb was checked by an unexpected problem. A gendarme, spanning the entire width of the ridge, completely blocked the route. Its western side comprised a series of elongated cliffs rising sharply from the glacier, far below, to the pointed horn, above. On the right a shelf led to the east face, ending in a six-hundred-metre drop.

Kain climbed a short wall immediately before him and surveyed the gendarme on its west side. Only one available route seemed possible: a smooth slab about two metres in width with only a hint of a depression for the feet. Beyond was a small, slanting crack with a slight bulge. He looked for a rock projection to anchor the rope but there was none.[1]

As he saw no other plausible crossing, Kain stepped onto the steep, blank rock. With great attention to balance, he began to cross the slab. Each move threatened a slip which could end only in a disastrous fall.

On reaching the small slanting crack, Kain found his

[1] Rock pitons were not commonly used in 1916, the year Kain made this climb, and were scorned by purists.

position so awkward he was unable to get a good hold. Thinking he had started on the wrong foot, he retreated. On his second attempt he was surprised to find himself in exactly the same position. Balancing on the toes of his left foot, he reached up in the hope of placing his arm inside the crack and grasping a good handhold. That didn't work either. He retreated again.

On his next crossing he brought an ice axe with the express purpose of inserting it into the bottom of the crack in such a way that he could place his left foot on it and thereby gain a little height from which he might find the much-needed handhold. The axe was not only of little use, it became a nuisance. Kain realized the only way of disposing of it was to let it drop, which he would not do. He crossed back again to get rid of the axe.

On his fourth attempt he grew bolder, and, jamming his left arm into the crack, he found a hold higher up for his right hand. He made one uncertain move before pulling himself over the bulge. Much to his relief, Kain found it was an easy climb above to a safe stance behind the gendarme. He called down, "I make it." It had taken an hour and a half for him to gain no more than twenty metres.

This "bugaboo" gendarme, which gave the spire its name, was Kain's most difficult climb in Canada. The date: 29 August 1916.

About eighty kilometres southwest of Vienna, there is a rock cliff called the Raxalpe (2008). Below it lies the village of Nasswald, founded in 1731 by Protestant woodcutters. Konrad Kain was born there on 10 August 1883, the first child of a Florentine mother and an Austrian father.[2]

Konrad attended a separate school, where there was but one teacher for almost a hundred pupils. As a result, his seven years of formal education were nearly fruitless, and when he left school in 1897 at the age of fourteen, he could

[2]Kain's Christian name was Anglicized to Conrad after his arrival in Canada.

scarcely write his name. To make matters worse, his father had died five years earlier, leaving the then nine-year-old boy as the oldest male in the family. Without the father's support, the Kains lived a frugal existence.

After Konrad left school, he first became a goatherd and then a quarryman. In November 1902, when he was barely nineteen years old, he protested the wrongful dismissal of a friend from the quarry, and was himself fired from his job. Forced to leave Nasswald to find work, he experienced a hard winter. He stole bread to eat, was chased by dogs, was arrested as a vagrant, and injured his feet badly in worn-out boots. At home the burgomaster saw little good in the young man, speculating Konrad would "get mixed up with the Socialists and end up on the gallows."

Konrad was rehired at the quarry the following spring but decided to augment his meagre income by poaching on the weekends. In this pursuit he had bad luck. On his second hunt, the cliffs were in a treacherous condition, covered with hard ice and snow. Despite this he managed to stalk three chamois, and when the blast of his gun resounded, one of the animals fell in a cloud of smoke.

After he had skinned the chamois, the young poacher began his descent, heavily loaded with the wet skin, his rifle, and staff. But by now the sun had set and it was difficult to find a way safely in the dark. Cautiously, he moved downwards. Then, without warning, he half-stepped and half-slipped over a cliff into space.

In an instant, he came crashing to a halt against a tree. He got up, shook himself, and almost immediately lost control again, riding down the slope on the seat of his pants. When he came to a stop the second time, his nerves were shattered and the chamois skin was lost. To his immense relief, however, he saw lanterns on a road below and was able to find a path to safety.

Shortly afterwards, Konrad made a sober review of his short poaching career. He wrote, "I came to the proper conclusion: *I sold my gun."*

The Raxalpe is a rock formation which offers a wide variety of short climbs all of which were familiar to Kain who grew up in the shadow of its cliffs. For more than a hundred years, mountaineers from Vienna have used this area to learn and practise rock-climbing techniques. Their ranks include many novices eager to employ local boys to guide them.

Kain took his first paid guiding job there at Easter 1903. The climb went well at first. But when he was about thirty metres up a chimney, he removed his rucksack and shoes to complete the last difficult section and, while preparing to continue, accidentally upset both his sack and his boots.[3] To his horror and humiliation, he watched them fall down and out of the chimney and fly over the heads of his clients. There was much embarrassment. Kain finished the route but spent the rest of the day hobbling among the rocks at the foot of the cliffs in search of his equipment.

After eight weeks of hated compulsory military training in 1904, Kain again returned to the quarry but was refused employment because of his frequent absences to go climbing. Forced to choose one activity or the other, he chose what he liked to do best.

Expending immense energy over the next five years, Kain trained himself as a guide and established his climbing reputation in the Alps. Most of the great mountains in Austria, Italy, France, and Switzerland were ascended by him. In Corsica, he made his first, first ascent on Capo Tafonato. During this period, Kain compiled a record which few mountaineers attain in an entire lifetime. On 10 October 1906, he was presented with his *FührerBuch* formally authorizing him to act as a professional guide.[4]

[3] During that period, climbing short difficult sections in stockinged feet was an accepted practice to increase the purchasing power of the foot, to say nothing of what it did to enhance the audacious image of the guide in the eyes of his client.

[4] The guide's book, or *FührerBuch*, is used as the official record of all climbs undertaken by the guide. Unfortunately, Kain's book with all accurate records of his earliest ascents was lost. We know of these activities only through his subsequent writings and the personal journal which he maintained.

Other events took place which greatly affected his future. Kain acquired one of his most important clients, Dr. Erich Pistor of Vienna, who took Kain on his first foreign tour and later assisted his entry into Canada. Kain, aware that he was undereducated, went to Vienna to study English with Mrs. Pistor, who was herself English-born. He was very lonely and homesick living away from his family but was dissuaded from quitting his studies by a young woman. Who she was no one knows, but his feelings for her were obvious. "I cannot thank her in words for all the good she did me. But I will hold her memory [dear] all my life."

And in 1906, at Gstätterboden in the Tyrol, Kain met Amelia Malek,[5] a young botanist. They became warm, lifelong friends. He sent her flowers from the different ranges in which he climbed as well as his journal, which she preserved until after his death. It is through this document we know the details of his early years.[6]

While climbing in the Alps in 1908, Kain nearly lost his life during a few dangerous moments. Returning from the Barre des Ecrins in the Dauphinè District of France, he chose to descend via an unfamiliar route which required the passage of a steep, narrow couloir about two hundred metres in length. As there was need to cut steps, he and his party were exposed to falling rocks for some time. Suddenly, without warning, rockfall began. Two members of the party had already reached a position of protection, but Kain and one other companion were caught in the line of fire. Kain wrote,

There was no protection at all for the last two climbers. I took an extra turn of rope around my anchored axe and lifted my rucksack higher against my head. At that very moment, the stone avalanche arrived. One stone struck me on the shoulder, then seconds later another hit me

[5]Amelia Malek lived out her later life at Reichenau, Austria. She died of starvation in 1945.

[6]Most of his writings appear in his book *Where the Clouds Can Go*, published posthumously in 1935 under the aegis of his friend and client, J. Monroe Thorington.

on the head, giving me a severe wound. Blood streamed; I could hold myself no longer, fell, and slipped down the length of the rope. I was unconscious for several minutes, and they carried me beneath a rock and bound up my injuries.

Despite his wounds, Kain guided his party to safety.

At the end of the 1908 season, Kain evaluated his life again. "I [am] just the same as in the year preceding — healthy, even contented, but with nothing in my pockets! What [will] the year 1909 bring forth?" With no increased likelihood of bettering himself at home, he decided to emigrate to Canada. He asked Pistor for help.

At first, Pistor wrote to the Canadian Pacific Railway Company seeking a guide's position for his friend at one of the company's mountain hotels. When this failed, he wrote to Arthur Wheeler, president of the Alpine Club of Canada, and introduced Kain with these words: "He is a fine fellow. With the ladies he is as gentle as a lamb, but with the men he is like a lion." A favourable reply was received, and Kain was engaged at a rate of two dollars a day plus two dollars for each mountain excursion.

In May 1909, Kain said goodbye to his weeping mother and, overcome with tenderness, wrote, "It was really a strange feeling to say goodbye to the mountains of my home. I stopped more than once and looked back. I could scarcely drag myself away."

In Vienna he said farewell to his friends. "To those who were dearest to me I went last of all. With some I had to hold back tightly lest I reveal my emotion."

He travelled to Liverpool and sailed on 4 June aboard the *Empress of Britain*. On his long train journey across the continent he recorded, "From Quebec to Winnipeg one doesn't see much of fertile Canada. Nothing but bushes and rocks." And, in Saskatchewan he wrote, "There begin those awful annoying mosquitoes, of which naturally no land agent in Europe informs a person!" He arrived at Banff in the middle of a dark, clear night and the next day met Wheeler, who put him to work on the construction of the Alpine Club of Canada's new clubhouse on Sulphur Mountain.

At the ACC's Annual Camp at Lake O'Hara that summer, Kain was commissioned to be the club's first official guide. Before the camp opened he made his first ascent in Canada, climbing Mount Odaray (3098) with Wheeler and Val Fynn, and a week or so later climbed Mount Victoria (3464) alone.

Aside from making many ascents, the summer of 1909 was a great learning period for the young Austrian. Porcupines, he discovered, would eat his boots even when he was sleeping on them, and he noted that "every climber [in Canada], male or female, must carry for himself . . . the guide is not looked on as a beast of burden." Engaged by Wheeler for survey work around Rogers Pass, Kain made solo climbs of Avalanche Mountain (2864) and Mount Sir Donald (3297).

When the 1909 season was over, Kain received his summer's pay, amounting to $410. Equal to two thousand Austrian Kronen, it was a king's ransom to him. He counted the money over and over and set aside $100 to be sent to his mother. In his mind's eye, he imagined her joy at receiving this sum. He began to weep. "My eyes dissolved in tears, for I knew my mother loved me and that I was the only one upon whom she could depend."

Kain now had to find work for the winter. In January 1910 he was employed by an Austrian farmer in the Beaver Hills, near Fort Saskatchewan, Alberta. It probably would have been a typical prairie winter except for one thing: the farmer wanted him to marry one of the local girls and settle down. The farmer even had someone in mind.

When Kain met Marie, he found her young and attractive, with a strong body well developed by farm labour. Her family treated him to whisky, homemade roasted sausages, and sauerkraut and then went to the barn, ostensibly to view a new colt. Kain was left alone with Marie. The two shared a friendship toast, and to Kain's surprise, she embraced and kissed him. Becoming flushed, she opened her eyes widely and suddenly burst out, "Do I please you? Do you love me?"

Nearly overwhelmed, Kain fought a growing desire to return her embraces but thought to himself, "One must be a man, not a fool." When Marie's parents returned, he was greatly relieved, but as he left the house he was unable to avoid a noisy parting kiss from her.

In the weeks that followed, pressure from all sides was put on Kain to marry Marie. He resisted firmly and fortified himself by reading his diary and letters from those at home whom he loved. If he married her, he realized, his life would be greatly altered, and he wanted to avoid that at all cost.

A month or so later after a Sunday church service, Kain received a courteous invitation from Marie's parents which he felt could not be declined. He returned to their farm, and when evening came the girl's parents insisted he stay the night. While being shown to his room by Marie's mother, Kain was told pointedly that her daughter slept next door, while she and her husband slept downstairs! "Well, everything is understood now!" Kain thought to himself.

At the appropriate hour, Marie retired to her room. But soon there was a knocking on Kain's door, and she presented him with an extra blanket. Her room, she said, was much warmer. Kain convinced her to return to her bed but admitted to himself he was increasingly tempted to follow her. How easy it would be to give in to his weakening flesh and declare his love. And the night had only begun!

Marie would not let up. Once more she returned to Kain's door, this time concerned about noises. She asked him to comfort her in her room. It desperation Kain explained they were not married. "But there's another bed," she said. Resigned, he got up and went with her.

After she closed the door, Marie embraced her young man, made his bed, and put out the light. They retired separately — until Marie lit the lamp again. This time Kain was "fit to be tied" and, growing angry, chided her for her behaviour. She started to cry and asked his forgiveness. She realized he was a good man who was trying his best to protect her. They both fell asleep.

When Kain went to the kitchen for breakfast the next morning, Marie's mother asked, *"Were you with her?"* "No!" was his reply. The mother could have wept, but Kain "was proud of having been master over [him] self."

In the spring he worked with a railroad gang northwest of Edmonton for a short time and then attended the Alpine Club camp at Consolation Valley, ascending Mounts Fay (3238), Bident (3084), Temple (3547), and Eiffel Peak (3076), all easy climbs of long duration. In August, on his twenty-seventh birthday, he climbed Des Poilus (3161), and in September he made his first hunt in the Bugaboo Group of the Purcell Range.

Kain was very enterprising and continually experimenting with new things. In February 1911, he set up a small ski jump on Tunnel Mountain at Banff and interested local people in the sport. It was the first jump ever constructed there, resulting in the start of recreational skiing in the area of Banff.

That same year Kain joined the Yellowhead Pass expedition, a survey party led by Arthur Wheeler, which included Donald (Curly) Phillips, an outfitter; Ned Hollister from the U.S. National Museum; Byron Harmon, the photographer from Banff; and George Kinney, who had earlier made several unsuccessful attempts on Mount Robson. Kain and Kinney made the first ascent of Pyramid Mountain (2766) near Jasper before the expedition, and once in the Robson area Kain was employed to carry topographical equipment and to do camp chores. But there was no real climbing. Kain and Harmon were permitted to make the first ascent of Robson's neighbour, Mount Resplendent (3426), but the grand prize, Mount Robson itself, remained as remote as ever. Wheeler was saving it for an Alpine Club ascent some time in the future.

One afternoon, Kain, bored with his work and disappointed by the climbing opportunity which was being lost, left camp alone. He planned to climb Whitehorn Mountain (3395), located some kilometres to the west of Robson. Eventually he reached Whitehorn Pass, crossed it, and descended the west side to a glacier, its yawning crevasses dangerously poised to accept a sacrifice. When he reached Whitehorn's southwest ridge he heard thunder. Pausing a moment to appraise the situation, he decided to go on. It was his only chance to gain the peak and his objective was near. He climbed quickly to the virgin summit.

Kain was unable to build a cairn on the top because of deep snow, so he descended about fifty metres to some exposed rocks, built a stone man, and left the following record in a match holder: "Conrad Kain, Führer von Wien, Bei Sturm 11-8-1911 ("Conrad Kain, guide from Vienna, in a storm 11-8-1911"). It was actually 10 August, his twenty-eighth birthday. By the time he had finished, it was almost night, rain was falling, and the mountain conditions were deteriorating rapidly as he began his descent. He wrote,

The route of return was the same but more dangerous. Before I came to the pass, the sun sank behind the mountains. I should have liked to see the sun two hours longer.

I thought that I could get across the glacier by daylight. To my astonishment, I found that the snowbridge, which had brought me on the rocks, was broken. I had hard work to get on the glacier. I was quite helpless in the rain. I wanted to stay on the glacier overnight; but I could not stand it longer than ten minutes, and the cold warned me that I must go on, whatever happened. My one bit of good fortune was the lightning, which showed me the way. Step by step, I had to feel with the axe to find whether I [was] on the edge of a crevasse. Very often the axe fell right through and, more than once, I thought: "This is the last step." I tried again to stay overnight on the glacier, but in five minutes I would have been frozen stiff from head to foot. I felt indescribably glad when I found rocks underfoot; I yodeled with delight.

Once on the rocks, Kain was safe. At daybreak, he reached camp in a pouring rain and went to bed. A little later, Kinney woke him, and, without saying a word, Kain pointed in the direction of Whitehorn. They both grinned.

Two days later, Kain returned to the glacier and looked for his tracks. He was shocked. The glacier's entire surface was a scene of rot and decay. Rain had softened the snowbridges, leaving them slumped and weblike. He had taken tremendous chances. A fall into a crevasse would have been fatal. If the plunge had not killed him, exposure to cold would have. "I was appalled when I saw the dangerous crevasses," he wrote. "It was one of the craziest and most foolhardy undertakings that I ever made in the mountains."

Kain spent the winter of 1911–1912 trapping along the Moose River near Robson. Nature brought him both frustration, danger, and reward. In November he spent a whole day following the tracks of a bull caribou up and down a treed mountainside without ever seeing his prey. By nightfall Kain was totally exhausted and barely made it back to camp. But the following day he was at it again.

In a neighbouring valley, while searching for goats, Kain found some fresh tracks in the snow which led to higher ground. The snow was deep and became deeper with altitude, but the hope of a kill kept him climbing. At last, on the highest slope, he caught sight of a billy goat. The goat had had trouble reaching the pass ahead because of cornices, but after succeeding it stopped on a small lookout from which it could watch its pursuer.

The snow slope Kain was climbing was very dangerous, and there was every chance the hunter would start an avalanche. Just as he came below the pass, where the goat watched, there were several loud reports, and cracks opened up everywhere across the slope.

Kain tried desperately to keep his balance in the moving mass, but snow blocks broke, tilted, and spun. Underneath, the powder snow gave way, and the whole surface started to seethe. In an effort to save himself, Kain quickly turned, faced downhill, and, sitting, placed his rifle across his knees. Images flashed through his mind as the avalanche quickly gained top speed. At the edge of a precipice, he closed his eyes and was hurtled through the air in a torrent of snow and blocks. He came to a dead stop; the avalanche was over.

The sensation of recent moments faded quickly. All was quiet. Kain's head was above the surface, but he was suffering a sharp pain in his back and he could not move his legs, which were packed tight. After fifteen minutes or more, he managed to free himself and, looking down, saw blood in the hole where he had been. Feeling his aching back, he confirmed that it was his blood. Above him, he saw the six-metre precipice over which he had just plummeted. He was lucky to be alive.

Kain emptied his collar of snow and glanced across the avalanche debris. A distant black spot caught his eye. His interest was aroused. Struggling towards the spot, he thought he heard a faint groan. The hunt was not over. The goat, too, had been in the slide.

Buried by the avalanche with his horns and ears just above the surface, the doomed billy goat was fighting for his life. When he reached the imprisoned animal, Kain drew his knife and cut its throat admitting later he "did not feel like a sportsman . . . but the law of nature in the woods is a strong one — kill or starve."

In camp that same afternoon, Kain treated his wounds with Zambuck ointment, fixed in place with a clean piece of floursack stuck around the edges with melted spruce gum.

The hunter-trapper spent four months on the trapline that winter, sometimes travelling forty to fifty kilometres a day. He slept forty nights in the open and survived life and death struggles when all he had to eat was roasted squirrel, whisky-jack, or soup made from a discarded marten carcass. He had learned how to survive in the wilderness.

In the spring, Kain received an invitation from Ned Hollister, who wanted him to join a scientific expedition to Siberia to collect small vertebrates in the Altai Mountains. Kain thought it was a long way to go "to trap mice," but he couldn't resist the adventure or his affection for Hollister. When the expedition was over, he went home to Austria to see his mother. It was to be for the last time. He never saw his homeland again.

Kain's desire to see more of the world caused him to forego trapping the following winter and voyage to Australia and New Zealand. He trusted his luck to find employment. But by January 1913, he was still unemployed and virtually destitute. As if in answer to his prayers, he received a letter from Arthur Wheeler. "I want you for Robson Camp. There will be several attempts to make the ascent of Robson. How does that prospect strike you, old boy?" Without hesitation, Kain embarked on the next ship.

The Indians call Mount Robson *Yuh-Hai-Has-Kun*, "The Mountain of the Spiral Road." Robson (3954) is located in British Columbia immediately west of the Alberta provincial boundary near Jasper. The snows of this great mountain flow into the nearby Fraser River and travel sixteen hundred kilometres to empty into the Pacific Ocean at Vancouver. When seen from the west, Robson is an impressive sight. Its southwest face rises in a gigantic wall of terraced rock, divided by a great couloir topped with ice. Its summit is often shrouded in mist. Few mountain walls compare to this face as it soars, dominating everything three thousand metres below it.

Before 1913 five attempts had been made on the mountain, four of which were led by the Reverend George Kinney. The highest point reached was the Dome (3078), an ice-covered buttress positioned at the head of the Robson Glacier, but Robson's summit still remained untrodden. Kain recognized its difficulties and wrote to Amelia Malek, "I expect to have hard and possibly dangerous work . . . Mount Robson is a wicked peak."

On 30 July 1913, after an ascent of Mount Resplendent, Kain returned to the tree line above Robson Pass. There, as arranged, he met two strong and able climbers, Bill Foster, the deputy minister of Public Works for British Columbia; and an American from Summit, New Jersey, Albert MacCarthy, known as Mack. Carrying blankets and firewood, the three men camped at the base of the Extinguisher, a rock tower on the Robson Glacier shaped in the form of a candle extinguisher. As they sat sheltered next to a stone wall that evening, they discussed the next day's assault on the north-east face of the mountain.

The party left camp at 4:30 A.M., 31 July, under a clear, starry sky. Proceeding up the Robson Glacier towards the Dome, they climbed the heavily crevassed icefall which descends the Dome's east side. Once at the Dome, they walked easily across the snow to the foot of the northeast face, which now, at close quarters, soared ominously above them.

Robson's southeast ridge is interrupted only by a shoulder, a relatively flat section between the point of attack and the summit itself. From the shoulder, a glacier hangs down the face to the Dome snow-field. The remainder of the face is unbroken, steep rock crowned by cornices.

Kain believed the ridge could be gained by climbing the rock to the left of the hanging glacier. His plan appeared feasible provided the bergschrund could be crossed; its upper lip was separated from its lower counterpart by a considerable margin.

Kain led off and found a snowbridge which had collapsed into the bergschrund. Using some awkward manoeuvres, he gained the upper lip and sighted a line of ascent which alternated between the ice-glazed rock on the left and the edge of the hanging glacier on the right. The ice slope stood at sixty to sixty-five degrees and promised a lot of laborious step cutting. Swinging his heavy axe with one hand Kain cut more than a hundred steps in a zigzag pattern to a ledge of rock.[7]

Thereafter the face alternated from icy rock walls to mixed snow and ice slopes, tracked by falling stones and studded with projecting rocks. The exposure to falling rock was continuous and nerve wracking. Above them, the cornice threatened to break and sweep everyone down the face. Kain could not help but recall guide Moritz Inderbinen's

[7]The long-shafted ice axes of that period were meant for use with both hands when cutting steps, but on a slope of this angle the use of two hands was impossible.

comments when he attempted the climb with members of the Alpine Club in 1909: "We should all have been kilt." Kain lengthened the rope to his companions in a hope it would increase their protection, but it was doubtful if any security was possible in such an exposed position.

Meanwhile, there was nothing that Foster and MacCarthy could do but stand in their guide's steps, unable to move until he had completed each section. In the shadow of the mountain the cold was intense, and the wind and flying ice chips bit into their flesh. The crest above seemed far away and dangerous, while below all could be lost in a spinning, body-destroying fall. At noon Kain gained the top of the ridge, and their first great obstacle was behind them. The face, four hundred and fifty metres high, had been surmounted for the first time. They stopped to rest.

The climbers followed the ridge. On reaching the shoulder, they looked upon a configuration of steep ice walls, fifteen to twenty metres high, rising in a series of snow-filled terraces. As Kain started to chop steps, the freshly cut ice appeared green, and snow sifted across the incline, blown by a constant wind.

For some time the peak of the mountain was obscured by the steep terraces, but as soon as the slope gave way to a more moderate angle, the summit appeared. A difficult final wall was outflanked by Kain, and as he came to the last, short slope leading onto the top, he turned, smiled, and said, "Gentlemen, that's as far as I can take you." In a moment, the three climbers were the first to stand on the apex of Mount Robson, monarch of the Rockies.

The peak itself was mildly disappointing. It comprised merely two cornices of snow meeting at an angle. But the panoramic view it offered was magnificent. The sky was clear. At an elevation six hundred metres higher than any other mountain in the area, the climbers could see a limitless number of peaks.

After savouring their achievement for about ten minutes, the three men began to shiver. Their clothes, damp from the day's exertions and now caked with snow, were hardening.

The rope was also stiff, it was more like steel cable than a length of hemp. About six o'clock in the evening they began their descent.

At the shoulder Kain chose to descend by the unknown southwest face, which he believed would be less dangerous than their earlier line of ascent. Without knowledge of the route, they made an error in going down too far and were blocked by a precipice. Climbing up again, they found an ice couloir overhung by ice cliffs. Descent via the couloir was very risky, but it seemed the only way.

Foster expressed his confidence in Kain, "Conrad, if it is not too dangerous for you, cutting steps, then don't worry about us. We'll trust you and fortune." On reaching a place of safety, they rested briefly but soon were driven on by the thought of a fire at the tree line. Unfortunately they were still on the ice when the sun set.

About ten o'clock that night, the party reached bare rock. They elected to bivouac on a shelf about two metres wide. The men removed their boots and placed their feet into their rucksacks. Foster and MacCarthy shared a sack as they only had one between them. Tying his two companions to a rock anchor, Kain made himself as comfortable as possible and quickly fell asleep. He dreamt of a forest with plenty of firewood.

A few grey clouds were reflecting early morning light when Kain awoke. He sat quietly entertaining his thoughts while his companions slept. Every now and then the silence was torn by an avalanche which slipped its moorings and headed for the abyss.

When Foster and MacCarthy awakened, they complained their eyes were swollen shut and very painful. Kain applied some cold poultices to ease their pain, and their eyes partially opened.

Cautiously they started down again. Every few hundred metres, a vertical wall of rotten rock had to be bypassed. A hanging glacier required more than three hours to negotiate. Finally they reached Kinney Lake. For five hours more they toiled uphill back to the camp at Robson Pass. As they strolled in quietly among the tents, they were greeted with joyous congratulations. The victory was complete. But Foster knew it would not have been possible except for Kain. He wrote, "The primary factor in the success of this expedition was . . . the marvellous resource and skill of Conrad Kain."[8]

Kain was a man of slightly less than average height. His brown eyes were his most notable feature. They had depth in colour and expression and reflected instantly his every mood. His clothing always appeared rumpled. He did, however, frequently wear a neck tie on climbs in deference to his clients, who always appeared to him to be of a higher social status than his.

Few paid as much attention to these matters as he did, however. His personality was so vibrant that he captivated everyone who met him. Women referred to him as "dear Conrad," and men saw him as the epitome of what they might like to be — an independent spirit admired for his achievements and loved for his warmth and humour. He was a merciless wit, and when he told stories around a campfire he could render his audience nearly sick with laughter.

Socially amenable, his success with people was strangely contradictive to another dimension of his character. He spent a lot of time alone, thinking about life and conveying his thoughts to only a few close friends. They noted it was his sincerity and good will which were his most distinguishing traits. He had the ability to make lasting relationships with men like Curly Phillips and Byron Harmon. They swore by him.

As a guide he was unsurpassed, imaginative, and inventive. His achievements were made when technique was largely self-developed, equipment very elemental, and

[8]Kain had cut about six hundred steps, a feat of immense strength and endurance when considered in addition to the other hardships of the climb. The northeast face of Mount Robson later became known as the Kain Face. It was not ascended again until 1961.

clothing little more than that worn on the street. About his skills he was self-effacing, saying, "I am better as some, and not so good as others," although no one could determine who was better than he. One client wrote, "He seemed to have an almost uncanny aptitude in ascending apparently inaccessible places," to which remarks Kain usually answered with amusement, "I am used to this game, but people who do this sort of thing for the first time describe it as a very funny sensation."

Kain added greatly to guiding lore, giving it many colourful facets; one is more remembered than others. He once put down a set of guiding principles which stands today without amendment. They are:

> First [the guide] should never show fear. Second, he should be courteous to all, and always give special attention to the weakest member in the party. Third, he should be witty, and able to make up a white lie if necessary on short notice and tell it in a convincing manner. Fourth, he should know when and how to show authority; and when the situation demands it, [he] should be able to give a good scolding to whomsoever deserves it.

The ascent of Mount Robson heralded a new expansive phase in Kain's life. During the Canadian winter of 1913-1914, he spent the first of three summer climbing seasons in New Zealand. In three consecutive years, he completed a total of fifty-nine ascents, of which twenty-nine were firsts. In addition he made a large number of other excursions in the Southern Alps which resulted in new or first traverses of mountains already climbed. Some of his New Zealand adventures brought him fame, and one brought him notoriety.

On 22 February 1914, a party composed of Sydney King and two guides, Thompson and Richmond, were killed by an avalanche on the Linda Glacier of Mount Cook (3764). Kain, who had been simultaneously traversing the mountain in the opposite direction to the ill-fated party, immediately joined the rescue, even though he had been without sleep for many hours. His services in recovering Richmond's body were described as herculean and indispensable. The bodies of King and Thompson were not recovered until fourteen years later. Their badly mutilated remains appeared at the toe of the glacier in 1928.

Kain's mountaineering activity during his last New Zealand season brought great controversy. On 31 January 1916, he undertook a grand traverse of the three peaks of Mount Cook[9] with a woman client who was fifty-nine years old. This route had only been done once before, and then with two guides. Kain's success was greeted by criticism as well as cheers. The grand traverse was hailed as "a marvellous feat unequalled for daring in the annals of the Southern Alps," but even Kain's closest admirers judged him imprudent for undertaking such a dangerous expedition with a woman client of that age.

Nineteen sixteen was the last season for Kain in New Zealand. The tourist department would not reissue licences to private guides. No reason was given for their decision, but Kain believed it reflected wartime prejudices. Although he was now a Canadian citizen, he was regarded as an alien in New Zealand because of his Austrian origin. He was very hurt and disappointed by this experience. He wrote many years later about this period of his life, "It was wartime. I could tell some very interesting stories in connection with this patriotic sentiment, but it is better to forget it."

Meanwhile, each summer Kain returned to Canada. In 1914, he and Albert MacCarthy made the first ascent of Mount Farnham (3457), in the Purcells, thereby establishing the first ascents of the highest peaks in both the Rockies and the Purcells in two successive seasons.

[9]Mount Cook is the highest peak in the Southern Alps of New Zealand. A grand traverse is one in which all peaks of a single mountain massif are climbed by following the summit crest, linking the peaks together in one continuous climbing effort.

By 1916 Kain was working exclusively for MacCarthy. On 19 July of that summer, the pair made one of the most memorable first ascents in the Rockies, that of Mount Louis (2682). Close to Banff but hidden in a side valley, this spectacular limestone tower of closely packed, vertical slabs rises more than a thousand metres above Fortymile Creek. When viewed from the south, the mountain appears as a pair of hands held upwards in supplication.

The day was intended to be only an outing on horseback, but when Kain started searching the lower cliff for a route, MacCarthy followed. The reconnaissance developed into a climb. When the two men returned many hours later, they stopped at the tree line and, looking back, Kain exclaimed, "Ye Gods, Mr. MacCarthy, just look at that; they never will believe we climbed it."[10]

It was the beginning of an unforgettable summer. Kain, MacCarthy, and others headed for the Purcell Range to explore the headwaters of Bugaboo and Vowell Creeks. At the source of these glacial streams rises a compact group of grey granite spires, natural cathedrals against the sky. The towers are vertical and challenging; the rock is clean and solid; and the setting is one of great beauty. Kain called it "one of the most beautiful and charming spots I have seen." None of the great pinnacles had been climbed.

The highest peak in the group, Howser Spire (3399), was ascended and traversed, and two days later Kain led Albert and Bess MacCarthy and John Vincent on the first ascent of Peak Three, later to be known as Bugaboo Spire (3185).

When Kain entered the bush along the Simpson River that fall, he began a period of isolated melancholy. He saw no one for months, living in a small log cabin which he shared with his dog, Bruno, sixteen mice, and a snake called Satan. He read the Bible and wrote to close friends. His letters were filled with introspection which reflected per-

[10]A detailed account of this climb is given in Chapter 3.

[11]Howser Spire was not named at the time of its first ascent. This climb is reported in Chapter 3.

sonal doubt about the value of his guiding career. To one friend he wrote,

> I have now decided to give up mountain guiding. . . . My life as a guide was a life of romance. . . . Don't address to the Alpine Club. You see I must forget them all, otherwise I might go climbing again, and I must not make myself a fool again.

It was true that, except for his mountaineering, Kain did not have much to show for his thirty-three years. And he was tired of bachelor life. When he returned to the Columbia Valley in June 1917 he married Henriquita (Granito) Ferreira, an attractive, dark-haired woman with a slim and graceful figure. His marriage was to be a source of great happiness to him after so many years alone.

Hetta Kain was born near Georgetown, British Guiana, in 1884. She was educated in a convent where she learned to speak Portuguese and some Hindustani, as well as English. Upon graduation, she married J. Ferreira, and they had a daughter. In 1913, after her husband died, Hetta emigrated to Canada. She worked at different places around Wilmer, British Columbia, and for a while was a maid at Karmax Ranch, which was owned by the MacCarthys. It was there she met Kain.

For three years after their marriage Kain and Hetta lived on MacCarthy's ranch. Then, during the summer of 1920, they purchased 8.3 acres of sloping land above the village of Wilmer, a lovely setting overlooking the Columbia Valley. The land was bisected by an irrigation ditch, and the slopes below it were fertile and green. Here, next to a prominent poplar tree, Kain built a small, two-room, white clapboard house, which, under Hetta's care, was soon covered with columbine and sweet peas.[12]

Kain recovered from his bout of melancholy, and his working life continued as before — hunting and outfitting in the fall (including a trip to Alaska), trapping all winter, and

[12]The Kain house accidentally burnt to the ground in 1975, severely damaging, but not destroying, the now mighty poplar tree.

gardening and guiding in the summer. Never a good shot, he was a better trapper. Once he even snared a bear in its den. Occasionally a traveller would find one of Kain's inscribed blazes along his trapline: "A hell of a trip — soft snow," or, "Wind blowing hard; snow drifting in: what a romantic life this trapping game is!"

Perhaps because he knew he would not be a leader in the mountains indefinitely, he continued to make first ascents and to repeat old ones. In March 1919 he climbed Jumbo Mountain (3399) in the Purcells, alone and on snowshoes. It was the first winter ascent of any Canadian peak over 3350 metres (11,000 feet). Kain made the climb from Farnham Creek in an amazing four and a half hours. By this time his reputation as a successful guide had spread throughout the entire mountaineering community of North America.

"Conrad Kain [is] perhaps the best guide that has ever been in the country," wrote Jim Simpson to Roy Thorington in 1923. Thorington accepted his advice to employ Kain and thus began an important friendship. That summer at the Columbia Icefield they climbed Mounts Castleguard (3077), Columbia (3747), Athabasca (3491), North Twin (3684), and Saskatchewan (3342). The latter two climbs were first ascents.

Similarly in 1924 at Athabasca Pass, they climbed Mounts Hooker (3286), Kane (3048), Brown (2791), and Oates (3115). In the Ramparts southwest of Jasper they were the first to gain the summit of Simon Peak (3322). And that season also, Kain, now forty-one, returned as chief guide to the ACC at Robson Pass Camp. Robson had not been climbed since his first successful attempt in 1913. From a high camp on the southwest face, he led four new parties to the summit, which included ascents by the first four women to climb the mountain. (Phyl Munday was one of them.)[13] He concluded this amazing year with a new route of Mount Edith Cavell (3363) via its east ridge and the first ascent of Mount King Edward (3475) at the Columbia Icefield.

[13]See Chapter 6.

The year 1924 was Kain's last great season of climbing, although he remained active every year. "I had to record my first defeat," was how he described his failure to climb Snowpatch Spire in 1925. Five years later at forty-six he attempted his second ascent of Bugaboo Spire and also failed due to lack of physical conditioning and his state of health, to which he paid little attention. On his fiftieth birthday, however, 10 August 1933, he made the third ascent of Mount Louis with Henry Kingman, an American, and was delighted not only with his success but with finding the record of his first ascent which he had made seventeen years earlier. His last climb occurred on 8 September 1933 in the Purcells, when he made the first ascent of a peak later to bear his name, Mount Conrad (3252). In a photograph taken that summer, he did not look well.

Meanwhile, the Great Depression had reached the Columbia Valley, and it was felt by everyone. Kain was tired of battling for his living. With little economic security and his best physical years behind him, he wondered what would happen to Hetta and himself. He wrote to Thorington, "The depression has hit me hard, last summer [1932] I had no work for myself and the horses"; then again in January 1933 he wrote, "I am having a hard winter, no luck at trapping or anything. There is no money in farm products, which have to be sold at or below cost of production."

About this time Hetta was found to be suffering from a bowel obstruction. She was driven to Cranbrook, where an operation was performed at Saint Eugene's Hospital. Infection set in. She died on 7 February at the age of forty-eight. Kain was grief stricken.

When he returned to Wilmer, he found things very different. In a letter to Thorington he wrote, "I feel sorry to say that my little place does not look so nice as it did when my dear old girl looked after it in my absents *(sic)*." And a few weeks later, "At times I get so damenable *(sic)* lonely. I miss my dear old sweetheart more than ever."

And loneliness was not his only problem; other things were going wrong. In October, Kain began to experience severe headaches. He was advised to go to Calgary for diagnosis; the doctors there found nothing serious and merely extracted a tooth. But they were wrong.

His niece, Vera (Hurst) Wikman, recalled, after he returned to Wilmer, "Uncle began to frighten us. He would suddenly get up and wander around talking to himself. He became delirious and rambled on about who was going to take care of his horses." On 11 November 1933, Kain wrote his last letter to Thorington:[14]

Dear Doc,

Thanks for letters and pictures. I have been sick for over six weeks and feeling not to (sic) good right now. Did you receive the rucksack?

With kind regards,
Sincerely yours,
Conrad Kain

The next month, Kain was hospitalized in Cranbrook. As his headaches increased, he developed left hemiplegia, a paralysis of the left side of his body. He became intensely drowsy. As the disease progressed, his swallowing became more difficult, and it was nearly impossible to arouse him. Another niece, Enid (Hurst) Hanson, described him at that time: "He has become very weak, and childish, he does not know anyone, he does not understand to eat, he really does not know anything." Kain's family thought he was suffering from spinal meningitis, but his physicians diagnosed his illness as encephalitis lethargica, sleeping sickness, and one wrote to Thorington, "Poor Conrad's days are numbered." He could not last. The great guide of a thousand expeditions was dying.

Conrad Kain passed away at 12:30 A.M. on 2 February

---

[14]Kain corresponded with Thorington for ten years. Thorington, who was editor of the *American Alpine Journal*, gathered documents relating to his friend and other noted climbers. When Kain died, Thorington, who was fluent in German, wrote to Amelia Malek and thus gained access to Kain's earlier records. Since then, Thorington's collection has been donated to Princeton University.

1934. He was buried the following day at Cranbrook. When news of his death became known, tributes flowed from Canada, the United States, New Zealand, and Austria. They spoke as "the tribe of Con," a single voice bearing him praise in every way. As might be expected, it was one of his old trail companions, Jim Simpson, who praised him best:

> Conrad gave every ounce of his best at all times. He would die for you, if need be, quicker than most men think of living. No matter what his creed, his color or his nationality, he was measured by a man's yardstick, no other. We shall all miss him.

Chapter Five

Ed Feuz
1884 –

*There is no greater glory for a man . . . than
that which he wins by his own hands and feet.*

Homer

It was still early in the season, and guests had yet to arrive at
Chateau Lake Louise. The three guides, on a routine inspec-
tion of the Abbot hut, had promised some of the younger
cooks from the hotel to take them on the climb provided
they carried wood for the hut stove.

The party was well up the Victoria Glacier and making
good progress when they heard a sharp report, then a
rumble, then a roar. Instinctively they stopped, frozen in
their tracks, trying to determine the source of the sound. As
they looked quickly about, a chill of frightening realization
rushed down their backs. They had no doubts — a giant
avalanche was rushing towards them, and they were in its
path.

Ed Feuz shouted urgently to the others and ran for the
wall farthest away from the danger. Near the rocks he tried
desperately to plant his ice axe in the snow slope to anchor
himself against the onslaught of the slide, but he could not
hold the axe in place. A great icy blast of wind in advance of
the avalanche lifted and buffeted him, tearing at his clothes
and body. Struggle as he might, there was nothing he could
do to resist the overwhelming force contained in the great
cloud of thundering snow as it engulfed him. He tried to
swim upwards to stay on the surface, but it was all in vain. Its
weight was too great, its force too primordial. It piled about
him, immobilizing him, and burying him alive. In the last

seconds he was able to extend his right arm above his head. By good fortune, and that alone, the fingers of his hand projected above the snow.

Meanwhile at the Plain of Six Glaciers Teahouse, Feuz's wife Martha and their two little girls saw the airborne mass tumbling from Mount Victoria into the Death Trap. Terrified, they watched the avalanche's uncontrolled descent towards the climbers.

It stopped as suddenly as it started. Guide Rudolf Aemmer and his men, who were far below, had been unaffected. Aemmer's party climbed up, searching the debris for victims. Most of the group were located and seemed all right, but Feuz and two others could not be seen. Looking carefully, someone spotted fingers sticking out of the snow. Weeping with both fear and relief, the rescuer dug and scratched the hardening snow from Feuz's face. The rest was more difficult; his body seemed set in concrete. When finally he was dug out, Feuz went to the help of the others.

There was still one man missing. In the desolate mass of broken snow blocks, Feuz peered into a hole formed by two chunks of ice. He could just make out the outline of a hat. With a shout to the others, he quickly excavated the victim's face just as the suffocating climber was about to lose consciousness.

With the last man accounted for, they assessed the damage. Guide Christian Hasler was bleeding from the face as a result of being hit by falling ice, but he would recover. There were other minor injuries, and some of the packs had been swept away, but that was all. Their survival was a miracle. In later years, Ed Feuz would often exclaim about the Death Trap, "That is the most dangerous place there is in the Canadian Rockies!"

Edward Feuz[1] is the eldest son of a Swiss guide and was born in the canton of Berne at Interlaken on 27 November

[1]Canadians pronounce Feuz as "foits."

1884. There were eight children in all, five sons and three daughters, of which two sons, Ernest and Walter, were also to have mountaineering careers in Canada. All the boys were handsome, and Edward was more so than the others.

In 1898, when he was thirteen, Edward climbed his first mountain, the Jungfrau (4167), a major peak in his home mountains of the Bernese Oberland. He was the youngest ever to make the ascent up to that time. The party with which he climbed was made up of tourists and was led by his father. Approaching the mountain from its north side, the climbers came to a steep, broad ice flank, below which lay a deep crevasse. The tourists crossed over, but young Edward, very frightened at the prospect of jumping the gap, started to cry. His father, obligated to his clients, had to get his son across. He shouted and cajoled but, in the end, he simply yanked on the rope to which his son was tied, forcing the boy to make the leap. As he did so, Edward let go of his alpenstock, which went bouncing down the slope out of sight. He never forgot the yank on the rope and used it skillfully on others on a number of occasions during his career.

That same year, 1898, the Canadian Pacific Railway decided to engage some Swiss guides at their mountain hotels. Through Cook's Travel Office at Interlaken, the company put a proposition to Feuz senior, who was chief guide for his district. Details were worked out, and in the summer of 1899 two Swiss guides arrived in Canada. They were Edward's father and Christian Hasler, Sr.

Edward left school after nine years of training and followed his father's plan for him to enter the hotel business for which a good working knowledge of languages was essential. In 1902 Feuz senior arranged for his son to live on a farm near Lausanne where French was spoken.

On the farm Edward lived over a piggery with another boy and hated the long hours of work and the hardships he was forced to endure at the hands of a "crazy" master. Still young and small in stature, he was required to perform tasks which were demanding even of a grown man. When his father[2] returned in the fall of 1902 and saw the conditions under which his son was living, he resolved to take him to Canada. Edward pointed out however, he could do so only after he had completed his one-year contract with the farmer.

When the contract expired in the spring of 1903, Edward applied for a Swiss porter's license which entitled him to train as a guide. That summer, with his father, he arrived in Canada. He was first sent to Field and then to Glacier, where his father was chief guide.

Edward's first recorded Canadian climbs were made in July 1903. With two climbers from California and his father in the lead he climbed Castor Peak (2779), Pollux Peak (2800), and Eagle Peak (2854), all mountains in the Selkirks, close to Rogers Pass. The clients found their porter's conduct to be of the highest order, and Edward seemed to be off to a good start, but some minor pitfalls awaited him.

At that point Edward spoke very little English. One day his father sent him with a honeymoon couple to explore the lower reaches of the nearby Illecillewaet Glacier. As Edward led his clients among the towering seracs of the icefall, the groom kept asking his guide if it was safe to go on. Edward whose command of English was very rudimentary did not understand the question and kept answering "no" but all the while he continued to lead the couple into the maze. The question was repeated and always answered in the same manner. The response raised the groom's alarm, and finally he pulled the rope and signalled to Edward to take them down. This Edward did but he was puzzled. On reaching Glacier House he questioned the head porter about his client's strange behaviour, and the word "safe" was explained to him. For the remainder of the couple's visit he could not look them in the face because of his embarrass-

[2]Edward Feuz, Sr. was a carpenter and worked his trade during the winter months; guiding was a full-time job in the summer. His father, in turn, was a stonemason, specializing in the construction of public fountains and cemetery headstones.

ment. His father insisted he remain in Canada that winter to learn the language.

When Feuz senior returned to Switzerland in the fall of 1903, Edward was alone in a strange country for the first time in his life. He did odd jobs around the hotel, shovelling snow, carrying baggage, and helping in the kitchen. But he was lonelier than he had ever been before. At night he felt so homesick he sometimes went down to the tracks and looked eastward toward Switzerland, where warmth and security lay.

In February 1904, a minister from Calgary, the Reverend John Herdman, wanted to climb Mount Abbott (2466), a minor peak near Glacier House. He engaged Edward to accompany him. There was an "unfathomable" quantity of snow on the route, and the two men carried both alpenstocks and ice axes for balance on their snowshoes. The climb was made successfully. It was Edward's first winter ascent and likely the first ever recorded in Canada.

The following summer, Edward acquired a new client, Joseph Hickson, a young philosophy professor from McGill University. Edward was taken aback when he observed Hickson's "crooked leg," his left being shorter than his right, but it did not hamper his climbing. The first ascent of Mount McGill (2678), west of Rogers Pass, was achieved by Edward and Hickson a few days later. The porter and the professor became best friends and shared long coincident careers.[3]

After another winter at Glacier, Edward entered his third season, climbing many peaks in the area and meeting a variety of people from such widespread places as Calcutta, Honolulu, and New York. From the latter city, his client was publisher William Randolph Hearst. Hearst had come to Glacier with a number of "pretty, jolly girls." They created quite a stir. The first evening, camping in the Asulkan Valley, a storm gathered, with lightning seen and thunder heard at

[3]Joseph Hickson employed Feuz for twenty-five climbing seasons during the period 1903–1956. Hickson, a bachelor, died at the age of eighty-three.

a distance. Although the young women went to bed with giggles and laughter, they shortly called Hearst to their tent. He listened quietly and then approached Edward. The girls, he said, were afraid, not only of the approaching storm but also of bears. Would Edward mind sleeping with them? Twenty-one-year-old Edward could hardly believe his ears. Smiling, he answered, "It would be a pleasure, Mr. Hearst!" As one might expect, the storm faded away, and it turned out to be a quiet night — without bears.

After more than two years in Canada, Edward was glad to be home in Interlaken in the fall 1905. For three weeks he visited his friends and relations and then took a job at a resort teaching skating and looking after the rink. He repeated this winter employment every year for seven consecutive years until he moved to Canada permanently.

When Edward and his father left Switzerland in 1906, they were accompanied by Gottfried, Edward's cousin, who was a carpenter as well as a qualified guide. On arriving at Montreal they received a welcome designed to publicize the CPR's western hotels. For two weeks the Swiss attended publicity functions. They wore knickers on the street in Montreal and were requested to show their skill by climbing in stone quarries. Everywhere they went, they were photographed. By the time they reached the mountains, a full month had elapsed.

After an expedition to the Waputik Range north of Field and the first ascent of Mount Tupper (2816), close to Rogers Pass, Edward and his cousin attended the first annual camp of the Alpine Club of Canada. What promised to be a rewarding experience proved to be an aggravating one. At first, the ladies of the club expected to climb in skirts. The skirts caught on rocks and parties were constantly held up. Then there was the matter of pay. Although the guides were on loan from the CPR to the ACC and each received his standard five dollars a day from the company, they were denied their special pay, or tips normally received when guiding from a hotel. Ten dollars was given at the end of the camp to each man, a sum similar to that awarded to dishwashers.

This financial dispute developed into an intense, lifelong dislike between Edward and Arthur Wheeler, the first president and director of the club. However, Edward went on to serve the ACC faithfully for many years.[4]

In 1907 Edward made the first ascent of Mount Begbie (2730), near Revelstoke, with Herdman, and after the annual camp made his second attempt to ascend Pinnacle Mountain (3067), above Moraine Lake. Its turreted summit repulsed his efforts for a second time, and he was angered by his failure to get his client, Hickson, to the top.

The next spring at Interlaken, Edward wrote and qualified for his guide's licence, which was issued on 15 May 1908. A description of him was entered in his guide's book, which read in part as follows: height 161 centimetres[5], brown eyes, fair hair, no distinguishing marks. Edward awaited his first client to make an entry in his book.[6] He was Frank Marshall from Jamestown, New York. On 19 July 1908 they ascended Mount Rogers (3214), north of Rogers Pass. It was Edward's last summer at Glacier.

In 1909 he was stationed at Lake Louise where he was joined by two new guides, Ernest, his gymnastic younger

[4]After camp one summer, a party guided by Feuz climbed The President (3139), northwest of Field. On the descent, Wheeler, who was a member of the party, refused to put on the rope and slipped on a patch of bare ice. Feuz was leading below him and, on hearing Wheeler's cry, looked up to see the director flying towards a precipice. Alertly, Feuz cast himself across Wheeler as he passed and prevented his fall to a certain death.

Although Feuz disliked Arthur Wheeler very much, he was fond of his son, Oliver, whom he regarded as a very good climber.

[5]Even for that day, Feuz was a short man; 161 centimetres is 5 feet 3 1/4 inches.

[6]The red leatherbound book, the *FührerBuch*, was issued to each guide, authenticating his profession and stipulating the regulations under which he was to work. Each page was numbered, and commencing on page 44 there was a series of blank pages on which a client could enter his comments about the services of his guide, commending him to future patrons. The book also served as a record of the guide's activity during his career.

brother[7]; and Rudolf Aemmer,[8] an ivory carver and child-hood friend from Interlaken.

Climbing activity that summer was intense. With Hickson and Aemmer, Edward made the first ascent of Pinnacle Mountain, an accomplishment which had eluded him twice before. On the third attempt the weather was not promising as the three climbers started out in a drizzle of rain from Paradise Valley. Reaching the tower by way of the Eiffel-Pinnacle Col and the southwest ridge, Edward traversed cautiously around the treacherous base of the precipitous tower for two hours before finding a large couloir on its north side. Partially filled with snow and ice, it led to a shale slope and the summit. When they rappelled down on their return, Aemmer knocked a rock loose, which fell, struck the rope, and severed it several metres from its end. In later years, the guides fixed ropes in place to aid future parties.[9]

The ACC camp of 1909 turned out to be a gathering place for guides. The Swiss were there, and so was one Austrian, Conrad Kain. They made profound impressions on the guests.[10] Ethel Johns, a novice who attended the camp, wrote,

> While we were waiting one of my long cherished dreams came true. I saw a Swiss guide in the flesh. So many of one's dreams are spoiled on the realization; but that

[7]Ernest Feuz, four years younger than Edward, had been an outstanding gymnast while at school. This skill he used very successfully while rock climbing.

[8]Rudolf Aemmer became interested in climbing as a result of Feuz's urging. As a young boy Aemmer had delivered newspapers in Interlaken and after graduating from school trained three years as an ivory carver.

[9]When, in 1922, Albert MacCarthy found out about these fixed ropes, he vehemently opposed their use as nonsporting.

[10]Early in the century, North Americans had little, if any, alpine tradition. Mountaineering was a new sport, practised principally in the Alps.

guide was, as the Virginian put it: "better than I dreamed." He wore the official badge on his coat lapel. He even sported the Tyrolean feather. His boots were as thick and as full of nails as I had hoped. He carried an ice-axe, a rucksack, and a coiled rope. I walked around him at a respectful distance and regarded him from every angle. He was a most satisfying person.

That September, again with Hickson and Aemmer, Edward made the second ascent of Deltaform Mountain (3424), in the Valley of the Ten Peaks at Moraine Lake, before accompanying Hickson to Glacier, where he led his client on Mount Sir Donald. Returning quickly to Lake Louise, Edward undertook his third serious climb in five days. On 4 – 5 September he and Aemmer took young George Culver on the first traverse of Mount Victoria travelling its crest from north to south. The exposed route, over crumbling rock, required unceasing care and attention. By the time they returned, exhausted, to the chalet, thirty hours had passed.

When Edward returned to Interlaken in the fall of 1909, he married Martha Heiman, the daughter of a notary public. The Heiman family had lived across the street from the Feuzes for a number of years, and Edward often observed his neighbour, admiring her neat appearance, her good figure, and her rosy cheeks. She was a woman who kept to herself, liked to read, and prided herself in her knowledge of several languages. She became a good wife and dear friend to her husband, and with him shared many adventures over the next sixty-five years.

Returning to Canada in 1910, Edward was again employed by Hickson. Together they climbed Mount Hungabee (3492) from Lake O'Hara and Mount Assiniboine (3618) south of Banff. Assiniboine was made in the company of Felix Wedgwood, a direct descendant of the famous English potter, and Gottfried, Edward's cousin. It was a smoky, hazy day, very warm and with no wind. When the summit was reached, Hickson proposed a traverse of the mountain, but

111

Edward replied, "Nothing doing, Doctor. I'm not going down there. Look at the weather. There's something wrong here. Maybe before we get down we will have all we can do to get home." Gottfried nodded, and Hickson accepted their advice.

The descent was uneventful until they passed the lower rock band and began to cross the broad slope leading to the glacier, later named the Wedgwood Glacier. Suddenly there was a great bang as lightning struck, and all four men were knocked flat on their backs. Edward's alpine hat was gone, discharged from his head by the force of the lightning. Miraculously, no one was seriously hurt. A tremendous storm began, partly hail and then rain. By the time the men reached the grass slopes, the ropes were so wet and swollen they were unable to untie them. The soaked, exhausted men returned to their camp with the ropes still on, where the rain had turned to snow and lay on the ground several centimetres deep.

After Assiniboine, Edward and Hickson made the first ascents of Mount Quadra (3176), near Moraine Lake, and Cyclone Mountain (3042), and Mount Saint Bride (3314), northeast of Lake Louise. On Saint Bride, Hickson engaged Edward Feuz, Sr., as a second guide. Feuz senior had attempted the mountain before, unsuccessfully, and his earlier knowledge was thought to be useful for this climb.

Not far below the summit of Saint Bride there is a difficult, bulging wall. Feuz senior was convinced the only solution to overcome this obstacle was to carry a pole and jam it into a crack in the wall. Near Baker Lake, some distance from the mountain, Edward found a jack pine of the right size, cut it, and nailed it with spikes to prevent it from turning. While his father looked after Hickson, Edward carried the pole on his back up the mountain.

After five hours and twelve hundred metres of glacier climbing, the party reached the last cliff and its difficulties. The first problem was a short chimney of about five metres which was overcome by using the three-man trick. With

Hickson at the bottom of the column and the elder guide on his shoulders, Edward climbed over them both and completed the pitch.

The second problem was the wall about eight metres high, "quite vertical and bulging forwards at the top." To one side, there was a straight fall-off, "an awful hole." The pole, so arduously brought to overcome the place, proved useless; there was no secure foundation on which to place its butt. Set back by the failure of his first "solution," Feuz senior then donned his rope-soled climbing shoes and twice attempted the chimney and was twice defeated. Edward immediately took the lead, and, for the longest time, he fingered the small holds and sought a way upwards. Each time he tried to move, the rock pushed him backwards over the adjacent abyss, putting his body into a critical state of imbalance. He thought to himself, "If only I had a piton or two to help me." In the meantime, his father was calling up to him, "Come down! Don't be silly!"

Without a word to the others, and barely knowing what started it all, Edward screwed up his courage and abandoned his fears. Using all of the strength in his fingers and arms, and guessing a good hold would come to hand as soon as he climbed, he made several deft moves and quickly reached a safe stance. To this day, he says, "I don't know how I did it." Soon after, the summit was theirs.

As it turned out, 1910 was the last Canadian season for Edward Feuz, Sr. He returned to Switzerland that autumn, where he remained for the rest of his career. After twelve summers in Canada, he had successfully launched the Swiss guide program for the CPR and had indelibly marked Canadian mountaineering with his family stamp.

About that time the CPR wanted Swiss families to emigrate to Canada to ensure a reliable supply of guides and create the nucleus of a Swiss colony. To this end they built a community at Golden comprising six houses, each replicating, but not duplicating, alpine dwellings as might be found in Switzerland. Built on a sloping hundred-acre site north of the town and in plain view of the railway, each house possessed one or more large balconies and had a spring-fed water supply. The community was named Edelweiss but became known more commonly as the Swiss Village.

When the 1911 season concluded, Ed Feuz, as he was now becoming known, had taken his father's place as the senior guide in Canada. In this capacity he was asked to inspect the Swiss Village site and return that fall to Interlaken with a message: married guides who wished to emigrate to Canada on a five-year contract would be assured of a rental house for ten dollars a month. The contract guaranteed both winter and summer employment.

This opportunity was welcomed by some and not by others. Gottfried Feuz did not want to emigrate and decided to make 1912 his last season. Others, like Rudolf Aemmer and Ernest Feuz, were keen to come, but they had to get married to take advantage of the offer. When they detrained at Golden in June 1912, all of them were wed except Christian Hasler, Jr., who had brought with him a fiancée from Interlaken. She was Rosa, one of Feuz's cousins. Hasler and Rosa were married at the hotel the day of their arrival.[11]

Feuz was assigned the topmost house on the hill, as he was now the spokesman for the group and also because he had a wife and one daughter, his first, Gertrude. Yet all was not happiness. When Martha Feuz saw Golden for the first time she cried, and Ed felt "very bad." It was not like Switzerland at all.

During this hectic domestic activity, Feuz was met, almost as soon as he got off the train, by Howard Palmer and

[11]Also in the party was Walter Feuz, ten years younger than his brother Ed, as well as Hanni Heiman, Martha Feuz's youngest sister. They were too young to be married that year. Both worked at Glacier House in the beginning. They were married at Golden in 1914 and have lived there since that time. A few years ago, Walter bought Swiss Village from the CPR. His son-in-law now manages the community.

Although Walter never became an official Swiss guide because he did not return to Interlaken to qualify, he was regarded as a very competent guide by the CPR and was assigned many important clients.

Edward Holway. Palmer had made a series of explorations in the northern Selkirks in recent years, had twice attempted Mount Sir Sandford (3522), the monarch of the Selkirks, and had twice been defeated. This year he wanted to try again and needed two guides. Feuz and Aemmer were the obvious choices.

The party set off in very hot weather, taking the train to Gold River. After canoeing and bushwhacking for five days, they reached the mountain. By lantern light on 24 June, they left their camp and crossed the Ravelin Glacier, approaching the peak from the north. The chosen route varied from that used in earlier attempts, and it proved successful.

The principal difficulty came only after they reached the summit ridge. They came to a double cornice, which in the heat of the day was melting and dropping pieces of ice. Palmer did not want to go on but the guides started to speak Swiss-German purposely so the clients could not understand. Then Feuz belayed Aemmer as he left the crest and crossed below the cornice on the south side of the mountain. Immediately on his right was a vertical rock face with a tremendous drop. "That's too much, Ed," said Palmer. "It's not safe to go on."

Ignoring Palmer, Aemmer completed the bypass of the cornice and took a good stance in the snow, belaying with his axe. When Palmer hesitated, Feuz gave him a push and forced him to step into the track. After that Holway followed "like a lamb," and the mountain, which had defeated six previous parties, was won. "One of the finest ascents I made," said Feuz many years later.

The climb had been physically demanding for so early in the season, and the guides slept until midmorning the next day, behaviour noted carefully by Palmer and Holway. Nonetheless, a few days later the party travelled north over the Adamant Glacier and, in one long day, made the first ascent of Mount Adamant (3356). Upon reaching its south face, they climbed a prominent gully which led to the southwest ridge. Because of the long approach and the high temperatures, the guides decided to reduce weight and leave much of their extra clothing and equipment at the bottom of the couloir.

It was a long, direct climb, slowed in places by steep ice of sixty to seventy degrees. Much time was consumed, and meanwhile a storm was building as a result of the heat. Freezing rain had begun just as they reached the summit, and they stopped only long enough to build a cairn before descending. The steps made during the ascent filled in with sleet, and great care was needed to avoid a slip. But any hesitation by the clients was met with an exhortation from the guides to keep moving as they were without their jackets. By the time they reached their rucksacks, the weather had moderated, and the four men made off for their camp near Sir Sandford. They arrived about one o'clock the next morning.

For the rest of the summer Feuz attended the ACC camp, made a traverse of Mount Victoria, and finished the season with climbs around Lake Louise. But the first winter with his family did not please him. He and the other guides had no winter employment as promised by the company. Instead they were forced to get by with part time work, piling wood slabs and hauling fence poles for the local sawmill. The following winter the situation continued and was only corrected after Feuz wrote the Swiss consulate in Montreal. After that, the guides were given winter work caretaking the CPR hotels, clearing roofs of snow, and cutting ice from the lakes for summer refrigeration. But this employment, although reliable, still worked a hardship on the men and their families. They were required to stay at the hotels during the week, while their wives remained in Golden.

During the summer of 1913, Feuz was engaged by Hickson to make a fifteen-day trip northwards to the North Saskatchewan River, leaving from Laggan. They crossed the Bow, Howse, and Baker Passes and returned via Field. They marked one first ascent en route, Mount Chephren (3266), a peak located above Waterfowl Lakes on what is now the Icefields Parkway. The trip was Feuz's first excursion north of Lake Louise.

In 1914 Feuz was engaged by an experienced Scottish mountaineer, James Young. Together they showed what a good guide and an experienced climber could do in a short time. During a three-week spell of fine weather in August, the two men made a total of twelve-ascents, including two firsts: at Lake Louise, Victoria (north peak), Victoria (south peak), Deltaform, and Hungabee; at Glacier, Uto (traverse), Sir Donald (traverse), Tupper, Rogers, Grant Peak, Swiss Peak, Findhorn Peak (2882, first ascent), and Tomatin Peak (2911, first ascent). The latter two lay at the head of Van Horne Brook and were reached through trail-less bush heavy with devil's club and slide alder. In Feuz's guide's book, Young wrote, "I soon found that Edward possessed qualities quite unusual in a Swiss guide . . . he proved a good woodsman, camper, cook and packer."

At Golden, mountainside living at Swiss Village was posing some problems. It was too far for Gertie Feuz to go to school, too difficult to push baby carriages up the hill, and gardening was impossible; and Feuz, for one, wanted his wife to be happy. He purchased two and a half acres from the CPR along Hospital Creek and left the village. For forty-five years of his life he lived on this land, property which he bought in 1915.

Among other climbs that summer, Feuz and Hickson accomplished the first traverse of the south tower of Mount Goodsir (3562) south of Field. It was early September and quite cold at night, and on the descent they were forced to bivouac. Inadequately equipped for a night in the open, Hickson shivered and shook, and Feuz, seeing this, did what he could to relieve the situation. He lay close to Hickson so that their body warmth could be shared and intermittently lit a candle for psychological reasons, if nothing else. Both men were glad to see the dawn.

Despite differing backgrounds, events such as this brought the two men close together, and they came to know one another as friends. At the same time, they could not avoid observing one another's faults. Hickson often saw Feuz as impatient, and Feuz thought Hickson was stubborn. Feuz also noted his client's propensity for falling into streams as a result of his short leg which unbalanced him. Hickson would not cross even minor streams without first having a log in place, no matter how narrow the crossing might be; and after Feuz had obliged his client, Hickson always fell into the water anyway. It seemed to happen without fail.

Hickson's habit of getting wet this way became a topic of conversation among the guides. One day Ed bet his brother Walter that Hickson would fall into a small creek en route to a climb, and he, not fully believing Hickson's reputation, gamely took the bet. Predictably, Hickson did it again. While Ed smiled smugly and muttered, "I told you so," Walter could only shake his head.

On another occasion, while returning from Paradise Valley, Hickson fell into a stream, and Feuz did what he had not done before — he laughed. This made Hickson damned mad, and when they returned to camp that evening he retaliated by refusing Feuz his customary shot of whisky. Even after Feuz asked for it, he was refused. But the next morning all was forgiven, and they laughed over the event.

Feuz and Hickson were the first climbers in the Bugaboos in 1916, but their visit there turned out to be only a camping trip. Heavy snow fell, and they were forced to abandon their plans. Their next big trip came three years later, when they journeyed to the British and French Military Groups, south of Banff. Their first objective was the unclimbed highest peak of the British Military Group, Mount Sir Douglas (3406), named after Sir Douglas Haig a noted British commander in World War I. On 11 August they set out from their camp located about two kilometres north of Palliser Pass and took a route up the northwest glacier to the west ridge. It was relatively easy climbing all the way, but on the sharp shale of the final rock section, they wore out their rope-soled shoes which they had donned in the event of difficulties.

Crossing Palliser Pass on 13 August en route to the French Military Group, they encountered the Fynn-Aemmer party going north. The boisterous gathering of twenty-five horses and a dozen people was long remembered by those present.

The trail south was a terrible ordeal for both men and horses. They made camp at the northernmost of the Kananaskis Lakes and proceeded on foot to Hidden Lake. From this point Mount Joffre (3449), highest of the French Military Group, could be sighted ten kilometres to the south. On a fine, warm day Feuz and Hickson commenced the long bushwhack, eventually reaching the Mangin Glacier on Joffre's north side. Via the glacier and the northeast ridge, they reached the summit and returned without mishap. They travelled northwards again, but before returning home they fulfilled Hickson's dream of traversing Mount Assiniboine, ascending by its northwest face and descending by its southwest flank.

In 1920 Hickson engaged Feuz for twenty-six days in August to accompany him on a journey to the North Saskatchewan Valley and to Mount Forbes (3628), southwest of Saskatchewan River Crossing on the Icefields Parkway. Their ascent of Forbes was the second ever made. At its third and final buttress, about a hundred metres below the summit, the ridge narrowed, with a sharp drop on one side. The buttress wall was steep and crumbling, with only a few safe holds. Feuz stopped momentarily and wondered how the first party had ever proceeded beyond that point.

Looking across the wall to the right, he discovered a hole which led into the mountain and appeared to exit above the buttress. The hole was narrow, filled with snow at the bottom and with ice at the top. Craning his neck, Feuz peered upwards and saw daylight at the top of the tunnel. There was just enought room for a body to pass through. Entering the opening, he climbed to where it became constricted, then jammed his body between the ice and rock and wedged himself in. It was a strenuous effort for about ten metres until he worked out of the hole and onto the ridge. It led easily to the summit.

After aiding in the recovery of Dr. Stone's body on Eon Mountain in 1921,[12] Feuz made a quick trip to the British Military Group and added another first to his record — Mount French (3234). He returned to Banff and joined Hickson and Louis Crosby in the first ascent of Mount Fifi (2621), the sister peak of Mount Louis.

An important event of 1922 was the construction of the highest building in Canada, the new climbing hut at Abbot Pass. It was built with rock walls and a timber roof and was divided into sleeping and dining areas. The cost was thirty thousand dollars, and the CPR guides were employed to transport the materials and furnishings to the site. Horses were used as far up the Victoria Glacier as crevasses would allow. Beyond that point the guides carried two tons of materials and furnishings to the site on their backs. Larger items were hauled by sled and hand winches. Unfortunately, one old mare led by Feuz slipped backwards into a small crevasse and then sat down, its hindquarters wedged between the walls. Feuz went for help, but, before guides and outfitters could effect a rescue, the body heat from the horse had enlarged the crevasse. The poor animal settled in between the icy walls and perished.

That summer Feuz, Roy Thorington, and Howard Palmer made the trip to Mount Freshfield, climbed it, and then completed four first ascents in the immediate area, along the divide. The next year, 1923, Feuz made two more firsts, this time with Hickson.

In 1924 Feuz guided the Field brothers, Osgood and Fred, of Massachusetts, to the Columbia Icefield. In the group was a new guide from Switzerland, Joseph Biner. While the pack train was crossing the Howse River, the outfitter, who was responsible for the group on the trail, wheeled his horse and rode back to speak with Feuz.

"What the hell is the matter with your partner, Ed? Look at him — he is standing still in the water."

Feuz was himself sometimes apprehensive when crossing rivers on horseback and nervously looked back at Biner,

[12]See Chapter 3.

who was sitting astride his horse with water streaming rapidly across its flanks. The rest of the outfit was drawing away, and yet Biner was immobile. Feuz urged his horse down the stream to see what the trouble was.

"What's the matter, Joseph? Aren't you coming?"

"What do you mean, I *am* coming!" replied Biner as he stared hypnotically at the water flowing past his motionless horse.

"You are *not* moving, Joseph!" replied Feuz and gave his partner's horse a kick.

The expedition was a success. They made the first ascent of the South Twin (3566), the second of the North Twin (3719) and Mount Andromeda (3444), and the third of Mount Columbia (3747), the highest peak in Alberta. Other first were made of an unnamed peak in the Columbia Icefield Group, Mount Outram (3252) in the Forbes Group, and Mount Patterson (3197) and Epaulette Mountain (3094) in the northern Waputiks. These climbs were becoming typical of this period of Feuz's career; he had to work farther and farther afield to find virgin peaks for his clients.

East of the Continental Divide, at the confluence of the North Saskatchewan and Alexandra Rivers, lies Mount Amery (3335). It was named after the Right Honourable Leopold Stewart Amery, former secretary of state for Dominion Affairs for the United Kingdom. In 1929 it had not been climbed, and Amery arrived in Canada to be the first person to do so. Because of his fame, it was an occasion of considerable importance, and Arthur Wheeler, always in evidence on such occasions, took charge of the expedition. Feuz, who had been selected as guide, immediately differed with the ACC director over the placing of campsites. Unaccustomed to having his authority questioned on these matters, Feuz confronted Wheeler, who, under pressure from the assertive guide, gave in.

On 20 August 1929 Feuz led his distinguished charge and his companion, Brian Meredith, onto the slopes of Mount Amery. The weather had been deteriorating, and a storm was almost certain before the day was out. Feuz considered abandoning the attempt, but Amery insisted on continuing. Before they reached the summit ridge, the storm had broken and was raging against them. Once there, they caught the full blast of the wind and snow stuck to their eyelashes. They could not see more than five metres ahead, while below the valley was black. They struggled into the storm and made their way to the top, where Feuz constructed a cairn on what he believed to be the highest point. Without other formality, they turned and worked their way downwards. When they reached the trees, it was dark.

Feuz lit his lantern. The bush was heavy with snow and very wet, and his client was extremely tired from the day's efforts. Feuz proposed that they stop and bivouac. At first the Englishman refused and only when he realized how tired he was, gave in. Feuz made a fire, and beside it he laid a bed of boughs, on which Amery lay down and was soon asleep. The next morning they returned to camp.

The party remained there for a few days, as the weather continued stormy, and Feuz noticed that his client was disquieted. Considerate of his welfare, he approached Amery and asked what was disturbing him. Amery was worried they had not reached the summit of the mountain. The storm had been fierce, visibility low, and they could have easily missed the high point. Another party might find their claim to a first ascent unsubstantiated. Feuz, however, disagreed. He was certain they had been on the true summit and suggested, to prove the point, that they climb Mount Saskatchewan (3342), immediately to the north. From there they would be able to see the cairn on the summit of Mount Amery. The next day the weather broke, and they made the ascent. Using Feuz's "glass," Amery scanned the neighbouring peak and spotted the pile of rocks on the very highest point. "You were right," he said smiling, "we did climb to the top."

They made other ascents around Maligne Lake, and one evening in mid-September Amery bade farewell to Feuz. From his personal equipment he took his ice axe and gave it to his guide as a gesture of good will and appreciation. They never met again.

By 1930 Feuz had made many first ascents, and in August he added the fiftieth to his list, while Hickson, who was with him, completed his thirtieth. They counted only those peaks over 3050 metres (10,000 feet), excluding all climbs of lesser elevation. Feuz's achievement might have been even greater, but at no time did he, or any other Swiss guide, make a first ascent without clients. It was for them to claim the record.

In the late thirties Feuz started acquiring some notable women mountaineers as clients, who, like men, wanted their share of the big peaks. Among these were Lillian Gest from Philadelphia and Kati Gardiner from England. In 1937 Feuz led Gardiner on the first ascents of Queant Mountain (3109) and Trident (3000), south of the Columbia Icefield; Mount Murchison (3333), south of Saskatchewan River Crossing; and four unnamed summits north of the Pipestone Valley, northeast of Lake Louise. Other climbs included as second ascent of Mount Bryce (3507), a major massif with a trio of peaks, which lies adjacent to the Columbia Icefield. On three of these excursions, Gest was in the party.

Gardiner was a climber of considerable note, with experience both in the Alps and New Zealand, as well as Canada. High on her list of objectives was an ascent of Mount Robson (3954), the majestic monarch of the Rockies, west of Yellowhead Pass. She had made a number of attempts with the two Canadian National Railway guides at Jasper, Hans and Christian Fuhrer, but they had been unable to get over the icefall of the southwest glacier. She appealed to the CPR to let her have two guides from Lake Louise who might improve her chances.

Feuz heard about the request and asked the manager of the Hotel Department to let him go. The manager refused, insisting that Robson was a CNR mountain as it lay close to the CNR railway and Robson Station. Feuz argued that Gardiner was a good customer of the CPR, travelling on its steamships and using its railways and hotels. The Fuhrers could not lead her up Robson, but he believed he could. It was a fairly strong position to take because, so far, Feuz had not even seen the mountain, let alone climbed it. Eventually he won his argument on the condition that he would not announce his plans publicly. The agreement was sealed with a drink.

In 1939 the climb was on. Christian Hasler, Jr. was engaged as the second guide and accompanied the client to Hargreaves Ranch, while Feuz studied the mountain with binoculars from Robson Station. He determined a route, and a few days later Robson was climbed without marked difficulty. When it was over, Gardiner returned south with her guides and made ten other ascents, including the virgin White Pyramid (3277) at Waterfowl Lakes. At the end of the season she was extremely pleased with her success and with the man who had made it possible.

Unfortunately this remarkable summer of 1939 was marred when, after their return, Hasler made a late September trip to Sherbrooke Lake and was mauled by a female grizzly.[13] Feuz visited him in hospital two days later and witnessed the awful damage caused to his friend's arms and shoulders. Although Hasler survived the attack, he was grievously injured and did not fully recover. A year later, while doing some work on the roof of his house in Golden, he collapsed and died.

After the start of the Second World War, guiding activity decreased, but Feuz still had some clients and made four first ascents. When the United States entered the conflict, activity further decreased. Feuz managed to make two firsts in 1944 with Thorington: Aries Peak (3018) and Stairway Peak (2999), both in the Waputiks at their northern extremity. It was a suitable celebration for Feuz, who was to be sixty years old that November, but in his home town of Interlaken a sad event took place. Edward Feuz, Sr. died.

[13]The bear mauling was one in a series of tragic events in Hasler's life. In 1937 his son Billy was killed in a chemical explosion at school. Later the same year his wife died.

Feuz continued to guide for another five years, but the time for first ascents in the Rockies was over. Most big mountains had been climbed, and young people, normally attracted to an adventure sport like mountaineering, had had enough adventure during the war. They were keen to return to peaceful, less dangerous pursuits.

In September 1949 a party was held at the guide's house at Lake Louise, honouring Feuz and Aemmer. Both men were retiring. For forty-six years Feuz had been a member of the Hotel Department of the CPR and had made over seventy first ascents and countless other climbs. He was proud also that fifty years of guiding by the Swiss guides (1899 – 1949) had resulted in a perfect safety record. The policies set by his father and Christian Hasler, Sr. had been followed: "Find the easiest route up the mountain. Go the safe way. Always keep to the ridges."

After his retirement, Feuz accepted an invitation from Hickson to visit Montreal and one from his dentist, Bert Wiebrecht, to visit Milwaukee. Two years later, Wiebrecht came to Golden and made an entry in Feuz's *FührerBuch* that expressed the feelings of many of the guide's mountain friends. In part it read,

> Fortunate indeed is the man who has had the privilege of climbing with you, as I have, for no guide has greater ability, skill or judgement. But above all of this I cherish your friendship, your incomparable comradeship, through which you have instilled in me the ability to appreciate the peace and contentment that only the mountains can bring to the soul of man. . . . Believe me it has been an honour to be called your friend.

When Joseph Hickson died in Montreal in 1956, Feuz felt the loss, but, in his wisdom, he accepted it and reflected on his good fortune of having excellent health. His robustness continues to amaze his family, his friends, and the public.

In 1964, the year of his eightieth birthday, Feuz climbed Mount Temple (3547), the highest peak in the Lake Louise Group. He made it by the "tourist route," but the ascent showed his astonishing durability and physical strength, built up since childhood. Two years later he crossed Abbot Pass, leading the son and grandson of Henry Kingman, one of his clients in 1906; and in 1968 Feuz guided a family across east Mitre Pass. The group was nearly struck by rockfall, and their guide gave them a warning shout. But after the incident it occurred to Feuz he might not be fast enough to get out of the way next time. He decided his mountaineering days were over. But three years later in 1971, at the age of eighty-six, he was featured in the TV program, "This Land," and was filmed climbing in the Moraine Lake area.

Since his wife died in 1974, Feuz has lived alone in Golden in a bungalow next door to his daughter, Gertrude, and her husband, George Marr. His home is characteristic of the man — neat, tidy, and full of mementos. Although he is ninety-four, he possesses excellent health and is full of vigour and vitality. Conversations with him are lively. Only in recent years has he become aware that he has been an important part of Canadian mountain history, and he finds sometimes that "it is a damn nuisance," because visitors interfere with his gardening. His garden, of both flowers and vegetables, is his principal occupation in summer, and polishing woods for lamps and other uses is his hobby in winter.

The Feuz years span almost the entire period of the golden age of Canadian mountaineering — the years of exploration, pioneering, and first ascents. Feuz is himself a living record of these years.

Illustrations

I

II

III

IV

V

VI

VII

VIII

IX

X

XI

XII

XIV

Chapter Six

Phyl Munday
ca. 1898 –

A strong woman, as strong as any man.

Ed Feuz

Over the Pacific a storm had been gathering for many hours. The three climbers — Phyl Munday, her husband Don, and her sister Betty — decided to turn back late in the afternoon. The first ascent of Mount Waddington would have to wait for another day. As they hurried down the ridge, they were enveloped by haze and darkness.

Thunder had begun rolling across the sky when suddenly "the night burst into crashing flame" and the mountain came alive with electric fire. Devil's lightning stabbed the air, its blinding glare thrown back by snowy rocks. Hurrying and stumbling downwards, the frightened climbers found themselves encapsulated in light, their groping figures weaving and bobbing like marionettes on some ghostly stage. Their hats were fringed with flame; their ice axes flickered a blue light.

At the pass thunder and lightning came together, and the wind drove horizontally through the gap. All around, darts of light shot out from the rocks, stones falling from the cliffs trailed red sparks into the depths below, and avalanches slipped away, adding their voices to the din. A tempest of doom was on the mountain.

Once below the pass, the climbers escaped the fury of the wind. Little by little they went down, and gradually their axes burned less brightly, the rocks glowed only dimly, and the onset of snow gave way to rain. They stopped, pulled a tarpaulin over their heads, and waited for daylight. It was 19 August 1927.

The parents of Phyllis Beatrice James were both English. Her father was manager firstly of Lipton's and then Ridgway's tea estates in Ceylon (Sri Lanka), where she was born. Her birthday falls on 24 September, but the year of her birth is uncertain due to the loss of records. It is generally accepted to be 1898. There were two other children, Esmeé, also born in Ceylon, and later known as Betty, and Richard, who was born after the family moved to Canada.

Phyllis received her education in Vancouver. In 1909, she joined the fledgling Girl Guides Association and later the B.C. Mountaineering Club. Her first personal ascent was Grouse Mountain in North Vancouver, a feat which at that time was considered an achievement for a teen-age girl.

Towards the end of the First World War she was employed as a clerical worker in the Military Annex of the New Westminster General Hospital, where she also served as a member of the Voluntary Aid Detachment. Here, in 1918, she met Don Munday, a twenty-eight-year-old soldier and mountaineer.

Don started climbing before the war, and, when hostilities broke out, he joined the Scout Section of the Canadian 47th Infantry Battalion. He was wounded at Passchendaele when a bullet entered his left wrist and exited from his elbow. He was invalided home in 1918 after being awarded the Military Medal.

Phyllis did not like him very much at first, but he was "very persistent." Soon, however, his love of the mountains and his quiet, gentlemanly ways won her over. When they were married in February 1920 it was the beginning of an unique union; no similar husband-wife partnership has ever existed in the annals of mountaineering. They spent their honeymoon in the Mount Robson area, climbing Lynx Mountain (3170) and making a first ascent of the north ridge of Mount Resplendent (3426).

The following March, 1921, their only daughter, Edith Phyllis, was born. Her birth, however, did not deter their outdoor activities, Phyl and Don, as they would be known for decades ahead, made their first climbs in the Selkirks that same summer. During the next three years, they explored Garibaldi Park and the Chilliwack area of southern British Columbia, making six easy first ascents of moderate elevation. Their first major climb came in 1924.

As members of the Alpine Club of Canada, Phyl and Don were attending its annual camp at Robson Pass and had just returned from an ascent of Mumm Peak (2962) when it was announced they would have the opportunity to climb Mount Robson. The party would include two other men and one other woman, Annette Buck. Conrad Kain would guide them.

The weather had been very hot and dry, and the trek to high camp parched their thirst. The camp comprised three tents, a stove, cooking utensils, and bedding and was located at the timber line on the southwest face, above Kinney Lake.

There was some rain the night before the climb, but the weather held, and before daylight Kain woke them. By mid-morning they had reached the ice wall at the head of the great couloir. Its cracked but silent towers threatened those who passed below it. To minimize the danger, the party moved quickly and silently across the wide, curving ledges. Phyl traversed first and then watched anxiously as Don, with the second rope, made the same perilous passage.

Once above the wall and on the glacier, they worked steadily towards the main ridge, held up only once when Kain's assistant guide fell through a snowbridge and lost his axe, which took an hour to recover. After reaching the ridge, they followed a weaving course amidst ice terraces which reminded Phyl of "breakers on a rough sea." From the terraces, dripping icicles glistened in the sun like ballroom chandeliers.

Late in the afternoon Phyl waited while Kain negotiated the last, short, face section, disappeared from view, and then pulled in the rope quickly. She climbed onto the summit and was greeted by the guide, who extended his hand and said, "There, Lady! You are the first woman on top of Mount Robson."

Fifty years later Phyl would remember the beautiful windless day, the myriad of peaks, and the vision of tiny Berg Lake, thousands of meters below. "It's something I shall never forget if I live to be a hundred. I wish I could do it again."

Meanwhile, in North Vancouver, Don had built a log cabin on Grouse Mountain, where the family lived. It was in a fortunate location for those who came up the mountain and got into trouble. Once Phyl put an injured teen-age girl on her back and carried her down to safety. On another occasion, she nursed a young man in the cabin for several weeks after he had fallen down a cliff, suffered head injuries, and could not be moved. For this service she was recognized by the Girl Guides Association and awarded their Bronze Cross for Valour.

Before the big mountains were in condition for climbing in 1925, a friend, Tom Ingram, invited the Mundays to join him on an ascent of Mount Arrowsmith (1817), just east of Port Alberni on Vancouver Island. While stopping for lunch during the climb, Phyl scanned the mainland Coast Mountains across the channel with binoculars. She spotted a high peak gleaming through a break in the clouds. Pointing it out to Don, he took a compass bearing. It lay almost due north in a line passing just west of the head of Bute Inlet. They guessed it to be about 240 kilometres away, in an area virtually unknown and yet unmapped. Judging from its sister peaks, it could be a monarch, never before discovered. They determined to find out. Don wrote later, "It was the far off finger of destiny beckoning." But for the moment, destiny would have to wait.

In July the Mundays went to the Premier Range of the Cariboo Mountains, west of Yellowhead Pass. They made a first ascent of Mount Sir John Thompson (3277) and a second ascent of the highest peak, Mount Sir Wilfrid Laurier (3520).

The trip was plagued with porcupines. One molested their campsite at every opportunity, followed the Mundays to the snow line when they went climbing, and was waiting for them when they returned. When not so amused, the porcupine spent its time observing the climbers from high in a tree alongside a creek by which they camped.

Don, who was an excellent axeman, decided to put an end to that one day and felled the tree. The head of the evergreen and its inhabitant crashed on the opposite bank, where the Mundays hoped the animal would remain. They had no such luck. The porcupine merely plopped in the water and swam back. "A perfect pest," said Phyl with an emphasis on her p's.

Later, from the ACC camp at Lake O'Hara, the Mundays climbed both Mount Hungabee and Mount Victoria before returning home to plan their fall expedition to what they called "mystery mountain."

As the name implies, the Coast Mountains lie along the Pacific Ocean, extending north of Vancouver about fifteen hundred kilometres. Heavy glaciation in this chain results as moist sea winds are forced up, chilled over the mountains, and precipitated as wet snow at high altitudes.

In September the Mundays made a reconnaissance of mystery mountain via Bute Inlet, northwest of Vancouver. Aboard the steamer to the logging camp at Orford Bay, located half way up the east shore of the inlet, was their friend Ingram and a new man, Athol Agur. A trapper motored them by boat to a point from which they climbed Mount Rodney (2390) with the purpose of viewing the terrain which lay up the valley of the Homathko River. They were not encouraged by what they saw.

The valley is a deep trench about fifty kilometres long with steep flanks twenty-four hundred metres high. Its head seemed blocked by a large glacier. The approach to the mountain would be rough. But they were encouraged by the fact that the peaks lying west of the trench rose to thirty-six hundred metres, and therefore mystery mountain which they believed exceeded four thousand metres, was truly a new monarch. "It was obvious nothing could equal it," Phyl stated later.

The Homathko River was first explored by employees of Alfred Waddington, who in 1862 held a charter to build a toll road to the Cariboo gold fields. The road was nearly completed two years later when a band of Chilcotin Indians, badly treated by Waddington's foreman, massacred nine of a twelve-man work party camped on a sand bar along the river.[1] The Waddington project collapsed as a result, and sixty years later, when the Mundays and their party arrived on the scene, no vestige of the road remained.

Two advance groups took provisions up Bute Inlet early in May 1926 to prepare for the first attempt to reach the mountain. On the thirtieth, the entire party gathered at Orford Bay. In addition to Phyl and Don, there was Bert Munday, Don's brother; Agur; Ingram; and a newcomer, Johnnie Johnson. The next day, with a five week supply of provisions, they entered the mouth of the Homathko Valley. The "trench lost itself in a cavernous gloom as unwelcoming as the dark lair of some unknown beast," wrote Don soon after.

The valley floor is a place of indescribable turmoil. Its high flanks serve to collect copious rainfall, raising water levels a metre above normal overnight. At high speed in the narrow gorge, the water undermines trees, giants and dwarves alike; acres of logjams impound water which silts to form beds of quicksand; root systems are flooded and choked of life, leaving giant spears of deadwood as sentinels of destruction; alder groves rot and fall in tangles; devil's club, a thorny, diabolical plant, shoots up from the ruins in a detestable snarl.

But the worst hazards were the glacial creeks which feed the river on both sides. They were, according to Phyl, "too wild, too deep, and too swift to ford." Bridged by trees cut to span their width, the half-submerged logs shuddered and churned in the turbulent water. Many times Phyl crossed

[1]Mountains in the area have been named for Otto Tiedemann, Waddington's engineer, and for Tellot, one of several Indians hanged for the massacre. The sand bar where the incident took place was subsequently named Murderer's Bar.

under a heavy load, her eyes firmly fixed on her footing, her hand grasping a taut handline.

For thirteen days they battled this "heart-breaking barrier" to a point close to the mouth of Coola Creek, forty-eight kilometres up the valley. But they were still little more than a hundred metres above the sea. A short distance up the creek, however, they caught their first glimpse of Waddington Glacier. It appeared very low in the trees. On 19 June they followed the glacier northwestwards and climbed a twenty-seven-hundred-metre mountain from which they discovered a pass leading to their objective. The pass appeared to be the possible key to success.

Phyl paid a price that day. Without goggles in glaring fog, she became snow-blind and had to be led back to camp. Although the pain was severe, the infirmity was only temporary. Few in the group realized she was also suffering from arthritis. That night, as with most nights over the years, she wrapped her knees in cold towel compresses and covered them with light rubber sheets to keep the swelling down. "A bit of a nuisance," she would often remark.

Short of rations, the climbers had to hurry if they were to reach the base of the mountain. On the evening of 23 June, they left Johnson in camp and set off under brilliant moonlight. The snow was soft and deep. To make a track was exhausting. As they reached the top of the pass, however, the sun rose, glorifying the scene. At 5:15 that morning they saw for the first time the mighty bulk of mystery mountain, revealed at last from its base to its crest. Its flanks were cloaked in a mantle of glaciers which spread out like roots to entwine lesser mounts; its top was crowned by a soaring, snow-feathered tower.

The eager group crossed the pass and then turned upwards in a northeasterly direction, climbing to a col along the mountain's southeast ridge. From there they could see on the other side of the ridge another vast east-west glacier, bounded on its north side by a chain of statuesque peaks. It was all virgin territory; they had "outrun the mapmakers." But for now it was as far as they could go.

By nightfall they returned to camp. On 4 July the party, homeward bound, reached Orford Bay, but some would not see the mountain again. Phyl and Don knew they would be back.

Early in 1927 the Mundays were confronted with a tragedy involving their two friends who had shared so much with them. In February Johnson and Agur were caught in an avalanche on Grouse Mountain. Johnson's foot snagged in a cypress tree at the edge of a cliff and he was saved, but Agur was swept two hundred and fifty metres to his death. The Mundays and others tried in vain to recover his body but were thwarted until the snow melted five months later.

After the trials of the first approach to mystery mountain, Phyl and Don hoped for an easier route and chose one roughly parallel to the first. On 30 May 1927 they sailed from Vancouver to Glendale Cove in Knight Inlet, a point approximately sixty kilometres west of Orford Bay. Knight Inlet, fed by the mighty Klinaklini River[2] and the outwash of the Franklin Glacier, would lead them, they expected, to mystery mountain from the southwest. They hoped this approach would improve their chances for success.

It was a spectacular boat trip fifty-six kilometres up the inlet, where cascades a thousand metres high spilled from precipitous cliffs into the sea. From a ridge at the head of the inlet the Mundays viewed the Franklin Glacier for the first time. It "curved back impressively...a dim, white, secretive aisle." In the next few days they cut trail from the shore along the northwest bank of the Franklin and then returned to Vancouver for supplies and a third member of the party, Phyl's sister, Betty McCallum. Packing loads half their body weight, they reached the glacier snout again by 26 July and, the following week, worked loads twenty kilometres up the icy passage.

Standing off the southwest face of their objective was a low mountain in the middle of the ice stream. On the mountain's left they named Dais Glacier and on its right Corridor

[2]Klinaklini is pronounced "kleen-a-kleen."

Glacier. Via the Dais they made one attempt to more than thirty-three hundred metres, and via the Corridor they made a second effort, during which Phyl was injured by rockfall. Undeterred, a day or two later she insisted on making a third try along the northwest ridge from a low gap which led to the other side of the mountain. They climbed to an altitude just under thirty-nine hundred metres but turned back in the face of the most impressive electrical storm any of them had witnessed. Afterwards, they always referred to the pass as Fury Gap.

On 20 August, in calmer weather, they left their bivouac and returned to camp. From there, Betty McCallum gladly prepared to travel home. She "hated the mountains" and had only come along to appease her mother, who did not want her to be left alone that summer. After she boarded the steamer at Glendale Cove, Phyl and Don went back to the Franklin again but were stormed in for a full week. Under a new blanket of snow, the mountain was inaccessible.

In the inlet low tides and head winds held up their return passage. It was a fortunate occurrence. The Mundays became the first to receive news from a survey party that the altitude of the mystery mountain had been calculated to be 4042 metres, very close to Don's estimate.[3] Mystery mountain was definitely the monarch of the Coast Mountains. Within months the peak was named Mount Waddington and a nearby sister peak named Mount Munday.[4]

Their experience in 1927 taught the Mundays that the Franklin Glacier route was the best way to Mount Waddington, and in 1928 they returned with Don's brother, Bert.

[3]Arthur Wheeler, director of the Alpine Club of Canada and surveyor of the Great Divide, did not believe any mountain in British Columbia could be higher than Mount Robson, which he had surveyed. He was convinced of Waddington's altitude only after being permitted by the British Columbia Department of Lands to check the surveyor's calculations.

[4]The Canadian Permanent Committee on Geographic Names suggested to the Mundays the highest peak be given their name, but they felt the name should reflect the history of the area and suggested Mount Waddington.

Twenty-two days after leaving Glendale Cove the three established a camp below Fury Gap, and on 8 July they began their most successful attempt on the mountain up to that time.

From the gap, the northwest ridge of Waddington is a succession of peaks, heavily caked in ice and windblown snow. The Mundays had named them the twin Men-at-Arms Peaks, Bodyguard, and Councillor. They bypassed the first pair by traversing on the north face. After steps were cut up Bodyguard, they descended to the col at the foot of Councillor and rested. Phyl produced a tin of grated pineapple, which they spooned into their mouths with rock flakes.

The ice cap on the ridge ahead overhung the rock, and, returning to the climb, they were forced onto the face again. Anchorage was poor, so they were cautious. On regaining the ridge, they encountered a crevasse some four hundred metres long which interrupted their path. In deep powder snow they floundered among seracs to a narrow passage over the opening. When a second crevasse halted them, they found a three-metre block which had fallen to bridge the gap. It was hanging on two knobs of ice, one on each wall of the crevasse.

Phyl led all these sections. She was the lightest and was expected to test the bridges which were fragile and thin. She crossed gingerly. Sometimes they cracked audibly and settled under her weight.

By then they were at an altitude where the air was noticeably colder. Soggy boots stiffened with frost, and wet mitts adhered instantly to their metal axe heads. Rising in front of them still was a five-hundred metre slope of wind-slabbed snow. It was brittle and dangerous, and the risks it presented were enormous. As they climbed it, blocks broke away and slipped down the mountain. Any moment a major slide could develop and carry them to the depths.

Around supper time a final slope rose upwards to the sky. Like the one earlier, it offered no certainty of safety. The snow was granular, coarse, and cohesionless. At each step it crumbled. Don cleared it away and cut steps in the ice beneath. So steep was it in places that he had to cut hand-holds as well as vertical slots for his knees as he moved up. Abruptly the incline fell back and was transformed dramatically into two flared and opposing cornices. There was barely enough room between them for the party to stand. They were aghast: they had not reached the summit of Mount Waddington.

The ridge continued down, and there, across a short gap to the east, was the soaring main tower of the mountain, its rocks adorned with ice feathers. Merely sixty metres higher than where they were standing on the northwest summit, it was still out of reach. The weather was deteriorating, and it was late. Because they were soaking wet, they realized it would be imprudent to go on and be forced to bivouac at that altitude. It was too great a risk. After three years of effort, they made a hard but wise decision. They would have to come back. More than five years would pass before they tried again.

In 1929 Phyl's mother, Beatrice, died, which precluded any climbing activity. In 1930, Phyl and Don returned to the Franklin Glacier. After making four first ascents of lesser peaks close to the glacier, they determined to attempt the ice-capped mountain bearing their name, Mount Munday (3505). Using skis for travel for the first time, they expected to make the ascent in one long day, as opposed to three days if they travelled on foot.

Soon after starting out in the early hours of 22 July, a brilliant morning sky forecast a perfect day. From their Franklin Glacier camp near the main icefall, they reached the Corridor Glacier, crossed it, and turned up Ice Valley below the peaks of Mount Munday.

Mount Munday is a major mountain on the long southeast ridge of the Waddington massif. It has several peaks. Narrow steep glaciers cling to the rock of its irregular south face, which forms one wall of Ice Valley.

The Mundays climbed to the head of the valley to Mystery Pass, which they had gained in 1926 from the opposite direction. From the pass they skied up Munday's moderate slopes until they came to the bottom of a cirque. They chose to climb directly up its face to the saddle between the mountain's middle and east peaks. A bergschrund spanned the cirque from side to side and was bridged by a thin crust of loose, honeycombed snow. Would it hold?

On the bridge, one of Don's skis suddenly settled but did not go through. He watched anxiously as Phyl came onto the crossing. Instantly one of her skis broke through completely, leaving her foot dangling aimlessly in the void beneath. She caught her breath, expecting the worst to happen, but the bridge held. Awkwardly she freed herself, and together they side stepped up the steep snow curtain to the saddle, where they removed their skis.

Once on the middle peak they saw easily that Mount Munday's west peak was the highest. As it was getting late, they hurried onwards and reached the main summit of the mountain, two small pinnacles separated by a sharp snow ridge. It was a pleasant victory, slightly overshadowed by the fact that to the northwest was an unfinished project. There in clear view stood the dominant pyramid of Mount Waddington, about six kilometres away.

It was now five thirty in the afternoon. A cold wind came up, whining through the rocks. Phyl and Don hurried back to their skis and schussed spread-eagled over the snow-bridge which they had crossed earlier. Well into the night they travelled, arriving back at their camp twenty-four hours after leaving it. The day had been a long but victorious one.

In 1931, the Mundays abandoned steamer travel and voyaged the entire four hundred kilometres from Vancouver to the head of Knight Inlet in a five-metre open boat with a kicker on the transom. Their daughter Edith, then eleven, accompanied her parents and was left on an island to stay with friends. As fate would have it, Waddington was inaccessible due to unusually heavy snowfall, but they did make two first ascents of lower peaks and started to build a cabin along the lower reaches of the Franklin River.

After another brief visit to the area in 1932, the Mundays

received an invitation for 1933 from Bostonian Henry Hall. He and his guide, Hans Fuhrer, were going to make an attempt on Waddington from the northeast via Scimitar Glacier. Hall believed a plausible route existed from the col between Waddington and its sister peak, Mount Combatant. The approach would be tough, but by now the Mundays were accustomed to it.

The party, which included Alf Roovers[5] and Don Brown, crossed the Chilcotin Plateau from Williams Lake to Tatla Lake, British Columbia, in an open truck. Twenty kilometres southwest, at Bluff Lake, they met their outfitters. They were notable characters. One objected to taking a woman beyond Middle Lake, and another, Valleu, carried a loaded revolver in his shirt and slept with a sawed-off shotgun. The others complained that he tried to exercise ownership over the entire valley.

With seventeen horses they set off along the upper banks of Mosley Creek,[6] a journey of forty-five kilometres, before they reached the snout of the Scimitar Glacier. Tributaries flowed into the creek, and at each crossing the packers sat astride their horses in belly-deep water, ready to rope any pack horse that got into trouble. Despite precautions, some animals nearly drowned in the swiftly flowing icy water.

On reaching the Scimitar Valley, they found it had been ravaged by fire. The blaze resulted in windblown deadfall which posed tremendous trail-making problems; five men cleared only five kilometres in five days. Footing was treacherous; Fuhrer scarred his face when he slipped and fell on his axe blade. In the rocky sections, where stable footing was infrequent, the horses suffered badly under their loads and stumbled awkwardly. One fell upside down, was badly bruised and cut, and was barely extricated as it lay on its packsaddle.

[5]Alf Roovers, a young American, was killed in a fall from a cliff at Arden, New York, one year later, 14 December 1934.

[6]At the time of this exploration, Mosley Creek had not been named officially and was known as the west branch of the Homathko.

At the Scimitar Glacier, it was necessary to cut a staircase for the horses onto the ice. The animals did not like it at all. Phyl carried gravel to cover the steps, and the frightened beasts were eventually led through. Once they became used to it, two horses easily carried loads along the ice to the party's base camp close to the foot of Mount Hickson. Three full weeks had passed before they reached this camp.

When the party, excluding Brown, approached the Waddington-Combatant col on 14 July 1933, they discovered that Waddington's northeast side "put on a most impressive face," its upper half a series of ice walls, its lower, a precipice scoured by avalanches. Disappointed, they all agreed the mountain could not be approached from this direction. The climbers turned instead to the col joining Mounts Combatant and Hickson. From there Combatant (3701) was climbed, a first ascent. They bivouacked on the summit and spent the night on a shelf trying not to push one another into space. It was a relief to get moving again in the morning.

During the expedition, Phyl's strength and endurance were greatly admired by the men, who found they had nothing to worry about having her along. Not only was she a big woman, but she was strong as well. Certain duties befell her which were "womanly," and she took a ribbing about her camp baking. Baked bread was nonexistent in camp, and biscuits were in short supply. A primus pressure stove was all that was available for cooking above the tree line, and Phyl was charged with the making of a flour substitute. What she baked was not exactly like pancakes and not exactly like bannock either. The men first called it "pannock" and, later, "panic." An appetite and strawberry jam were all that were needed to make the "panics" go down. Phyl was somewhat miffed: as if the men could have done better!

Four days after the first ascent of Combatant, a sleet storm struck their camp about one o'clock in the morning. The Munday's tent was torn apart at the seams. They joined Fuhrer in the cook tent, but by daybreak it, too, had split open. Everything was soaked. And Waddington was deep in a new mantle of snow. After making an unsuccessful attempt on Mount Geddes (3353), they abandoned the Scimitar and turned homewards.

Four parties entered the Waddington area in 1934. One of them ended tragically: on 26 June the party leader, Alec Dalgleish from Vancouver, fell more than two hundred metres to an instant death. It was the first fatality on the mountain.

Later in the season the Mundays, with Hall, Fuhrer, and two young men, Pip Brock and Ron Munro, arrived at Waddington via their traditional route, the Franklin Glacier. By mid-August they had completed two attempts to climb the mountain's main tower. The first was by way of the Dais Glacier. Deep, unstable snow turned them back at thirty-five hundred metres. The second attempt brought them onto the northwest summit for the second time. They studied the final tower at close range. It was very close and only a little higher, "a great spire poised in a void." But, unlike most mountains, Waddington offered its greatest difficulties at its apex.

Encrusted with ice feathers, the sharp crest made a direct approach too dangerous. They climbed down from the northwest peak and traversed onto the northeast face. A closer look at the climbing problems revealed a bergschrund below them, its upper and lower lips separated by a menacing vertical gap of fifteen metres. It guarded the base of the cliff. They might scale the face from their traverse position, but what they saw above them diminished their resolve. The short face was steep and exposed; the rock was rotten, loose, and intermixed with ice. Security was at a minimum without pitons and extra rope. For the last disappointing time, they turned back. On 17 August they made a first ascent of a lower peak and named it Mount Finality (2743).

The Waddington glacial region lies between two great river systems which roughly parallel one another; on the east is the Homathko, on the west the Klinaklini. To the west of the

159

Klinaklini River is an ice cap of about seven hundred and fifty square kilometres, a remnant of the last continental ice sheet. The principal summit of the region is Silverthrone Mountain (2957). No one knew a way to the peak, and the Mundays hoped to find it by way of the Klinaklini Glacier.

Over the winters, Don Munday had been building a six-metre boat with a cabin to replace the skiff used on earlier voyages up Knight Inlet. In 1935 it was launched and christened the *Edidonphyl.* They used it on their trip that summer to the head of the inlet.

The route up the Klinaklini Valley proved to be tortuous by reason of its terrain and the wasps prevalent that summer in southwestern British Columbia. Following the river north to its junction with Tumult Creek, the Mundays could find no safe way to cross the creek and thus reach the Klinaklini Glacier. After exploring westwards some distance, they returned home.

In 1936 the Mundays came back for a second try at Silverthrone and this time they were ready to deal with Tumult Creek. They carried thirty metres of light wire cable. Walking up its south bank to the glacier, the party crossed the ice, and then trekked down the north bank of the creek. With the help of two teen-age boys, Sherry Chase and Bill Hinton, they rigged a wire crossing above the creek, using poles set in rock piles as shear legs. A pulley system was devised for hauling, and soon all loads were across.

By previous arrangement, the Mundays then went downstream to meet Hall and Fuhrer who, they found, had just successfully climbed Monarch Mountain (3533) to the north and brought news also of the first ascent of Mount Waddington.[7] With their hopes for the achievement now finally gone, Phyl and Don could not help but reflect on their

[7]The first ascent of Waddington's main summit was accomplished by Fritz Wiessner and Bill House on 21 July 1936 with the use of pitons and extra rope. They climbed the mountain's southwest face. House was an American and Wiessner was a Swiss living in the U.S. who subsequently joined an American climbing expedition to K2, the second-highest mountain in the world.

years of frustrated effort. They put their disappointment aside and turned to the work at hand.

Bears and wolves are inhabitants of the Coast Mountains, and the Mundays often sighted them or found traces of their nearby presence. Bears gave them no trouble except on one occasion during the second Silverthrone expedition.

The party was packing loads to a camp beside the south tongue of the Klinaklini Glacier when they encountered a young grizzly and stopped to photograph it. Concentrating on picture taking, they were surprised when they heard a loud "whoof" behind them and wheeled quickly to see three other bears, a female grizzly and two cubs. No more than ten metres away, the curious bears were advancing at a rapid pace.

Everyone yelled. The female broke off with her cubs and joined the younger bear in a gully. Everything was quiet for a moment until the cubs, filled with unsatisfied curiosity, approached the climbers again. Without a sound the female charged off a large rock at Phyl. Don intervened, fanning his hat and throwing it at the bear. But as he backed away from her, he tripped and fell into some bushes at the top of a short cliff.

Phyl immediately sensed Don would be attacked in this defenceless position. "I was so mad at her [the bear]," Phyl said. She took her ice axe and, with it raised over her head, stood by her fallen husband; ready to do battle. The grizzly gave a bellow, broke off her charge, and left Phyl, "in possession of the field."

"It was a good thing she did, too," Phyl said later, "or we'd have been in real trouble."

A few days later, after a first ascent of Fang Peak (2347), they were able to spot Silverthrone Mountain and determine its direction over the icefield. On 14 August 1936 they travelled about eleven kilometres to a point east of the mountain, climbed a rock rib to the summit ridge, and followed its sharp, undulating crescent to the top. With their first ascent accomplished they turned to make the long journey back to Knight Inlet.

Directly north of the Klinaklini Icefield lies another group of Coast Mountains, known as the Monarch-Bentinck Group. They lie in an area south of the Bella Coola River, a long east-west valley cut into granite.

In July 1937 the Mundays voyaged more than six hundred kilometres in the *Edidonphyl* to Bella Coola via Queen Charlotte Strait and Fitz Hugh Sound. Their daughter Edith, then sixteen years old, accompanied them to climb for the first time. Together they made the first ascent of Stupendous Mountain (2728), named by Sir Alexander Mackenzie in 1793. Returning from the climb, they stopped at Stuie Lodge along the Bella Coola, where Phyl acted as hostess at a reception for the visiting Governor General, Lord Tweedsmuir. He was there to see first-hand the provincial park which had been named in his honour.

One year later the three Mundays, Hall, and Herman Ulrichs returned, this time by steamer. They made a first ascent of Bastille Mountain (2286), an outlier of Mount Saugstad, which they attempted a year later, 1939, only to be turned back by snow. It was not a favourite area, and instead the Mundays' attention was drawn back to the Cariboos in 1940 and to another great icefield, the Homathko, in 1941.

The Homathko Icefield comprises an area of about six hundred and fifty square kilometres east of the Homathko River, southeast of Waddington. In the early forties, the great frozen mass was unexplored, but some of its peaks had been named to commemorate the Pacific voyages of Sir Francis Drake. In 1941, the Mundays made the first ascent of Mount Grenville (3079), on the southern boundary of the icefield, and in 1942 the first ascent of Mount Queen Bess (3313), on its northern limits.

The Second World War had now entered the Pacific Theatre. Don tried to rejoin the army, but he had been wounded previously and was considered too old. To assist the war effort, he gave up much of his freelance journalism and took regular employment in a Vancouver shipyard. Available time for climbing was greatly reduced, but by 1946 he and Phyl were at it again. They ascended Reliance Mountain (3134) above the Homathko River close to its junction with Mosley Creek. It proved to be their last first ascent.

Their mountaineering continued, however, in both the Coast Mountains and the Rockies. Phyl and Don seldom missed the Alpine Club of Canada's Annual Camp.[8] Phyl gave much to the organization over the years and was recognized for her leadership ability, being awarded the club's Silver Rope Badge in 1948.

Phyl and Don shared their last camp together in the Freshfield group of the Rockies in 1949, where they climbed Mount Freshfield (3336). In November Don fell ill and went into the Vancouver Military Hospital. For six long months Phyl, who did not drive, took the bus every day from North Vancouver to visit him.[9] It was a forlorn cause. Overcome with pneumonia, he died on 12 June 1950 at the age of sixty. A month later Phyl chartered an airplane, flew over Mount Munday, and scattered her husband's ashes. It ended, in her words, "the best thirty years of my life."

For Phyl, the next thirty years have been filled with honours. Already an Honorary Member of the ACC since 1938, she was made the only woman Honorary Member of the American Alpine Club in 1967. The same year she was awarded the Centennial Medal and appointed Dame of Grace of the Order of St. John in recognition for her voluntary work with the St. John Ambulance Association. In 1971, the Alpine Club of Canada elected her as its Honorary President, a title she continues to hold.

"I was tremendously surprised," she said when in 1973 she was asked by letter if she would accept membership in the Order of Canada. Of course she would! In April that year Phyl Munday was invested by Governor General Roland Michener. She wore a beautiful light blue gown and looked every inch a duchess.

[8] Phyl Munday continues to attend the camp, her last being in 1979 at Glacier Lake in the Rockies.

[9] When she was about seventy, Phyl learned to drive and bought her first car.

Today in her small, frame, hillside house on Tempe Crescent, in North Vancouver, Phyl Munday lives among her mementos. She is highly respected and loved by all who know her. Despite her eighty years or more, she recalls with clarity and brightness the days when she was her husband's "chief push" and says, "Those were the good days, hard, but good."

Chapter Seven

Fred Beckey
1923 –

*My successes belong to me alone,...and
I have paid for them in person.*

Walter Bonatti,
great Italian mountaineer

Beckey and Marts settled in their bivouac sack and reviewed the day's events. First there was sighting the aircraft wreckage at the bottom of the east face, pieces of torn aluminium, a gear wheel, and something bright, perhaps a string of beads. Then, while they were roping up, a gigantic block of granite had slid off, sparking its way down a slab they had crossed only a few minutes earlier. The sound of its crashing and the acrid smell of its descent had made them shudder.

The initial climbing had been tricky, too, and steep. Unexpectedly Beckey had fallen off a layback when his finger strength gave out; a protection piton saved him injury, but the slip made him angry. Then there was the sensational exposure in the latter section, four long leads on a crest between the east and north faces. "No room for error," Beckey had said.

The two men pondered these incidents while chewing a mixture of candies, raisins, and nuts, and secured to the ledge by four solid pitons and rope anchors. Below them was the black chasm of the north face.

Imperceptibly at first, and then more noticeably, their dark world closed in. Was it wisps of cloud or fog which had begun to sweep their airy ledge? They watched as water droplets slowly condensed on the surface of their bivouac sack and then dripped from its edges. The mist grew denser and their position more eery.

Damp and chilled, they could not sleep. When dawn came, it revealed itself as "a grey murk." The features of the mountain dissipated in a white, ghostly vapour. They seemed to be aboard a ship without a bearing. They discussed what to do next.

To continue climbing under these conditions could mean getting lost — a plausible and reckless prospect. Retreat was a better choice, but it, too, would be dangerous.

Into the mists they began their rappels, one after the other, over moist and clammy rock. Each one was risky. In the gloom the climbers were no longer certain of their surroundings. Tense yet careful, Beckey was gravely concerned: "It would be a disaster to rappel into the wrong area and pull down the ropes, cutting off upward retreat." They had, in fact, almost made this dangerous mistake by starting a rappel into the chasm of the north face; only the discovery of a small stone cairn, built on the way up, indicated which way to go.

As they worked their way down, the fog eventually thinned and the descent became easier. A few hours later, the perils of Mount Slesse's northeast buttress were behind them. The date: July 1963.

Fred Beckey was born in 1923 in West Seattle, Washington, where he was also educated. At thirteen he made a holiday visit to the Olympic Hot Springs with his parents and scrambled up Boulder Peak (1828) alone. He was in search of "fresh adventure and [a] chance for bravery."

His parents, much concerned, later saw to it that their son joined the Boy Scouts, where such excursions were supervised. In Scout shorts with pajama pants underneath to shield their knees from the sun, Fred and other boys learned how to snow climb with the use of alpenstocks. These early trips made a deep impression on him as a boy. In his diary he wrote, "I solemnly believe that a man who hasn't his heart in climbing will never make a true climber."

This early conviction turned into a personal commitment which shaped his entire future. Mountaineering would be his profession, and he would pursue it with dedication. There would be no one else to equal him.

At fifteen Fred joined the Seattle Mountaineers as a junior member, and the following year, 1939, he was introduced to the technical aspects of climbing when he enrolled in the club's climbing course. In that season alone he made thirty-five ascents, including his first first ascent, Mount Despair (2210), in the Cascade Range of northern Washington. Quickly assimilating new concepts as well as knowledge, Fred discovered that a small, self-reliant team in good physical condition could achieve great feats in the mountains.

Shortly thereafter Fred, with his younger brother Helmy, began to experiment with new techniques. Hip-piton belays for leader protection; prusik slings tied to the climbing rope for glacier skiing and crevasse rescue; body slings for rappels; and double ropes for direct aid pitches all came into use. The two boys did their first direct aid climbing on a steep rock wall, carefully chosen because soft snow lay at its base. The snow, they thought, might soften a fall should their ambition exceed their technique.

Quite taken by these experiences, Fred made a large number of ascents in his native Washington in 1940—1941. When not mountaineering, he kept in shape playing football, running cross-country, and "climbing over the tops of pay toilets," the latter a subtle combination of exercise and practical economics.

Before 1942, Fred had only been out of the state on one occasion, to climb six peaks in the Tetons of Wyoming, among them the Grand Teton (4199). But at age nineteen, with almost a hundred ascents including many firsts, he was ready to tackle an expedition to Canada.

In July 1942, he and Helmy disembarked at the head of Knight Inlet in British Columbia; they planned to make the second ascent of Mount Waddington (4042). It had been climbed only once, in 1936, by Fritz Wiessner and Bill House after an all-out effort. Sixteen other attempts had failed.

Despite their youth, the Beckey brothers knew Waddington would be no pushover, and they prepared carefully. Food supply was packaged in paraffined bags, each containing rations for one man-day. They carried a pressure stove, 150-centimetre glacier skis, air pillows, cache bags, and a blizzard tent, as well as other equipment.

During the first half of July, it rained almost every day. The brothers moved thirty-kilogram loads, first through the bush and then up the Franklin Glacier to Icefall Point. From this point they skied supplies as far as the pass between Mounts Munday and Agur. There on 13 July they were caught in a storm and spent two nights, wet and slightly frostbitten, in a large, partly filled crevasse. A few days later, after packing additional supplies to the pass, they skied around the southeast slopes of Munday and down the icefall of the Splendour Glacier into the awesome valley of the Tiedemann Glacier. There they hoped to reach the great peaks on its north side, but Helmy had a sprained back and Fred a knee infection resulting from a neglected devil's club thorn. These reasons and a shortage of food eventually forced them back.

On 30 July they made a ski ascent of Mount Munday. It increased their confidence and renewed their determination to make an assault on their principal objective, Mount Waddington. By 5 August they had moved eight days' supplies from the Franklin through the Dais Glacier icefall to a shelf below Waddington's eight-hundred-metre southwest face. It was a spectacular high camp.

Their position at the upper edge of the Dais Glacier was separated from the rock face by a large bergschrund. The same day as they made high camp, the brothers reconnoitred the "schrund," found it in decayed condition, but discovered a bridge where it could be crossed. However, the crossing was far to the right of a couloir up which they intended to climb. Once on the upper lip of the bergschrund, they had to traverse back to a point above their camp. Here they rappelled down, leaving the rope in place for a direct start next morning.

They slept fitfully that night. A noisy wind snapped the tent walls, causing the boys to turn and toss. Each movement was coupled with anxious anticipation of the next day's climb.

At four o'clock in the morning, 6 August 1942, the two brothers shook off sleep. With heavy packs and straining arms, they hauled themselves hand over hand up the rappel rope. In moments they were on the top lip of the bergschrund.

Good snow in the couloir quickly gave way to snow over hard ice, followed by a steep, thirty-metre rock section glazed with frozen water. When the temperature warmed up, this part would be a waterfall. Higher, the couloir was scored by avalanche fans, and conditions became more treacherous. Where possible, Fred and Helmy climbed the side walls, but the frequent transition from ice to rock meant climbing the latter on crampons. The points scraped and caught, jarring their nerves.

Several hours were consumed ascending the three hundred metres to a rock band, which they climbed at a steep angle around a buttress and over several ribs. Then, for the first time, the brothers saw clearly the upper face and its triangular snowfield. It was a "forbidding view." Thoughtful, yet not deterred, they climbed the steep snowfield as quickly as they could. The face was beginning to cast debris from the heights.

It was four in the afternoon when Fred changed his nailed boots for tennis shoes, over which he wore a pair of homemade felt pullovers. Alternating leads, Fred on the rock and Helmy on the ice, the two boys tackled the next section. Fourteen hours after leaving camp, they reached the bottom of the final hundred-and-fifty-metre tower.

The mountain did not let up. The young climbers kept to more exposed high-angle rock to avoid icefall, and Fred's piton hammer was heard in the early evening as he protected the last steep sections. In an icy crack, slippery and wet, it took all the concentration he had to climb, layback position, to its top. Meanwhile, windblown ice feathers rained down on them from above. In time a short traverse into a chimney led them to the summit ridge. By eight thirty that evening the two young men had ascended Mount Waddington. The matchcan register of Wiessner and House was found in the cairn a few feet below the snowy top. Into the record, the Beckeys entered their names.

As the sun set, the brothers prepared to leave the spot they had so energetically sought. Rappelling down the upper chimney to a tiny ledge, they made a bivouac. Once the anchors were set, they settled in a tent sack, heated some food with Sterno fuel, and then catnapped the night away with their feet hanging over the edge. They had great reason for satisfaction.

In the morning the brothers started their rappels, setting each anchor carefully and pulling the rope cautiously to prevent snags and dislodgement of rocks. Eventually they reached the head of the large lower couloir and decided to wait for the sun to leave the slope. A drop in temperature would make it safer. They had plenty of time. All was going well.

At six in the evening they started down again. Helmy was partially shielded by an overhang and was pulling the rope down when a speeding rock struck him without warning. He cried out in pain, then seized his leg as blood streamed from a severed vein above the knee. They stopped immediately to attend to this emergency, but by the time it was under control it was too dark to continue in safety. As they settled down for a second bivouac on a short, steep slope of loose scree, they remembered it was Helmy's seventeenth birthday.

Very weary the next morning, the young men reached their high camp. Nine days later they returned to Knight Inlet.

When the news of Waddington's ascent by two teenagers reached the Canadian climbing community, it was greeted with disbelief. The monarch of the Coast Mountains had defied all comers until 1936. How could two boys do it? The initial shock eventually gave way to admiration, and Phyl Munday, whose life had become entwined with the mountain, declared, "Those boys did a marvellous job."

The United States was then at war, and Fred was old enough to enlist. He joined the U.S. Army Mountain Troops at Quandary, Colorado, in 1943 and served until the end of the fighting. Surprisingly, he climbed very few peaks while in the army.

When hostilities ended, Beckey was climbing again. In 1946 he made his first climbs in Yosemite Valley, California, and first ascended both Kate's Needle (3049) and Devil's Thumb (2767) along the Alaska-British Columbia border. Devil's Thumb, which Beckey described as "a truncated Matterhorn — only steeper," required three attempts because of a combination of recurrent storms and technical severity. The final descent included a spectacular rappel twenty-five metres long, five metres clear of the face.

Only twenty-four years old in 1947, Beckey, already heralded as a veteran climber, returned to the Waddington area. There several unclimbed peaks, the highest in provincial Canada, attracted a two-month expedition of the Harvard Mountaineering Club. Beckey decided to join the party as it would allow him to try those peaks which he and Helmy had missed in 1942. With others he succeeded in making nine first ascents, including Mount Asperity (3506). Unfortunately the triumph of the expedition was marred by the death of Charles Shiverick in an avalanche, high on the Serra Peaks.

Beckey tried to climb all year round, dividing his activities between Canada and the U.S. in accordance with the season and the opportunities presented by each mountain region. Thus he came to Canada in 1948 to climb Mount Louis near Banff and to make his first visit to the Bugaboo Group, west of the headwaters of the Columbia River. He ascended Bugaboo Spire, via Kain's route, noting with admiration Kain's courage in traversing the gendarme without protection and wondering "why he didn't use sneakers." Crescent and Snowpatch Spires were also climbed, and Beckey completed a new route via the northeast face on Pigeon. It was his most difficult endeavour in the group and marked the beginning of his preference for steep faces, many of which would be made in Canada's Bugaboos.

In 1949, at the age of twenty-six, Beckey published the *Climber's Guide to the Cascade and Olympic Mountains of Washington*, the first of a series of guidebooks which he would write over the next thirty years. It became known as "Beckey's Bible." During the ensuing years, scores of new routes and first ascents were added to his credit, all in the southern forty-eight states or Alaska. Highlights included an ascent of Mount McKinley, the continent's highest mountain for the TV program, "I Search for Adventure," and a first ascent of Mount Deborah in Alaska with Heinrich Harrer, a member of the first party to ascend the north face of the famous Eiger in Switzerland.

His interest in foreign ranges was indulged for the first time in 1955 when he joined the International Himalayan Expedition to Lhotse, the beautiful sister summit to Mount Everest. Although the expedition was not successful in climbing Lhotse, Beckey established a world high-altitude ski record for that period when he skied up Everest's Khumbu Glacier to an altitude of seven thousand metres. The expedition yielded three first ascents, all climbed by a party including Beckey. They were: the south summit of Lobuje (4930), Langcha (6297), and Kantega IV (ca. 6800). Before leaving Nepal, the group explored the Kwangde region and discovered one of the world's highest lakes. Beckey stopped in Africa on his way home and climbed Kilimanjaro alone, more concerned with the warlike-looking Kikuyu tribesmen than with the problems of ascent.

The next year he took a rest and climbed only three new routes. It was a short respite.

Renewed interest in the Canadian ranges came to Beckey in 1959. After several conditioning climbs, he and

Hank Mather, a German climber then living in Vancouver, drove to the Bugaboos. They had several new routes in mind, but one, the east face of Snowpatch, was the most daring and enterprising Beckey had ever contemplated.

Snowpatch Spire, identified by the great white snow eye which stares from its tower of monolithic granite, dominates Boulder Camp, a tiny, fairylike meadow of flowers, grass, and ice-cold rivulets. Huge boulders fallen from the heights litter the scene, and the Bugaboo Glacier tumbles into the valley below. It is a Tolkienesque setting, from which soars the great spire, its eastern embattlements proportioned vertically to fend off all invaders. It was, in Beckey's opinion, a "stunning" wall as great as any of the great walls found in the Alps.

After studying its problems through binoculars, the climbers conceded they were in for a siege. The length of the sheer face was six hundred and twenty-five metres. The lowest section of two hundred and fifty metres was massively defended, overhung by at least two major rock roofs and several minor ones. The middle section angled back somewhat in a shallow depression but was slabby and without visible cracks for more than two hundred metres. The only possible relief in sight was in the upper third, where broken rock, tilted slabs, and cracks seemed to offer steep but easier climbing. With no natural route to guide them, they chose to go straight up the centre of the face. As Beckey said, "There really was no route. We just picked a likely series of cracks...through the overhangs."

The big effort had to be carefully planned. Hours were spent examining the face, picking out belay points and bivouac sites, and choosing and preparing equipment. Their plan was to force the route up from the ice at the foot of the wall, retreating each evening and leaving fixed ropes to gain the same height the day following. When they felt it was safe, they would abandon their ground support and rely on their own stamina to push on to the summit. Snow, rain, and lightning they would leave to chance.

173

In the afternoon of 26 July, Beckey and Mather went to the face of the mountain to establish a starting point. Mather, almost laughing, was amused by the prospect of a climb which started with so much difficulty. They were separated from the rock wall by a bergschrund, and the first line of cracks was across a two-metre gap. Mather lowered Beckey six metres into the bergschrund and watched him swing giddily on the rope as he pushed off the ice wall in an effort to reach a crack in the rock face opposite. Eventually he succeeded in catching a crack and jammed in an angle piton, which he hammered and fixed with a sling on which he could stand. More angles and some self-tensioning brought him above an overhang, but he was still below where Mather stood. Climbing as far as he could, Beckey left in two more pitons and called it a day.

At dawn the next morning they were back at the overhanging wall. Beckey resumed his lead, prusiking with rope slings and aluminium stirrups to his last position. An overhang above was filled with moss; Beckey tore it out. An estimated fifteen kilograms of green clods littered the snow below. After placing forty pitons and climbing only fifty metres in six hours, he came to the last move below the first belay station. It required raising himself quickly with both arms as if onto a mantelshelf, while stepping out of his last aid stirrup.

As Beckey made the lift, his foot caught in the stirrup. Partially suspended through the crucial motion, he fought to retain his grip while kicking desperately at the stirrup to free his boot. An instant away from falling into space, he felt his foot come free. He pulled himself onto the ledge. It was over in seconds but his heart pounded for some time afterwards.

All equipment, food, and water were hauled up, and Mather took the lead. His section went more easily and in two hours the climbers reached a second ledge, large enough to take the side of one hip. They fixed two ropes and rappelled off for the day. So overhanging was the face that they swung free from the wall and landed on the snow, clear of the bergschrund. The day following they returned to their car for more pitons.

Two more days gave them two more leads, Beckey taking the third on a double rope and Mather the fourth. Bolts were placed at belay positions. The wall was almost flawless except for some sensationally dangerous cracks which were frequently insufficient or rotten. Moss chunks were sent whirring to the glacier below. The exposure was unrivalled as they toiled suspended over space. The worst section on the fourth lead was bypassed using wooden wedges and two small bolts, but when they roped down at twilight, the pitch was still not finished. Looking up the face after their rappel, they could see they had reached the lower edge of a great white overhang, a distinct inverted column of rock, landmarking the face.

The two climbers knew that sometime they would have to abandon their ground support and stay on the face to complete the climb. They rested a few days and, with Brian Greenwood and Elfrida Pigou,[1] put up a new route on the less difficult west face which would allow them a rapid descent once they reached the top.

On 5 August they went to the final assault. Mather, with a broken hammer, managed to finish the fourth lead using giant angle pitons and came to a stance in a smooth chimney. Standing in his stirrups, he belayed Beckey, who passed him in midafternoon and climbed the fifth pitch, which required a bolt, more aid pitons, and some free climbing to their first bivouac ledge. Slightly higher, from another hanging belay, Beckey brought Mather up. On the sixth lead, Mather led left across a vertical wall to a crack cutting into a black overhang. Large wooden wedges and two bolts were used. This pitch proved to be the most exhausting problem on the climb. Mather's hands, arms, shoulders, and back ached from the strain of the required effort. As there was no

---

[1]Pigou, with three fellow climbers, perished when an avalanche overran their party on the lower Bravo Glacier of Mount Waddington in 1960. Their bodies were never recovered.

certainty of reaching another ledge above for a bivouac that night, they left the sixth pitch unfinished and rappelled down to the lower bivouac site.

Tied to the mountain on their tiny ledge, they dozed off only to awake before dawn, shivering with cold. During the night the fixed rope above their heads had run with water and then frozen. Prusiking up the first ten metres was most painful as their bare fingers grasped the icy rope.

Mather finished his lead of the day before using direct aid, placed a bolt, and started hauling the loads. One rucksack and a duffel bag stuck on the overhang, requiring Beckey to extricate them as he prusiked. He tried to climb the obstacle with the loads tied to him, but it was too much. The ropes, heavy with friction had jammed in the carabiners. Beckey and Mather arranged a separate sling to get the loads over the projection. It was a slow, trying process and damaged their morale. It was four in the afternoon when they finished their sixth lead. There had been little progress.

Then the climb changed noticeably. There were some free climbing sections, and from time to time the summit could be seen three hundred metres above them. Recognizing that the hard technical sections were over, the two lightened their loads, tossing off bundles of climbing iron and rope, most of which fell clear to the glacier. In the remaining light they made five and a half leads over enjoyable class five rock, with some short aid sections.

Now far too high to turn back, threatening clouds reminded them that they had best make their second bivouac quickly. They settled down on a granite sand pile against a thirty-degree-angle slab. The first part of the night was not too bad; tinned fruit and other food helped. But later it was bitterly cold, and a flashlight at Boulder Camp signalled them to advise the barometer was falling.

It was dawn on the seventh day since their start when Mather led off again. Only four aid pitons were needed, as they encountered mostly free climbing. Eventually lots of breaks in the rock surface permitted faster progress, and shortly past noon, 7 August 1959, these two strong men stood on the summit of Snowpatch, happy it was over. Relaxing a while, they took count of their difficulties: 160 piton placements, 8 bolts, and several wooden wedges had been used. But now all they could think of was a good night's sleep. They hurried down the west face.

The next day, returning to their starting point, they climbed the first three leads and recovered their fixed ropes which they had carefully left for an emergency descent. Beckey wrote, "We were off the great wall for the last time."

As happened seventeen years earlier with his ascent of Mount Waddington, Beckey's east face route on Snowpatch drew disbelief and then criticism for its "madness." But it stood the test of time and established a new set of climbing standards in Canada.

The east face route on Snowpatch heralded the opening of a decade of intense activity for Beckey, almost entirely aimed at steep faces. At thirty-six years of age, he had already done more original ascents than most climbers could imagine in a lifetime. And his greatest efforts tended to eclipse what were to others major new routes; Snowpatch would overshadow the direct west face ascent of Bugaboo Spire and the northwest face of Mount Slesse, east of Vancouver, done in the same year.

By now Beckey was a master at living at minimum cost. Although he worked as a salesman in the printing, advertising, and associated businesses, his climbing activities occupied a great part of each year. Earning a living seemed incidental to the advancement of his mountaineering career. He had at his command a wide choice of partners, among the best in North America. For many it became a distinction to have made a new climb with him, and an invitation from him caused more than one climber to drop all other plans. Most partners found their experiences with him unforgettable, not only for the climbing, where his speed and single-minded pursuit of the objective left them panting, but for other events as well. Basically shy and secretive about his plans, he was found to be intelligent, widely read, and in possession of firm opinions. Those with the wits often discovered themselves in intellectual wrestling matches, hardly relaxing, but certainly memorable, encounters with the master mountaineer.

Many a climber still wants to know what plans Beckey has for the future, but any enquiries are generally answered with vague replies. Not content with hard or classic climbs only, Beckey's penchant has been to create new routes, his intensive research teaching him what was available, especially in the most remote areas. It prompted one cynical contemporary to observe with amusement, "If Fred gets in there, he'll climb everything is sight."

Never married, Beckey lived with his brother Helmy in southern California for the good part of a decade, until Helmy moved to Europe. Fred became a master at automobile living, constantly on the move in search of new climbs where the weather and the season permitted them. Sparing himself very little, he could drive all night if needed. This kind of regimen never allowed his medium frame to become paunchy or soft; he was, in fact, stronger and faster than most men ten years his junior.

Beckey returned to Canada in July of 1961, his first objective being the stone-pitted north face of Mount Edith Cavell (3363), the highest and most impressive mountain close to Jasper. Thousands of tourists gaze upon the face each summer as it stands, stark and forbidding above its wing-shaped Angel Glacier. Surely, they think, no one can climb it.

With Beckey was Dan Doody, an American who, two years later, would be the official photographer to the American Everest Expedition, and Yvon Chouinard, a Californian who manufactures climbing equipment designed for the granite walls of Yosemite Valley; he had brought some untapered pitons especially for this climb. Chouinard and Doody had tried the ascent a year earlier.

The weather had been poor for several days when, on 20 July, it cleared and, with a late start, the three climbers were on their way. From the Edith Cavell teahouse they walked briskly to the base of the face, to the left of the main tongue of the glacier. Over class four rocks they climbed unroped in order to move quickly up the lower third of the wall, which was dominated by an unstable ice cliff. Once directly below the fifty-metre cliff, Beckey led three pitches "in grand style" to the surface of the glacier itself. Immediately relieved to be out of danger, they were not surprised when later that day the cliff collapsed and covered their entire approach route.

The danger of rockfall on the upper face forced them to choose a line along a vertical rock rib directly up the centre. The rib stands out slightly from the wall and was thought to be freer from falling debris. Beckey crossed the bergschrund and led quickly up a difficult system of jam cracks. For the next three hundred metres they moved as fast as they could over steep, loose rocks which kept them alert. All belay spots were chosen under overhangs to protect against rockfall, and pitons, to save time, were used only for belays.

Chouinard called the face a "shooting gallery." Once when Doody yelled "Rock!" Chouinard pulled in his head, and a grapefruit-size piece speeding from above, smashed right where Chouinard's head had been. Soon after, a sheet of snow shot over them, filling their collars with ice crystals and grit and leaving all else white around them.

In the upper third, Beckey, who was in top form, did most of the leading over rotten but somewhat easier rock. At ten in the evening, he was forced by the angle of the slope to cross an avalanche-scoured snow couloir. Placing a piton for protection slightly above the crossing point, he traversed the steep verglas-covered chute with barely a pause. "A magnificent lead," Chouinard said. A little higher up, Beckey found three protected ledges on which they could bivouac. The day had gone by without a stop for food or water. It was midnight.

The three spent a reasonably comfortable night, but in the morning, just as they started to climb again, it began to rain. Gradually the rain turned to hail, pounding them with a thousand tiny blows. They could hardly hear each other's shouts, so great was the din. Lightning began to strike the summit two hundred and fifty metres above their heads. Clouds surrounded them, clearing intermittently from time to time to reveal awesome views of the great precipitous wall of which they were now a tiny part.

Three hours later they reached the summit ice slope, and Chouinard took his turn at leading. The ice was decayed and kept sliding under his feet. He cut big steps for security, while below him Beckey and Doody, soaking wet, could feel their feet getting colder and colder. Chouinard looked down between his legs at them and could see them huddled against the wall. Thirteen hundred metres lower was the valley floor.

The last pitch was horrendous. On loose shale, without protection, his feet insecurely placed, Chouinard got his hands above a small band of dirt and onto the summit slope. For the first time he could see the summit pole, only fifteen metres away.[2] But try as he might he could not pull himself up. His feet kept sliding down, and his hands dug deeply into the dirt. There was a stupendous drop below him; he was afraid. "Oh God, what a place to get it!" he thought.

Then, desperate to find a passage, he spotted a patch of good snow to one side and cautiously eased over to it. It was solid. He pulled himself onto the top, and the day was theirs. One of Canada's great mountain walls had been surmounted.

After the Edith Cavell climb, Beckey and Chouinard drove to Rogers Pass and made the first ascent of the north face of Mount Sir Donald, the Selkirk Matterhorn, as Beckey liked to call it. The face rises in one long curve. It was tense, nerve-stressing work over steep ice slopes at the base and perilously loose quartzite blocks higher up. Beckey complained of exposure nerves, saying, "One could not err on a single hold."

In the Bugaboos, a few days later, they climbed a short, new technical route on the north face of Pigeon Spire and

[2]A wooden pole marking a summit is uncommon in the Canadian ranges where rock cairns normally indicate the highest point. Poles and crosses are common to the Alps.

then turned their gaze to the south tower of the neighbouring Howser Spire, which had not been climbed for twenty years.[3] Beckey could not understand why. "A line up the sheer east face was a challenge too apparent to overlook....It is one of the most glamorous walls in the range." On the anniversary of Conrad Kain's birthday, 10 August 1961, he and Chouinard started the climb and finished it the next day.

Studying the opposite, west face of Howser's south tower a day or two later, the two climbers were greatly impressed by its proportions. "Looking upward, we knew that here was a climb of high Yosemite standards, almost 2500 feet [760 metres] in height, and subject to all the dangers in mountaineering in an alpine range. It was apparent that this climb was a classic." They planned to use some of Chouinard's special hardware, ranging from very thin knife-blade pitons of chrome alloy to ten-centimetre aluminium angle "bongbongs" to fit large cracks.

On the first full day, they climbed up the fixed ropes which they had put in place earlier for an easy start. On the second pitch, the leader made a heart-stopping discovery as he prusiked upwards. Two strands of the three-strand nylon rope had been chewed completely through by a rodent who obviously enjoyed eating synthetic fibre. The remaining strand had withstood the load of the climber hanging on it.

The face proved to be long and strenuous, requiring the best techniques. In sections, stark and exposed, it comprised twenty-three pitches and necessitated more than a hundred piton placements. They descended from the summit after two days of climbing, and Beckey noted the face now "looked more hospitable, but only the knowledge we had climbed it made it so."

In 1962 – 1963 Beckey visited Canada to climb in the Bugaboos and Rockies with a variety of partners, including Brian Greenwood. Perhaps his most notable first ascent of this period was that of the northeast buttress of Mount

[3]The first ascent of the south tower of Howser Spire was completed in 1941 by a party which included Helmy Beckey.

Slesse (2429), which he termed "the beauty queen of the North Cascades." Located east of Vancouver near Chilliwack, its south peak was the scene of a disastrous air crash in December 1956, when sixty-two persons were killed including some members of the Saskatchewan Roughriders Football Club. The wreckage fell six hundred metres to the glacier below, leaving steel control cables dangling from the east face.

Beckey had climbed the south peak as early as 1952 and, in 1959, made a new route on the northwest face with Hank Mather and Don (Claunch) Gordon. In July 1963 he and Steve Marts of Seattle set out to ascend Slesse's long eight-hundred-metre northeast buttress. They turned back in the face of unstable weather.[4]

In late August of the same year, the two men returned with Eric Bjornstad, who was "willing to undergo the necessary suffering." Travelling light with two forty-five-metre ropes, a ninety-metre hauling line, thirty carabiners, twenty-eight pitons, a bolt kit, plus a quart of water and a down jacket each, they were prepared to try again. At the end of the first day they bivouacked just below the high point of their first attempt. On reaching it the next morning they picked up some equipment but abandoned a sweater which had been chewed up by rodents for use as nesting material. The next section of the buttress was much easier, but then came the final grand sweep, the climax of the climb. It was a high class five route, taxing both strength and ingenuity and unremitting in its difficulties. Hours passed by.

At nightfall Beckey finally found a good ledge for their second bivouac. Bjornstad followed the rope line to Beckey in the failing light, but when Mart's turn came he could not climb in the dark and clean the pitch of pitons. He had no alternative; he would have to spend the night standing in his nylon stirrups. His partners, somewhere higher up, dozed off on the ledge, harassed by "snafflehounds," rodents

[4]This attempt is described at the beginning of this chapter.

which chewed their packs and boots while the men were sitting on them!

Marts shivered the night away and was first to move the next morning, happy to leave his lonely standing bivouac. As he climbed he knocked out each successive piton with his hammer fixing them on a sling for later use. Finally, after two days, two bivouacs, and a total of twenty-five class five leads, all difficulties were overcome and the trio stood on the summit. Beckey said they "had separated myth from reality" and created one of the finest free climbs in southern British Columbia.

The year of the Slesse ascent, Beckey was forty years old, a time when many mountaineers consider retirement from the hard routes, preferring instead to rest on their laurels and do shorter, less arduous climbs. Such was not the case with him; his activity did not let up. His widely varied successes over the next five years included the first winter ascents of Mounts Robson, Sir Donald, and Lefroy; the south face of Mount Tupper (2816), the checkered sweeping battlements by the highway at Rogers Pass, and Tupper's sister peak opposite, the north face of Mount MacDonald (2893); many new east face routes in the Ramparts overlooking Amethyst Lakes near Jasper; a host of new technical climbs in the Squamish area, on the Chief (652) and its outliers; and expeditions to the Coast Mountains. Broadly speaking, this list covers his activities in the Canadian ranges, but, at the same time, Beckey was active in Yosemite, Cascades, Sierras, Alaska, and many other American climbing centres.

His obvious credentials prompted the editor of *Appalachia*, America's oldest mountaineering journal, to write in 1966, "Fred Beckey is widely regarded as this country's most active climber today, and his all-around mountaineering accomplishments have been exceeded by no one in the history of North American mountaineering." The weight of his long career with more than five hundred new routes and first ascents made him one of the best in the world.

"So Uncle Fred has finally started his memoirs," wrote

Dick Culbert after The Mountaineers published Beckey's first biographical book in 1969, *Challenge of the North Cascades*. Beckey had already published three guidebooks, but this one surprised many climbers, who regarded him as being more mechanical than human; the book displayed his broader dimensions as a man and drew attention to his scholarly studies of mountain history.

For the last ten years Beckey's activity in Canada has diminished, although he has continued to do some new climbs almost every season. There seems to be no end in sight. Climbing now with partners who are half his age, he is still secretive about his plans, an enigmatic personality. Never unfriendly, but often elusive, he remains utterly individualistic, seemingly oblivious to the schedules of modern society. In blue jeans and checkered shirt, his modest frame is lean, hard, and weathered. A beard, mottled with grey, adds to the look of a man seasoned by sun and storm. His accomplishments have made him great.

Chapter Eight

Hans Gmoser
1932 –

A man should have wings to carry him
where his dreams go, but sometimes a
pair of skis makes a good substitute.

Hans Gmoser

Marmolata was normally a straightforward climb. Gmoser had reached the mountain the usual way, by crossing the Bugaboo Glacier, and had climbed to the upper lip of the bergschrund at a spot where the snow-covered ice abutted the face. He searched the wall above for a place to step onto the rock and belay his two clients.

Pausing for a moment, he looked back, across the glacier. There, some distance off but still within earshot, was another party led by his fellow guide, Ferdl Taxbock. In a gesture of greeting, he yodelled and heard his voice carry the distance across the ice.

The echo barely ended when it was followed by a surprising crash. The entire upper lip of the bergschrund collapsed, not only tearing itself from the rock face but pulling out several large pieces of granite with it.

Gmoser was swept away. He looked up once quickly to see what was happening but could do nothing whatever to stop himself. He landed on his back on the bottom lip of the bergschrund, ten metres lower, and was crushed by an enormous weight. A block of granite, the size of a coffee table, lay over him. His blood began to ooze into the snow. It was essential the second guide reach him quickly.

Taxbock hurried. When he reached Gmoser's side he was horrified at what he saw. Gmoser's left arm was swelling with blood, and his left leg stuck out at a grotesque angle under the granite. The damage done to Gmoser's chest and vital organs could not be assessed.

Fighting pain, Gmoser asked for a morphine syringe from his emergency kit and, in a typical effort, injected himself in the shoulder. The other climbers began to dig. The block was too large to lift or slide to one side, so they had to make a hole in the snow beneath the victim, lower him into it, and then slide him out. All the while Gmoser remained conscious. After he was extricated, he was able to eat some lunch and fell asleep in the sun. A helicopter flew him from the site an hour or two later.

Gmoser survived his injuries. After four weeks in the hospital he was discharged wearing a cast on one leg and one arm. With a speaking tour schedule immediately facing him, he went on the road, a sadly battered advertisement for his mountain holiday company.

Hans Gmoser[1] was born at Braunau, Austria, on 7 July 1932, the child of a love relationship between a house servant, Rosa Gmoser, and an Austrian soldier named Hans Resch. After his birth, Rosa, who was only nineteen years old, returned with her infant son to her family to live in Traun, near Linz on the Danube River. When Hans was two years old, his mother married a locksmith, Erasmus Hintringer, who accepted Hans as his son and raised him as his own, but Hans continued to carry his mother's maiden name.

His first interest in the mountains was stimulated a few years later when, at the age of five, his mother took him by train through the Eastern Alps to Graz. En route Rosa met two friends who were equipped with packs and ropes. The alpinists got off the train at a station where the peaks looked very big and steep. These two men, it appeared to Little Hans, were going to climb straight up them. He was very impressed.

[1]Gmoser is pronounced "moser."

Hans started school in 1938, the year of the annexation of Austria by Nazi Germany. As a boy the war did not affect him greatly at first; he started skiing and hiking and accepted conditions the way they were. Hunger was offset by excitement; by 1944 bombings were a regular daylight occurrence. He and his schoolmates were often sent home by ten thirty in the morning.

By December 1945 Austria's operating infrastructure broke down, and the schools closed for several months. Hans was enlisted to build tank barricades and fill bomb craters. Food became scarcer. He, himself, could not have been much thinner. Sent to the country to seek food from relatives, his journeys revealed the darker side of war when he saw corpses of deserters hanging from trees.

By the time the war was over, Hans had become, in his own words, "a thirteen-year-old black marketeer." As he had nothing, everything had a value. Linz had become a divided city, and business was to be made with American troops. For personal services such as polishing boots, sewing emblems on shirts, and contracting out laundry, Hans found he could obtain cigarettes, chocolate, and other assorted goods. These he could trade off for food and other necessities. Living by his wits and nerve, he became a street person. He might have made a "first-rate gangster" except for a chance encounter with a priest. At Christmas 1945, the priest took Hans and several other boys to the Dachstein massif, near Salzburg, for a skiing holiday. It was a critical experience. The following summer Hans returned to the Dachstein (3006) and made it his first personal ascent. He was fourteen.

Meanwhile, in Traun, Hans had completed his compulsory schooling to the grade eight level. His parents were too poor to send him for further education, and, disappointed, he enrolled as an apprentice electrician in the pay of one of the largest employers in the area, the United Austrian Iron and Steel Works. He disliked the work.

By 1949, his apprenticeship was complete. Hans took a holiday and toured the Eastern Alps by bicycle with Franz Dopf, a young cabinetmaker from Traun. Adventurers both, they climbed the Gross Glockner (3804) together, wearing army boots and using rented ice axes. When the ascent was over, the pair had gained immeasurable self-confidence. It was a milestone for them.

A gift of climbing equipment came the next year from a family whose mountaineer son had been killed in the war. The young men were grateful for this windfall, but they did not know how to use it. After practising a bit on local rocks, Hans and his friend finally screwed up enough courage to attempt a grade four climb. Armed with a guidebook, they set off for the Töten Gebirge, the "Mountains of the Dead," the nearest range, south of Linz.

Everything went fairly well until they reached the crux of the climb. The problem was a curving crack which pushed the climbers out from the wall. A piton was already in place to which the rope could be clipped to protect the leader. But up to this point in his career, Hans thought a piton was merely for use as a handhold and saw no relationship between it and the carabiners and rope slings he had slung about his neck.

Both climbers in their turn tried to cross the crux and failed. Hans tried again. He hooked one finger into the eye of the piton. The finger began to hurt as soon as he put pressure on it. He looked for a safe alternative but there appeared to be none, and he could not bring himself to let go of the piton and make the next move. There must be an easier way, he thought. Hans looked questioningly at all the equipment he had around his neck. A revelation came to him in a flash! If he put a carabiner in the piton and clipped the rope into it, he would be protected from falling. Confident, he went across "like nothing." "We were so pleased with ourselves!" exclaimed Hans later.

In fact the pair were so pleased with themselves on finding this "new" technique they could not wait to get back to the hut and tell the other climbers how clever they were. To their surprise and embarrassment, the announcement was greeted by hoots of laughter and general amusement at their naïvete. However, nothing could stop them now. They were getting bolder.

A few weeks later, again with no preparation and little knowledge of the difficulties they would be facing, Hans and Franz set off from the same hut, this time to a grade six climb. At four in the morning they walked up the trail and over the scree until they reached a forbidding-looking place with yellow overhangs. They climbed to where it became dangerously steep and stopped. By this time they were so frightened they sat on a small ledge for an hour, looking in opposite directions and not speaking to one another. Finally Franz said, "If you want to get up there, we'd better get going." Hans answered, "If we're still alive tonight, we'll never go climbing again!"

They roped up. What followed was a terrible job of climbing. "We massacred it," said Hans. Using a double rope, they had great difficulty overcoming the piton sections. The whole flow of the climb became a confusion of tangled ropes and false starts. Normally completed in about four hours, the route took them ten, but they did get down safely and had learned an enormous amount in the process.

In April 1951 Hans was crossing the main square in Linz when he encountered Leo Grillmair,[2] an acquaintance of some standing and a plumber by occupation.

"What are you doing these days, Leo?" Hans asked.

"I'm going to Canada."

"What do you have to do to go to Canada?" Hans asked again.

"Sign up at the travel agency across the square."

"Wait a minute. I'm going with you."

When Hans told the agent that he wanted to go where there was plenty of skiing, he was told to go to Toronto, but later, when he was interviewed by a Canadian visa officer, Winnipeg was suggested. Finally they agreed on Edmonton. Late in November 1951, Hans sailed from Genoa for Halifax. For the nineteen-year-old Austrian, that experience alone was "worth the price of admission."

Grillmair had preceded Gmoser to Canada, and the pair met in Edmonton in early December. They were assigned

[2]Grillmair is pronounced "grill-mire."

189

jobs near Whitecourt, Alberta, to cut pulpwood on a piecework basis. Inexperienced at this work, they wrecked their chain saw on the third day and were fired immediately. Back in Edmonton shortly before Christmas, things looked quite bleak. They didn't know English very well, the banks were closed, and they had only Austrian schillings for money. Who would help them? Gmoser remembered his friend Dopf had a uncle living there. They looked in the phone book and there he was, Louis Dopf.

Dopf took the boys in. In the new year Gmoser and Grillmair both got jobs. With money earned and borrowed, they bought two pairs of skis, boots, and bindings. On a sunny afternoon they went to Whitemud Ravine to ski. "We were beside ourselves. We were so happy. Here we were in this country. We had a job. The sun was shining. We were skiing." It was the high point of their arrival in Canada. The low point came about three in the afternoon when Grillmair skied into a tree and broke his right leg. Gmoser worked and paid room and board for them both while his friend recovered.

In May Gmoser hitchhiked to Banff and saw the Rockies for the first time. As he approached via Highway 1A, the first mountain he saw was Yamnuska (2405), black and sombre against the evening sky. The mountain rose straight up, and it appealed to his youthful idealism.

> I was fascinated. A beautiful rock face took shape. In one straight line it rose to the sky. My eyes were fastened upon it and as the mountain stood there, solemn in this May evening, a silent promise was made.

Within a couple of weeks, Gmoser made his first Canadian ascent, the Roche Miette (2316), in the Athabasca Valley near Jasper. A month or so later he moved to Calgary.

During the summer Gmoser interested Grillmair in the unclimbed south face of Yamnuska. A system of chimneys cut through the face right of centre and offered a possible route to the summit crest. They resolved to try the route as soon as Grillmair's leg had fully recovered.

On 23 November 1952, Gmoser, Grillmair, and a girlfriend, Isabel Spreat, toiled up the large scree apron at the foot of the face. It was agreed that Grillmair would take the lead, even though he was only wearing rubber-soled street shoes. Following their proposed route all the way, they found it offered no exceptional difficulties but was still sufficiently challenging and varied to be of interest. Gmoser recorded the climb as his first, first ascent, little realizing the Grillmair Chimneys, as they would later be known, marked the beginning of a new phase of Canadian mountaineering, the phase of high angle rock climbing. For the next decade, the young Austrians and their new climbs attracted a lot of attention.

In 1953 there were only two official guides in the Canadian Rockies, Walter Perren and Edmund Petrig, both licensed in Switzerland. But there were a number, like Gmoser, who had taken the guide's test required by the national parks system. It comprised ticking off answers to twenty questions on a prescribed form. On this basis and personal reputation, Gmoser began guiding.

During the spring he took employment with Elizabeth Rummel, who operated a lodge at Mount Assiniboine. Guests were to be flown to the lodge, but when the pilot was killed in an automobile accident, Gmoser began guiding the guests overland from Sunshine Village, some twenty-five kilometres away. That summer he did very little work as an electrician and chose to spend most of his time climbing around Banff and Assiniboine, where he made three ascents of the mountain in one week. Later, Gmoser realized it was a very formative period for him, not just for his climbing experience but for his general education. Rummel owned an impressive mountaineering library, and Gmoser spent most of his free time studying the history and tradition of the Canadian mountains.

In the spring of 1955 Gmoser organized his first ski tour in the Selkirks. His clients enjoyed themselves immensely, but it turned out badly for their guide. While waiting for the train at Glacier to take some of his clients home, Gmoser fooled around on his skis behind the station. This time it was his turn to break a leg. There was no climbing that summer.

Some time in the mid-fifties Gmoser became firmly committed to a life's work in the mountains. In 1957, with two other practising guides, Frank Stark and Heinz Kahl, he formed the firm, Rocky Mountain Guides Ltd. But only Gmoser wanted to practise guiding all year round. He made several new climbs that summer, ranging as far north as Mount Robson.

The ascent of Robson, by its southwest face, was completed under very trying snow conditions. On the upper slopes the snow was so loose and deep that a path could be made only by ploughing into the swirling, bottomless mass, elbowing and stroking against it. Nothing more than an ill-defined trench was left after the effort.

The party descended in the midst of a thunderstorm. Hail, driven by turbulent air, pelted the climbers about the head and shoulders. As the storm gathered on the slope, the hail hurried by, hissing and spitting on its way to the depths. Thunder crashed and rolled, and lightning lit their surroundings with shafts of light, making them look like "ghosts dancing madly under the open sky."

By the end of August 1957, snow had closed the big peaks to climbing, and Gmoser returned to Yamnuska. He had in mind a direct route on the face, a *direttissima*, a straight line from the base to the summit. It appeared as a series of interconnecting cracks and slabs, broken at irregular intervals by overhangs and rock roofs. Near the top, one big roof could be seen, its yellow underside an ominous barrier to ascent. The whole undertaking looked quite impossible, and Gmoser and his friends frequently questioned themselves, why? Gmoser answered for them all,

> We wanted to inhale and breathe life again. We were rebelling against an existence which human kind had forced upon itself. We were rebelling against an existence full of distorted values, against an existence where a man is judged by the size of his living room, by the

amount of chromium on his car. But here we were ourselves again; simple and pure.

Earlier attempts to climb this route by Gmoser and Dopf had twice failed. The latest attempt with Grillmair and Kahl had brought them to a point two hundred and forty metres up the face. On 15 September 1957, they tried again.

The lower part of the route was now known to them, and they climbed easily to the first bivouac. Gmoser took the first lead in the morning. Part way up he found himself at the bottom of a steep, blank twenty-metre slab. Concentrating hard on the rock surface in front of him, he searched for any nubbin on which he could press a finger or catch the toe of his boot. Nothing escaped his attention as his eyes and hands scanned each possibility. Every strenuous or delicate move made him breathe in gasps. Below, his companions could only wait, measuring his progress as the rope ran out slowly.

Some distance above the top of the slab, Gmoser came hard under the big roof they had seen from below. He was relieved to find he could bypass it by traversing slightly and climbing the wall where the roof edge intersected the face. But once above it he was astonished to see another seventy-five-metre chimney with five more overhangs! He led the first two and then Kahl took over and continued to the top.

The emotional strain imposed by gravity and vertigo was now over, and a great wave of relief overwhelmed them. They had done it. Kahl, a smaller man, lifted his lanky partner to his shoulder in an expression of strength and joy, while Grillmair, silhouetted against the evening sky, slowly and carefully coiled the rope. Then, without speaking, they turned down the ridge towards home, their minds and bodies enriched by their adventure.[3]

[3]During Gmoser's ascent of Robson and the Direttissima, he had taken some sixteen-millimetre film footage. From it he produced the first of ten films with which he promoted his guiding business. The films were unexpectedly successful.

That winter Adolph Bitterlich, who sometimes assisted Gmoser on his ski tours as a second guide, invited him to join an expedition to little-known Mount Blackburn (5037) in Alaska, 130 kilometres northeast of Valdez, a town on the Gulf of Alaska. It was a peak much higher than any other Gmoser had ever climbed, and it offered him an opportunity for high-altitude experience. He accepted.

In the late spring 1958, Gmoser drove alone up the Alaska Highway. Where the pavement ended near Onoway, Alberta, and the gravel road began, he parked his car. With his pack and skis on his back he hitchhiked the remaining hundreds of kilometres to the Yukon-Alaska border, only to be turned back for having insufficient funds to enter the United States.

He wired his bank in Banff to send his full account and received about two hundred dollars. It was enough to allow him entry, but when Bitterlich arrived he had no money either. Gmoser slipped him the same two hundred.

The other members of the party had notable reputations, and Gmoser felt himself to be a complete greenhorn among them. But he proved, as he had often done before, that he was equal to this task as well as anyone. Travelling mostly on skis and often snowed in for days by Pacific storms, the expedition completed the second ascent of Blackburn, the first in forty-six years.

Gmoser returned to Alberta. That summer he made the third ascent of the lengthy and reputedly difficult Mount Alberta (3619) in the Columbia Group of Jasper National Park. It seemed to be another astonishing feat to Canadian climbers, who knew the mountain had been climbed before only by crack parties under the best conditions. Gmoser's party seemed to do it easily.

Meanwhile a new, very enterprising expedition was conceived in Gmoser's mind. He wanted to make an ascent of Mount Logan, Canada's highest mountain, and to do it by a completely new overland route. If he could pull it off, it would be a landmark expedition. That winter, before going on a ski tour to Europe, he thrashed out the details with a new friend, Montreal architect Philippe Delesalle.

Their program in general was as follows: Starting from Kluane Lake, northwest of Whitehorse, they planned a ski approach via the immense Kaskawulsh and Hubbard Glaciers to the foot of Logan's east ridge; a second ascent of Logan's east peak (5944); and a ski return via the Hubbard and Donjek Glaciers back to the highway, northwest of their starting point. Two airdrops would be arranged.

Three factors made these plans inconceivably ambitious: more than three hundred kilometres of travel were required over difficult, untrodden terrain, and an elevation gain in excess of five thousand metres would have to be climbed. In addition, the totally self-supporting party would have to accomplish these feats in only thirty-two days.

The party members were chosen with care. In addition to Gmoser and Delesalle, they were: Willy Pfisterer, an experienced guide from Jasper; Karl Ricker and Don Lyon, two newly graduated students from the University of British Columbia; and Ron Smylie, a mountaineering equipment supplier from Calgary. Their average age was twenty-seven.

On 27 May 1959 the climbers got under way. Their first camp was along the braided streams of the Slims River, and the second was on the bare ice of the Kaskawulsh Glacier, a gigantic ice road some eight kilometres in width. The third day brought them to the junction of the north and south arms of the Kuskawulsh, where the two great ice streams joined to form a wildly contorted surface of ice waves. Battling heavy loads, the party negotiated the medial moraine between the two arms and came to the first snow. It was a welcome relief; the skis were taken off the packs and put on their feet.

The next morning, moist air canopied the broad, gently rising glacier, making it no more than a bleak tunnel under the sky. With no wind, the heat became oppressive, and mountain lassitude began to take its toll. But that afternoon the sky lifted, and the men saw their first landmark, Mount Queen Mary (3886), at the junction of the Kaskawulsh and the Hubbard Glaciers. It was still fifty kilometres away.

On 1 June Mount Logan came into view. Ahead of the expedition rose one of the mightiest mountains on the planet. As they gazed on it, each man silently measured his personal courage, guessing what was needed to endure its hardships.

With only two days of food supply left, they were now beyond the point of no return. To find their first airdrop in time it was absolutely critical they not lose their way. On a blistering foggy day, without landmarks, it took them two attempts before the route from the Kaskawulsh to the Hubbard Glacier was found. After six days of climbing, they welcomed the long downhill schuss on the Hubbard.

At supper that evening, the party discussed the black weather formations building in the western sky. A snowstorm seemed very likely. If it snowed, the airdrop would be buried forever. After eating, Gmoser and Pfisterer set out with light packs and travelled all night. By four o'clock the next morning they had found the drop and recovered all but one bundle. That evening, 3 June, the entire party assembled at the foot of Logan's east ridge. The first leg of the journey was over.

The first ascent of Logan's east peak by an American party had taken more than twenty days and nine camps to climb the ridge. And they had been flown to its foot. Gmoser's party, with rations for only twelve days, would have to be faster. What fat remained on their bodies would soon melt away.

On 6 June they skied to the south face of the ridge, changed to felt-lined mukluks and crampons, and climbed the first fifty-degree slope. By nightfall the second day, their first camp on the ridge was fully established.

Under a cloudless sky the next morning, the climbers reached thirty-five hundred metres and tackled a steep slope on the ridge, where drifting snow made the edge uncertain. Belays seemed impossible. Swinging his ice axe, Gmoser cut the top off the sixty-metre knife edge, kicked in steps, and fixed a handline for the others. The terrifying exposure on both sides of the edge caused each climber to move cautiously and place his feet well in the track.

Crevasses intersected the crest higher up and forced the men onto the south face, where they found it difficult to place proper belay anchors. Their fatigue did not help matters. Verging on recklessness, they relied heavily on the large, bucket-shaped steps Gmoser had cut into the slope. But progress was steady, and on the night of 9 June the second ridge camp was fully established.

With the gain in altitude it had become much colder. All men were now sleeping in double down bags and wearing their clothing to bed. Canteens of hot tea were placed at their feet inside the sleeping bags, and boots were kept in the bags as well to prevent the leather from freezing. By 11 June a third camp had been established at an elevation of 5075 metres. Their advance had been rapid compared to the speed of the first ascent party. But now the effort was exacting a price.

After a night of poor sleep, the six climbers awoke the next morning with splitting headaches. A breakfast of codeine pills did little to help. They considered taking a day's rest, but Gmoser insisted they go for the summit immediately, because the weather remained clear and windless. Thus decided, the terrible struggle to don boots, mukluks, and crampons began.

By the time they had reached fifty-seven hundred metres, the altitude had taken toll of their bodies. But, sick or not, nothing would deprive them of their goal. A few steps at a time, interrupted by breathing stops, they toiled upwards against fatigue and gravity. About one o'clock in the afternoon Gmoser and his party stood on top of Logan's east peak. The climb had taken seven days from the bottom of the ridge, less than a third of the time required by the first party.

After identifying surrounding peaks for an hour, the

climbers' headaches drove them from the summit, and by five o'clock they had returned to Camp Three.

The following day, in one long effort interrupted only by periods waiting for the snow to harden, they descended the entire east ridge. Some time after midnight they threw away their mukluks, now unneeded, and rested.

Ahead of them lay the outward journey. Some argument took place as to whether they should abandon the planned return route in favour of the established approach march. But again Gmoser insisted they follow their plan, and this time he was supported by Ricker.

On the night of 15 June, all equipment was loaded on an emergency toboggan and pulled up the slopes of the Hubbard. It was terribly hard work. Halfway through the night, Gmoser called a halt. Following discussion, a decision was taken to abandon all extra equipment and to backpack only the essentials needed for their journey to civilization.

The next day the party camped and rested, waiting for frost to harden the snow. Each man rigged his own individual sled, using his skis. That night they travelled quickly, covering thirty kilometres in ten hours. By daybreak they had reached the head of the Donjek Glacier.

Late in the evening of 18 June, they started down the Donjek. After a distance the unseen crevasses became dangerous, and three times Ricker fell through a snow bridge. Each time he was saved only by his forward momentum, induced by his heavy pack and his speed. With skis caught in the opening and his upper torso on the downhill lip, he required help from his companions to get onto his feet. About elevation twenty-four hundred metres, the snow gave way to bare ice, and the crevasses could be easily seen.

Eventually the group came to a massive jumble of seracs which forced them onto the marginal moraine. This meant carrying their skis again, and it was trying as they stumbled among large, loose boulders. Some joy was experienced when, for the first time in three weeks, they saw green grass at the edge of a little lake, but still the march went on. Fifteen hours later, after passing down the moraine, across washouts, up steep sidehills, and through dense bush, the men reached the nose of the glacier. They gathered wood and made a fire, expecting the worst was over. They could not have been more wrong.

Gmoser had arranged a second air drop of three rubber rafts. They were spotted on the other side of the river. When after some difficulty the rafts were recovered, only two were serviceable. The third had hit a tree and contained, by actual count, ninety-six holes. It could not be patched.

A combination craft made of the two dinghies and several air mattresses gave them excitement as it quickly ran down the river at twenty-five kilometres an hour. But then Gmoser's raft blew a hole. With shouts the crew paddled madly and, reaching shallow water, leapt overboard to rescue the craft. They decided to rearrange the remains of their float, fill it with equipment, and send two men with it the rest of the way. The rafts set off.

Gmoser and three others walked the remaining forty kilometres to the road. Before midnight, they encountered a bulldozed track and sighted lights on a hillside. Finally reaching the Alaska Highway at one o'clock in the morning, Gmoser awakened the proprietress of a store and asked for food and shelter. They ate like animals.

The next morning, 22 June, they were driven to the Donjek River bridge to find the two rafters, Pfisterer and Smylie. The sight of them told the others something was wrong. During the night, in a snarl of river snags, they had cut loose the equipment-laden float. Downstream it caught again, deflated, and sank from view. A rescue effort recovered three tents and a rope, but all equipment and the photographs of three of the climbers were lost to the water. It was the last blow.

The thin, ragged, sunburnt mountaineers made their way home. Their expedition had been unlike any other. As the famous Italian mountaineer, Reinhold Messner, put it, "A great climb of this nature is like a life onto itself."

The following spring, 1960, Gmoser undertook a two-hundred-and-ten-kilometre, high-level ski tour from Wapta Lake in Yoho National Park to Jasper, but it proved too ambitious. Heavy storms held the party up, causing food shortages which forced them to abandon the project south of the Columbia Icefield. But he was successful in making the third ascent of Brussels Peak (3167) the following summer. First climbed in 1948, the fortresslike mountain south of Jasper had a reputation for great difficulty, but Gmoser claimed there was only one short section which presented real problems. This gave rise to an article written by him, "How Steep is Steep?" which declaimed the peak's difficulties. It brought, in return, criticism of him for oversimplifying the climb to the average mountaineer.

During the early sixties, Gmoser continued to work hard at the development of his guiding business, maintaining a schedule of activities for ski touring, guiding, and film presentation. The pace would have killed most men, but Gmoser accustomed himself to physically demanding climbs and tours, interspersed with jet travel to distant cities where he spoke in glowing terms about the places he was about to rush back to.

But this was business. In Gmoser's head was another expedition which, like Mount Logan, formed part of the curriculum of his "graduate school" of mountaineering. The scope of the undertaking was monumental and dangerous. He wanted to climb the north peak of Alaska's Mount McKinley (5934) via its Wickersham Wall. The huge wall formed the principal obstacle on a face forty-two hundred metres high, a mighty precipice which had thwarted earlier attempts to scale it. The most recent had been defeated when an avalanche had swept away all supplies. Gmoser knew he would need good planning, good men, and plenty of luck to succeed.

In early 1963 a party was chosen. The roster read: Hans Schwarz, a guide from Jasper; Gunti Prinz, in the Warden Service from Banff; Gmoser's friend Leo Grillmair and Dieter Raubach, both from Calgary; Pat Boswell of the CBC from

200

Toronto; and two Americans, Tom Spencer and Hank Kaufmann.

Starting in late May, the party marched with very heavy packs to the foot of the mountain in four days. By way of the Jeffery Spur on the right side of the wall, they overcame a knife-edge ridge blocked successively by two gigantic ice towers, and bridged a major crevasse with a rope ladder. By the time they had established their third camp on a rock ridge at four thousand metres, the technical difficulties were below them. Full of confidence now, they made the first of several major mistakes.

Thinking a small snowfall was the harbinger of greater storms which would trap them, they decided the route should be pushed immediately to the top of the wall without an intermediate camp. While they were doing this, however, the effects of altitude, insufficient acclimatization, and hard work took their toll. Complaining of headaches, thirst, lack of appetite, and fatigue, the men needed rest.

The top of the wall was at an elevation of 5050 metres, but before a camp was fully consolidated there, Gmoser, Schwarz, and Boswell set out to break trail to an even higher camp from which they hoped to reach the summit. Boswell, who had slipped and fallen a hundred metres the day before, did not go far before his remaining strength left him. Gmoser took his load and, six hours later, reached the fifty-five-hundred-metre level, where he cached the supplies. Back at the camp that night, he promised the party a day's rest.

But next morning Gmoser reneged. The weather was fine and could not be wasted. He and Schwarz decided it best to move the party to the higher camp, even if it meant going without full provisions. It was an unpopular decision. Their start was slow, and even with light loads it took an extreme effort for all of them to reach high camp. With much of their food in a cache below, they would have to hurry.

To some it did not matter. Two climbers were already incapacitated. Spencer was vomiting, moaning, and staring blankly into space, and Kaufmann was also very ill.

In a sharp, cold wind the next morning, the remaining six started out for the summit. Unroped, as they were on easy terrain, they soon became separated and spread across the upper slope. By one o'clock in the afternoon, Gmoser and Schwarz had succeeded in reaching McKinley's north peak. They had barely made it, and they felt little elation. It was snowing quite hard, not much could be seen, and they were physically strung out.

After descending a short distance, they spotted Prinz struggling upwards alone, battling against the wind and fighting his inclination to quit. Gmoser and Schwarz waited for him to finish his ascent, and then the three turned and went down. The others had turned back earlier.

The climbers slept poorly that night. A storm was on the mountain. The wind was raging and the tents vibrated horribly. Spencer and Kaufmann were so ill, Gmoser thought they might die of dehydration. He judged it essential they get down immediately, and in the morning they broke camp.

But a descent was impossible. The ferocity of the storm was dissipating their energy too quickly. Only two hundred metres down the slope they pitched camp again, this time in the lee of the ridge, away from the wind. It was quieter now, but the snow was building on the tents, and by the time they had bedded down, their survival was uncertain. Gmoser expressed his fears later:

> I was quite worried. Would the tents stand up under this tremendous load or would they collapse? But we were too tired to do anything about it.

In the morning two metres of snow had pressed the tents onto their faces, but they were still alive. Schwarz started down first with Spencer, and Gmoser followed a half hour later with Kaufmann. Kaufmann was almost sleepwalking, partially delirious. Once he slipped, and Gmoser was yanked from his stance, shot over his companion, and landed in the snow below. Gmoser was very shaken by this and realized how tenuous their situation was. To add to their trials, the wind was driving snow into their mouths and nostrils, so much so that Gmoser thought they might suffocate. In what seemed to be an eternity, but was only a few hours, they reached the two boulders which marked the site of their camp at 5050 metres.

Schwarz and Spencer were already there. Still strong and dependable, Schwarz had dug a snow cave for his two ill companions. The snow was not deep, and the cave had to be finished with skis. To Gmoser the sight of it suggested a "big coffin."

In a snow hole they had dug for themselves, he and Schwarz talked with concern about the whereabouts of the others who had been left to clear the high camp. With them were all the tents. When they did not arrive the next day, Gmoser became deeply worried.

On the morning of the second day, two figures appeared on the ridge, slowly moving down. Where were the two others? When Prinz and Boswell reached the camp, they told a grim story. They had survived two nights in a snow cave, but Grillmair had temporarily lost his eyesight and gone into a coma. Raubach had stayed with him.

On hearing this news Gmoser and Schwarz did not hesitate. They started up the ridge. They found Grillmair propped in a corner of the cave. He looked terribly ill. Urgently Gmoser made him an energy drink and administered some codeine tablets. Getting Grillmair on his feet, Gmoser tied on the rope and started down. Schwarz and Raubach followed with the tents and equipment. Eventually all reached the camp.

Although the party was safely together again, the stress conditions displayed their every weakness. While setting up the tents, Raubach came to Gmoser and motioned; he was paralyzed on one side and had lost his speech. Then a brief argument set Kaufmann off; he was yelling and screaming in an uncontrolled way. Very close to his own limits, Gmoser wondered what other blows could befall them now.

But just then they could tolerate no more, the crises reached their peak and slowly subsided. That night the weather eased a little and the next day they reached the head of the regular route on McKinley's west buttress. Although snow had begun to fall once more, they made their way down the mountain to a point where they could rest in complete safety. Towards the end of June, fully recovered from their experiences, they were picked up by ski plane and flown to civilization.

This epic climb on Mount McKinley in 1963 proved to be the last such expedition for Gmoser. Ten years later he accepted the leadership of a Canadian Mount Everest expedition, but when its private financing fell through and the climbing permit was thoughtlessly cancelled by the Canadian government, the opportunity was lost. Gmoser was sadly disappointed. The next opening would likely fall to a younger man.

However, by that time, other major events had occurred in his life. In 1966 he married Margaret MacGougan, the daughter of a Calgary physician. Two years later, their first son was born and named after the famous guide, Conrad Kain. When their second son was born in 1969, he was named Robson. Gmoser took quite a teasing about this. "The kid is really lucky you didn't climb Assiniboine the week before!" was one observation.

After McKinley he had also broken new ground in guiding. The Association of Canadian Mountain Guides was formed, and he was a founding member and the chairman of its first Standards Committee. He also became aware about that time of the ski-touring opportunities made possible by the use of helicopters; he had used one in making his 1963 film. By 1965 he was experimenting with them as a means of transportation for his winter ski tours. The machines had tremendous potential.

This discovery was discussed among Gmoser's climbing friends, many of whom were businessmen. The helicopter could mean the development of skiing in beautiful remote areas where, until now, only a few ski mountaineers had gone. Funds were raised, and Philippe Delesalle was commissioned to design a lodge. It was built in the valley below Bugaboo Glacier and opened for the winter of 1967 — 1968.

The first two years of operations met with such enthusiasm that Gmoser felt encouraged to build an addition to the lodge despite a financial deficit. He went ahead without first arranging financing. Money was tight at that time. When the banks looked at his balance sheet, two years of losses failed to reflect Gmoser's enthusiasm. The banks turned down his loan application. Earlier backers knew the company had very little book value and were not prepared to invest more.

At the time of the accident on Marmolata, Gmoser's contractor was pressing for payment, and he was facing bankruptcy. He was saved when he found a partner with the vision to see potential in the company and who paid into it $50,000 for twenty percent of the business. It was the show of confidence needed to encourage other investors.

Gmoser survived this financial crisis as well as his injuries. Within a year he had opened another operation in the Cariboo Mountains and today has four bases from which helicopter skiing takes place, two from his own lodges.

Heli-skiing attracts those who want the best. Well-to-do Americans, Europeans, and Canadians come for the snow. Among them have been former Prime Minister Trudeau, who vacationed at Bugaboo Lodge in 1969. He returned again in the summer of 1972 to climb Bugaboo Spire with Gmoser as his guide. Gmoser found him shy, fit, and very determined.

In the seventies Rocky Mountain Guides Ltd. became known as Canadian Mountain Holidays Ltd. Well promoted, its growth was dramatic. But with expanding numbers of clients the inevitable happened: a skier was lost to an avalanche. Over a period of four years, six died in total, four in two different accidents in one disastrous week in March 1977. Then, after thousands of helicopter hours, a machine went down in February 1978, killing its pilot, a guide, and two skiers. Gmoser was greatly saddened by these tragedies. With his staff, he has devised every reasonable means to prevent recurrence of such events.

In the summer of 1978, after more than twenty-five years of continuous mountaineering, Gmoser took no personal climbing clients; he was too occupied with his business affairs. It may only be temporary. His love for the mountains is deeply rooted and always will be an essential part of his character. To him,

> the mountain … is a symbol of truth and a symbol of life as it should be. The mountain teaches us that we should encounter difficulties and not drift along the easy way, which always leads down.

Chapter Nine

Brian Greenwood
1934 –

I don't complain and don't explain

Dougal Haston,
great Scottish mountaineer

Their second bivouac, high on the east face of Mount Babel, slowly came to an end as the morning sun bathed the rock. From their small, stony platform about a metre square, Greenwood and Locke unlimbered, preparing their ropes and hardware. In the quiet dew-filled valley below, their preparations went unnoticed.

Above them soared the final seventy-five metres to the summit. The upper wall was overhanging the lower face by a considerable margin. Greenwood led off calmly and climbed diagonally as far as the underside of a rock roof, then returned, and Locke took over the lead. The one-metre roof forced him away from the face as he leaned back to drive pitons into down-facing cracks. Held in place by Greenwood's pull on the rope and the stirrups under his feet, Locke fought strenuously against gravity. His efforts were accompanied by the rattle of the iron hardware and the grunts of his struggle. After an hour or more, he was able to peer above the edge of the roof. Meanwhile, Greenwood watched carefully from his belay position, puffing a cigarette and grasping the climbing rope loosely.

Immediately above the roof, a short wall gave way to an inside corner. Locke found a crack behind a flake of rock and managed to drive a piton. He hooked a stirrup in place and, at last, brought himself to a vertical position. Three more pitons in succession were driven behind the flake, and Locke moved successively upwards from one to the next

207

with the aid of his stirrups. It was a strenuous way to start the day, but it was the only exit upwards.

As Greenwood watched attentively, his partner shifted his weight to the highest piton. It immediately pulled out. Locke plunged wildly. The next series of pins came out in rapid succession as he fell on them — ping, ping, ping. In a clatter of gear, he pitched head-backwards into space, heading for the scree about six hundred metres below.

Tensioning his belay quickly, Greenwood caught his companion on the rope with a jolting arrest. Locke came to an abrupt stop on the face about three metres below the belay ledge. The last protection piton had held.

Snarled and tangled in his gear, the fallen climber righted himself painfully and examined the damage. His left hand, where the weight of his body had struck the rock, was connected to his forearm by two right-angle bends. With his good right arm Locke managed to regain the ledge; then he started to pass out. Greenwood considered what to do next.

Descent from the face to get help would take twenty to twenty-five rappels, likely requiring a day and a half for Greenwood's descent; Locke would have to stay behind. Additionally, they had consumed all their water, having planned to make the route in two days, and only a small amount of butter was left to eat. Between spells of fainting, Locke agreed with Greenwood it was not wise to separate under these conditions, so they followed the only remaining avenue open to them — they yelled.

Two other climbers had been watching their progress from the valley and knew something had gone wrong. They set out for help. Meanwhile, Greenwood and Locke settled in for their third bivouac. On a ledge about a half metre deep, they secured themselves with a couple of knife blade pitons driven into shallow cracks behind them. To Locke, the "bedsores" were more uncomfortable than his dislocated wrist, but he wondered, during the long night, if this episode could lead to "the end."[1]

[1]Afterwards Locke joked that, during the night, he kept glancing at Greenwood's thighs, wondering how they would taste as a last meal — "very tough," was his conclusion.

On the morning of the fourth day of the climb, a helicopter and the mountain rescue team from Banff arrived and prepared to haul the climbers to the ridge. When the first warden appeared in view suspended on a steel cable, he passed them about about five metres from their ledge. It was necessary to lower him another twenty-five metres farther down the face before he touched the rock. Greenwood dropped a rope end, and the warden made it to their position. Gingerly they arranged themselves on the small ledge so that Locke could get into the Gramminger rescue seat on the warden's back. As the team winched in the steel cable, the two men spun and jerked their way upwards, hanging giddily in space. Then it was Greenwood's turn. Shortly afterwards they were flown from the summit in the helicopter.

Thus ended Greenwood's 1966 attempt on the east face of Mount Babel. Later he would state laconically, "It was just as well, really. As it turned out we were going the wrong way."

Brian Greenwood came from England to Canada in 1956, arriving in Calgary during Stampede Week. His home had been in Hebden Bridge, in Yorkshire's West Riding. He was born on 16 August 1934, the son of a cobbler who later gave up his shop to work as a hand in a local woolen mill. Greenwood's mother died when he was four, and, although his father remarried sometime later, his early years were, to him, without maternal counsel. His only sister, Alice, also came to Canada after the second war and took residency in Edmonton.

Shortly after graduating from English grammar school at the age of eighteen, Greenwood enlisted in the Royal Air Force regular service. Over a period of three years he was stationed on the Isle of Man, in Egypt, and on Cyprus, where from a mountain camp he was allowed plenty of opportunity to hike. He was discharged in 1955.

In the meantime he had found a couple of friends who liked to climb, and they began on the gritstone outcrops of the Lake District and in Wales. Those were the years when

British climbing was entering a new era under the leadership of such men as Joe Brown and Don Whillans. However, Greenwood actually learned little while in Britain, and when he arrived in Canada considered himself little better than a novice.

He made his new home in Calgary, close to the mountains, and there he met Dick Lofthouse, another English climber. Lofthouse was more familiar with the Rockies than Greenwood, and at first Greenwood followed his new friend's suggestions as to where they should climb.

His first recorded ascent was that of the east face of Mount Inflexible (2987), in the Kananaskis Range southeast of Banff. It was a virgin mountain, and, although not highly significant, it established a pattern for Greenwood where he abandoned traditional ridge routes in favour of the challenge of steep face climbs. The date was September 1956.

The following year Greenwood put up the first of his many routes on Yamnuska (2405), the steep limestone mountain overlooking the Trans-Canada Highway fifty miles west of Calgary. The first routes on this easily accessible, south-facing crag had been made by the Austrian-born Hans Gmoser and some of his friends. Greenwood's Belfry route was immediately compared to Gmoser's Direttissima, and although shorter it was considered more difficult. For protection, Greenwood used slings on natural rock projections and homemade "chocks" made from machine nuts with the threads bored out.

The same year, 1957, Greenwood's interest was drawn to a quartzite obelisk at Moraine Lake, called the Tower of Babel (2362). Although of lesser elevation than its neighbours, the tower's north face posed unsolved climbing problems. With his companion from the Belfry route, Ron Thomson, and Lofthouse, Greenwood put the first route on the tower, one rated very severe by British standards. Whether he liked it or not, Greenwood's first exploits became a topic of conversation in the fledgling Calgary Mountain Club of which he was a member, and in a few years he became the central force within the club.

By this time Greenwood had formulated in his mind an unwritten list of "must" ascents in the Rockies — a list shared, if not discussed, with other climbers. He and Lofthouse made the fourth ascent of Mount Alberta (3619) in 1958. Both men had qualified as professional guides, and, due to their extraordinary fitness and the snow-free conditions on the mountain, they were able to avoid the normal bivouac. This rapid ascent of a mountain, reputed for its difficulty, length, and rotten rock, drew further unsolicited attention to Greenwood.

Some weeks later the partners climbed Mount Hungabee (3492) by its standard route from Opabin Pass. When they reached the summit, it was snowing lightly, and they were surrounded by cloud. It had been an easy climb for them despite the poor weather, and they saw no reason to hurry down. While having lunch, however, they were puzzled for a moment by a buzzing sound. When the two men realized it was coming from their ice axes, they knew lightning was close by.

Greenwood seemed less concerned than Lofthouse, who quickly grabbed his belongings and started down the ridge. They were not far below the summit when a bolt struck Greenwood's ice axe, which was strapped to his pack. Both men were knocked flat. The ledge they were on was shattered with a crash, and they were nearly hurled down the face. Lofthouse got up, quite amazed he was unhurt, but Greenwood was unconscious and badly burnt. The current had passed down his back and through the leg which grounded him to earth. His sweater was holed, one leg of his corduroy knickers was in shreds, and one boot had been completely blown off.

Lofthouse started to build a stone shelter right away so that Greenwood would be safe while he went for help. But in the interval Greenwood had somewhat regained his senses. He was not going to stay on the mountain, he said. They worked some feeling back into his paralyzed leg and tied on his shattered boot with a sling. Into a rising blizzard of snow, Greenwood, safeguarded by his partner, started down and made it all the way back to Lake O'Hara. "It showed me just how tough Brian really was," remarked Lofthouse later.

For two and a half weeks thereafter, Greenwood was under observation at the Banff General Hospital. On discharge, he headed immediately for the Bugaboos, where he and Lofthouse climbed the standard route on Pigeon Spire (3124) and the Kain route on Bugaboo Spire (3185).

To others, Greenwood seemed almost oblivious to physical discomfort. Lofthouse noticed he frequently climbed carrying only a handful of sugar lumps for lunch, a habit he gave up only after a rainstorm dissolved the sugar in his anorak pocket and left his clothing a sticky mess. In the Bugaboos the following year, 1959, he forgot to bring a lunch during a climb, and, too proud to take from others, or humiliated by his forgetfulness, he wandered up the glacier while his companions ate. From this, he found he could climb without food during the day and after that generally concerned himself more with his cigarette supply, a habit he kept up so he would not "get too fit."

That same summer, 1959, Greenwood met Fred Beckey in the Bugaboos. With him, Hank Mather, and Elfrida Pigou, Greenwood put a new route on the west face of Snowpatch Spire (3063), a route which required a pendulum traverse and seven bolts for its completion. The route served as the descent passage for Beckey and Mather after their landmark climb of the spire's east face. In the fall Greenwood met Beckey in the Tetons of Wyoming, where they climbed the north face of the Grand (Grand Teton).

At the end of the fifties, Greenwood acquired another new partner, a relative novice to climbing, Glen Boles of Calgary. Boles looked on Greenwood with respect and was delighted with their first experience together, a new north face route on the Tower of Babel.[2] "I was proud just to go out with him," Boles recalled later. Eventually they became partners in a mountaineering equipment business, operated from the basement of Greenwood's house. But the partnership did not work out. Greenwood's carefree at-

[2]Al Washington, another Englishman, was also on this climb.

titude concerning details conflicted with Boles's more meticulous way of doing things.

Still, it did not spoil their climbing partnership. In January 1961 they tried something different — the first winter ascent and traverse of Mount Rundle (2949), at Banff. The weather was mild, and they bivouacked comfortably for a long sixteen hours the first night. But, at the end of the second day, after crossing the main summit, they ran out of time and were forced to abandon their traverse.[3]

During the summer they ascended the unclimbed north ridge of Mount Babel (3104) and the unclimbed northwest ridge of Deltaform Mountain (3424) close to Moraine Lake. The Babel climb was the first of a series of exciting adventures for Greenwood on that mountain. The most remembered climb of 1961, however, was the first ascent of the north face of Mount Edith (2554), located near Banff. The face presents a technical climb of about three hundred metres on exposed, clean limestone; its upper section requires direct aid. Unawed by its difficulties, Greenwood impressed Boles by the manner in which he solved each problem as he came to it. Greenwood explained drily, "Climbs are only difficult before you do them, not after you've done them."

But Greenwood and Boles also made some mistakes in judgement. Once they tried to climb the North Twin (3719) at the Columbia Icefield without skis or snowshoes. They thought the snow would remain firm for twenty-four hours, but before they could reach the summit the snow turned so soft they sank to their knees. Progress became impossible. It was a terrific struggle to recross the wide icefield back to the road.

In 1962 Greenwood discovered the pursuit of aesthetic routes, those which were classic in reputation and enjoyment. If he could make new ones, all the better. He wrote, "While all the major summits in the Rockies have long since

[3]The complete winter traverse of Mount Rundle was completed by teen-agers Charlie Locke and Don Gardiner in December 1964, with two bivouacs.

been climbed, there is a very noticeable lack of good classical secondary routes, routes that require a little more of the climber than a basic technique and strong legs." Of the climbs he did that summer, two successful ascents and one failure would fall into this category.

The first of these successes was the long east ridge of Mount Temple (3547), which had been first climbed in 1931.[4] The second was in the Ramparts, west of Jasper. A continuous chain of peaks, the Ramparts form one curving embattlement of gigantic proportion. They were unclimbed on their steepest flanks.

Greenwood had been invited by Beckey to join him and Don Gordon on a climb of the thousand-metre east face of Oubliette Mountain (3094) one of the dominant faces in the Ramparts. They admitted later they had mistaken Oubliette for another peak and found out what mountain they had climbed only after the ascent. But, correct name or not, the climb was what mattered. The lower third of the face was remembered for a pitch directly up and through a waterfall. The upper two-thirds followed along a rock rib. Here they interchanged leads, and Beckey remembered, "Brian made a spectacular lead from a notch on a thin arête for a full lead of vertical and beyond vertical." Only the best received such praise.

For the next three years, Greenwood turned most of his efforts to guiding, but he did one new major route with Beckey in August 1963: the west buttress on the north tower of Howser Spire. It was considered at that time to be one of the outstanding remaining challenges in the Bugaboos. Requiring two bivouacs, Greenwood thought the route was "rather unaesthetic" because it followed no clear line. It was the last ascent he made with Beckey, after climbing regularly with him for five consecutive years.

Closer to home, there were great unclimbed faces in the vicinity of Lake Louise. Greenwood had examined the lower

[4]The evening before their ascent of the east ridge of Temple, the party had participated in an alpine rescue at Moraine Lake, bringing back a man who had fallen on the Tower of Babel.

cliffs of the east face of Mount Lefroy but had backed off because he could not find an obvious line of ascent. "It didn't take my fancy," was his remark. But he and Leo Grillmair, a guide from Banff, did establish a route on the left of Mount Babel's big east face. They climbed a rock buttress and wall to the scree slopes north of the summit. It gave Greenwood an excellent opportunity to examine a direct line up the centre of the face, which led to his first attempt of this route three years later with Charlie Locke.

Yamnuska, the Calgary rock climbers' practice ground, is a low peak located on the eastern edge of the Rockies, north of the Trans-Canada Highway. Its south face is very steep and skirted by a broad apron of scree which has fallen from the face. About three hundred and fifty metres in height and fifteen hundred metres long, the prominent south wall contains many routes of varying difficulty.

Climbing the face began in 1952, and by 1965 nine of the seventeen established routes had been made by Greenwood and various partners.[5] Moreover, many other routes had also been started by him but were left uncompleted.

In June 1962 a new phase of development occurred. Prior to this date, all the obvious weaknesses in the face had been followed to the top. Then, with Lofthouse and Heinz Kahl, Greenwood established the Red Shirt route, which opened the second phase of Yamnuska's development and became a "classic of its kind," combining pleasant rock work of moderate difficulty with tolerable exposure. In the years ahead, Greenwood came to regard it as the best route on the mountain because "anyone should be able to get up it."

By that time there was a body of climbing anecdotes relating to Greenwood's career, and this latest route added one more to the list. Greenwood had worn a red shirt for a number of years which had become faded and tattered. He took a lot of kidding from his friends about it, as everyone who knew him was familiar with the garment. According to

[5]The 1977 edition of *A Climber's Guide to Yamnuska* by Urs Kallen, lists thirty-three routes of which twelve are Greenwood originals.

Boles, Greenwood said he would throw it away if he could make this new climb on the "Yam." The red shirt was discarded by Greenwood somewhere near the bottom of the route, thus giving it its name.

Despite its training ground reputation, Yamnuska has provided climbers with many thrills. Summer ascents often become nightmares when repeated in winter. Greenwood recalled a winter ascent of the relatively straightforward Grillmair Chimneys route.

The month was January, and, as Greenwood began the ascent, snow started to fall. It piled up quickly, and, by the time he had reached the middle section of the climb, it was almost impossible to find a hold. Thirty centimetres of snow hid the rock completely and was difficult to sweep away. The climb was completed with jangled nerves. Greenwood had to admit it was one time when he thought he had overstepped his limits. "That's when you really have an experience to remember. You decide you're going to come off anyway, so you might as well climb."

Greenwood's name became synonymous with Yamnuska. Routes there could not be discussed without mention of him. But he had not always been successful, sometimes experiencing both physical and psychological difficulties. After many years of climbing the face, he chose the Forbidden Corner route as his personal favourite, although his friends reported he was once "psyched out" while attempting his first ascent of it.

Greenwood was injured in 1965 while attempting the first ascent of the Bowl, another Yamnuska route. During a very hard move he dislocated his shoulder. Rather than fall off, he persevered, climbing as far as the next stance, but it took toll of his shoulder. He got off the face and descended the scree with his arm at an awkward angle. In the hospital the doctor had tremendous difficulty resetting the shoulder, partly due to swelling but also due to Greenwood's tightly-knotted shoulder muscles. He laid off climbing several months after that to recover.

Until the summer of 1966, Greenwood had been employed by Texaco Canada Ltd. in its production department in Calgary. Family tradition taught him a man was respectable only if he held down a full-time job. One morning, after a long period of brooding, he called his office to say he would not be in that day — or any other day, for that matter. He quit and from then on committed almost all his energies to climbing. He had a major route in mind for a start.

During his early career, Greenwood had reconnoitred the lower north side of Mount Temple (3547), the highest mountain in the Lake Louise Group, to find a possible route up its gigantic and forbidding face. Its fifteen-hundred-metre rock wall was capped with an overhanging glacier. On his first, half-hearted attempt, he "chickened out."

In late July 1966, however, he was ready for another try. He recruited Heinz Kahl and a young, enthusiastic Calgarian, Charlie Locke. Locke felt honoured to be invited. To join the party, he, too, quit his job.

The sunless north face of Temple consists of three sections. The lower, less demanding, half of the wall inclines about sixty degrees and features a prominent ice couloir named, because of its shape, the Dolphin. Above this couloir is an awesome concave rock wall called by Greenwood the Depression. This feature is crowned by steep, overhanging ice cliffs which threaten any ascent of the Depression. To the left, or east of it, hangs the summit glacier.

The goal of the party was to climb the face "direct," that is, following a line directly as possible to the summit. Greenwood and Kahl could not agree on a plausible route above the Dolphin and the decision was put off until they reached the prominent ledge halfway up which ran across the face.

On Wednesday, 3 August 1966, the three walked to Lake Annette, a small alpine pool which lies at the foot of the face. That night it stormed and rained heavily, but by four o'clock in the morning the sky cleared. Without breakfast they

217

started immediately, moving as quickly as possible to avoid stonefall, which was expected to scour the lower face later that day when the sun warmed the mountain,

Climbing unroped up a couloir which led to the Dolphin, they found firm snow and made good time except for Kahl, who began to fall behind. Not at all well, he quickly became too fatigued to continue and decided to turn back.[6] As they re-sorted his food and equipment, there was a general feeling of disappointment.

After watching Kahl start down, Greenwood and Locke continued climbing up a small rock ridge to the right of the Dolphin, and near its top, they roped. To their right was another couloir, which bordered the foot of a steep buttress.

Skirting the bottom of its cliffs, they climbed the upper edge of the couloir. It was not exceptionally difficult, but for three rope lengths they were nagged by the fear that the overlying snow might not adhere to the ice beneath. Pitons placed in rotten rock along the bottom of the buttress did little to reassure them. The fourth rope length led them up a chimney which penetrated a rock cliff to the right of the buttress. This brought them to the prominent ledge which they had seen from below. The decision as to route now had to be made.

Greenwood wanted to inspect the face of the Depression and carefully traversed left along the sloping ledge, which was filled with forty-five-degree ice and covered with a layer of snow of varying thickness. Sometimes carefully pressing his boot in the snow and other times sweeping the snow away to cut steps underneath, he reached the upper edge of the ledge. With his hands on the rock and his feet on the ice, he traversed some sixty metres towards the Depression. Pitons gave little protection. Soon the thought of continuing under these conditions became intolerable.

Preferring the rock above, Greenwood climbed diagonally upwards and immediately encountered excellent limestone. Locke followed, and they exchanged leads until they reached the edge of the Depression.

[6]In the autumn of 1966, Heinz Kahl died of leukemia.

This feature was worthy of its name for other than topographical reasons. Its ledges were short, steep ice slopes; its rock steps were down-sloping; and what were thought to be chimneys when viewed from the valleys were nothing but waterworn corners. Nowhere was a crack system distinguishable, and at the top of all this, a twenty-metre ice cliff dominated, demanding direct aid ice climbing if it was to be scaled.

Greenwood speculated the entire Depression had once been filled with a hanging glacier which, having crashed down the face, had left only the ice cliffs behind. To move below them and pursue a direct line to the summit would be very dangerous. Reluctantly but wisely, the two men gave up the direct route and headed for the northwest ridge. What followed was a delightful high-angle climb requiring an occasional piton for direct aid.

In the afternoon an aircraft flew past the face several times, as if searching for them. Later, they learned it had been Kahl with a pilot friend, checking their progress.

Late in the day, it began to rain, and the appearance of the route grew more hostile. As luck would have it, a short while later Greenwood and Locke found a suitable bivouac site. Safe from the rain on a small platform, they made a supper soup. Suddenly a sharp report was heard above the roar of their stove. An enormous ice block had broken from the cliff above the Depression. Cascading silently through space, it struck the face with explosive force, sweeping across the Depression with a roar. As it continued downwards, it scoured the broad ledge on which the climbers had stood only a few hours before. Its terrifying force then quickly dissipated into the depths below, lost from sight and sound. Greenwood and Locke exchanged glances and reflected on their good judgement in abandoning that route. Both men ate their soup in silence.

During the night the rain turned to snow, and as daylight came they found themselves in a tiny, vertical world enclosed by fog. Stiff from the bivouac, Greenwood forced himself to take the initial lead. His wet fingers were cold, and snow continued to fall. The first crack out of the bivouac seemed difficult enough to require direct aid. Greenwood placed a piton, moved up on a stirrup, and then placed another. Locke was happy to see him in front. His lesser experience and the unrelenting high-angle climb, with no easy pitches, was beginning to affect his nerves. But the two men were now only one hundred and fifty metres below the northwest ridge, and, as they warmed up, the climbing, although difficult, became quite pleasant. With one final, strenuous pull on good holds, they surmounted the last overhanging bulge, traversed carefully upwards over snow and broken rock, and reached the upper edge of the face. Relieved at having scaled it safely, they unroped and climbed easily to the summit.

For young Locke, who was about twenty, the deviation from the intended route mattered little. For him, and everyone who heard of it, the climb as it occurred was a great achievement. Greenwood said little. A direct north face party would need a lot of luck, he thought, and "they shouldn't count on it."

The following December, Greenwood, Locke, and Chic Scott from Calgary made the first winter acent of Mount Hungabee. The climb was remembered for its superb bivouac on the face, made early in the afternoon because none of them wore a watch, and they did not know the time.

Although Greenwood never put much faith in climbing schools, he did attend the prestigious French Guides Course at Chamonix in 1967. He witnessed the state of climbing in the Alps. Routes were crowded and heavily pitoned, so much so that enjoyment was moderated, route finding eliminated, and the challenge reduced. It was not one of his favourite areas. But, as was often the case with him, he left a greater impression than he received.

In 1971 Lofthouse and Scott were at the Col de la Fourche hut near Chamonix and met the great French guide, André Contamine, who had in his company a group of aspirant guides. Contamine had climbed with Green-wood four years earlier. Told by Lofthouse they were from

Canada, Contamine's expression changed, he snapped his fingers, and everyone shouted "GREENWOOD!" The Canadian, with his mild eccentricities, blunt opinions, and empathetic manner, had left his stamp.

In 1968 Greenwood made the first winter ascents of the commanding northeast face of Mount Victoria and the south tower of Mount Eisenhower and during the summer scaled the sheer east face of Bugaboo Spire. The first party on this latter route worked its way up the six-hundred-metre wall with the use of about a hundred pitons and twelve bolts. The established time to complete the ascent was two days, but Greenwood and his partner, Oyvind Berle, did it in one.

The Yosemite Valley in California is one of the most highly regarded rock-climbing areas in the world. Its clean, soaring, thousand-metre granite walls have beckoned to greats and would-be greats for more than half a century. The height and grandeur of the faces inspire such names as the Wall of the Morning Light and the Royal Arches. Great technical advances have been made at Yosemite, and its challenges, supported by reliable weather, have made it perhaps the most important rock-climbing region in North America.

Greenwood discovered this mecca in October 1968. The camp life, the climate, the routes, and the people appealed to him greatly. He made at least half a dozen trips to Yosemite up to 1974 and completed some of the greatest routes the valley had to offer, including El Capitan's Salathé Wall and southwest face, the north face of Half Dome, and the south face of Watkins.

In his home mountains, Greenwood made another landmark ascent on Mount Temple in 1969. With James Jones, he completed the newest north face route, located west of his original track. The route was hailed as the easiest and safest on the face to that time, as it was completely free from falling ice.

It was during this same period that Greenwood met John Moss, who like himself had the stamina, nerves, and desire

221

to undertake long, hard routes. Moss, an Englishman, taught at the University of Alberta in Edmonton. In a few months in 1969, Greenwood and he made the second ascent of the Beckey-Mather route on the east face of Snowpatch, the first ascent of Balrog on Yamnuska,[7] and then the east face of Mount Babel, which had thwarted Greenwood in 1966.

Babel's steep, snowless, northeast face was an epic climb, classic in its line, and highest in its standard of difficulty. On a sunny morning, the two men left Moraine Lake campground loaded with ropes, climbing hardware, bivouac gear — and an ample supply of cigarettes. Following the trail below the slopes of the Tower of Babel, they reached Consolation Valley, where the northeast face dominates the lakes lying below it.

Toiling their way up a long scree slope which led to a steep snow couloir, they climbed to its top and stopped to sort out their climbing equipment. Greenwood pointed out the route to Moss, who had not been there before. First there was a buttress over a hundred metres high, above which was a blank, nonfeatured wall. Then followed a chimney and steep crack. Higher, above the crack, was a faintly visible line continuing almost to the top. Greenwood doubted it would go all the way, but, some hundred and fifty metres below the summit, a short traverse to the right led to another barely distinguishable line through the upper face. Here the crux would lie, the severest pitch of all. It posed itself at the end of the climb, when they would be physically and emotionally tired and stretched to the limit. On reaching that point, it would be very difficult to retreat.

Greenwood and Moss ascended the buttress and then roped up. Moss led the blank section, more detailed now at

[7]Balrog is considered to offer the most serious free climbing on Yamnuska. After many tries, Greenwood, with Moss and Nat Nicholas, succeeded and inscribed in the route book, "Balrog is slain!" As with some routes on this and other mountains in the area, this one is named after a mythological character in J. R. R. Tolkien's fantasy *The Lord of the Rings*.

close quarters, and Greenwood took the lead at the bottom of the difficult, steep crack, the key to the centre part of the face. He had climbed it several times before, but it was no easier this time. Greenwood called it a "thrutch" — a state of mind and body when the need to overcome gravity and imbalance becomes nothing less than gasping, heart-pounding, physical desperation. Moss followed with their climbing sack, and he, too, thought it to be one of the hardest free sections he had climbed.

At the top of the crack, Greenwood led up a great slab to a large central ledge which holds snow even in summer. Below this point, the hard climbing had been interspersed with sections of easier ground, but above, the face was relentlessly difficult — a world divided into two vertical halves, one of rock, the other of space. The climbers perse-vered past the central ledge to the shelf where Greenwood and Locke had bivouacked three years before. From this point on, the route would vary from the earlier attempt.

To prepare for the next morning and to use the daylight remaining, they traversed carefully around a corner under an overhanging wall. This airy section would require real skill. And the exposure to a fall was alarming. To some degree, history repeated itself.

Moss took the lead, pursuing a narrow crack suitable for pitons at its lower end but which widened considerably as he went higher. Heavily loaded with climbing iron and a hauling line, he moved up and drove in the first piton. Attaching a nylon stirrup, he tested the piton and then smoothly transferred his weight.

Progress was slow but steady. Moss drove in a bong as the crack became wider, followed by another piton behind a flake of rock. Above the piton, he delicately tapped in his next pin, but as he did so he noticed the crack was widening. The placement of the pitons was forcing the flake away from the wall. The pin from which his stirrup was hanging started to move. Quickly he reached lower to grasp the seemingly secure bong, but this moved also. Frantically he tried to get lower still, when suddenly, all the upper aid system pulled out. With a clatter and a shout, he started to fall. Simultaneously Greenwood took the strain in the rope and held his partner from possible disaster. One last piton had held.

Moss was uninjured. He reorganized his gear, clambered up, and redrove the bong. Moving up again, he thought it best to drill a bolt in the wall for greater security. From it they could reach another crack system. In the failing light Moss called for the bolt kit, and although he was only eight metres above the ledge, Greenwood had to reach well out to get hold of the hauling line which hung vertically from the overhanging face. Moss hauled up the kit, and after drilling a bolt descended to his partner's position.

After an uncomfortable night fastened to the face with pitons, the two were happy to see the morning sun. Greenwood took his turn to lead. The rope, tied off at the bolt above them, ran through the first and lowest piton. With his jumars attached, he ascended to the piton which kept him in proximity to the face. But to go higher it was necessary to unclip the rope, and free himself from the reassuring closeness of the wall. He was going to place all his trust in the bolt.

Greenwood pulled himself in, took a deep breath, and unclipped. As he let go he swung away from the face, dizzily spinning in space. The scree slopes seemed very far below. After seconds that seemed minutes, his breathing returned to normal, and his heartbeat slowed its pace. He jumared up to the bolt, spiralling in the morning light.

Once at the fastening, Greenwood reorganized the ropes and hardware before moving. Almost right away he found a hole for the next piton. With a series of pins and bongs for aid, and some free climbing, he finished the first lead above the ledge and found a belay station at the back of a chimney. This section of about thirty metres consumed four hours. He tied off the climbing rope to a piton and pulled up the rucksack on the lighter hauling line. Lighting a cigarette, he settled back and waited for Moss to jumar to his position, removing the line of pitons as he advanced. The continuing steepness made Moss wish, "Surely we can't be far from the top now."

They weren't. Moss led the next section, and Greenwood climbed the final steep pitch to the top of the face and onto the ridge. They had completed one of the most serious pure rock climbs ever done in Canada. The long descent down the northwest ridge could wait. For the moment, the mountain was theirs.

After this success on Babel, Greenwood and Moss, with two others, made the first ascent of the brooding northeast face of Mount Hungabee, which dominates the head of Paradise Valley. It took place in July 1970. They bivouacked in a cave, and rockfall cut Moss's rope, but other than that it was relatively uneventful, described by Greenwood as fourth-class scrambling, hardly needing a rope. Babel, he said, had been much tougher.

Greenwood's career about that time took an unexpected turn. He met Shirley Bridges, an energetic and competent climber with a colourful personality. Bridges hired Greenwood as her personal guide, and he, in turn, found her to be an ideal client with "enough money, time, and enthusiasm to do it properly." Over a period of four years they amassed an amazing record together: Mounts Robson, Louis, and Colin; some classic routes in Yosemite; Europe; North Wales; the sea stack, Old Man of Storr, in Scotland; the Italian Dolomites; and an expedition to the Cordillera Blanca in the Andes. As Greenwood put it, "With six clients like her, I could see being a professional."

In July 1972, Greenwood made his last serious face climb in Canada, the twelve-hundred metre north face of Mount Kitchener (3475), close to the Columbia Icefield. Following a series of pillars, he and three others found the rock conditions indescribably poor, so much so that adequate climbing protection with pitons was almost impossible. Paper shale was encountered in large sections and crumbled so badly that the climbers called the route Kelloggs, because the rock reminded them of corn flakes. The route took two bivouacs, and Greenwood's experience and leadership were reported to have been the major factors in the success of the party.

This climb was a turning point. Years of exposure to loose rock, stonefall, lightning, and avalanches were accumulating, and by 1974 Greenwood decided to quit climbing, "especially in the Rockies, because it's dangerous. I can remember so many instances when I could have been chopped — probably should have been," he recalled later. But it was more than that. He felt forced to compete with newer, younger climbers. The personal pleasure he derived from his ascents was diminishing. Climbs were becoming much the same, and his experiences were becoming repetitive. In October 1974, shortly after his fortieth birthday, Greenwood made his last major ascent, the six-day climb of the great Salathé Wall of El Capitan in the Yosemite Valley.

In 1975 Greenwood began a roofing business with a partner. An ironic accident occurred the following January. While working on a roof, he slipped from a ladder and fell heavily on his right leg, severely injuring his knee. An operation to repair the ligaments failed to provide full recovery. Greenwood was left with a permanent limp. He was forced to withdraw from hard climbing as his knee would no longer be reliable.

During his career, Greenwood dared to make the "impossible" climbs, constantly raising his own standards, thereby setting new levels of achievement in Canadian mountaineering. He serves as an inspiration to a host of younger climbers. For them he represents values which they hold to be true about the mountains.

Today Greenwood's hair is turning grey. Gazing into a styrofoam cup of Irish whisky, he muses over the past and says, "I know I wasn't a bad climber."

Chapter Ten

Dick Culbert
1940 –

Climbing would be a great, truly wonderful thing, if it weren't for all that damn climbing.

John Ohrenschall,
contemporary American climber

The snowfall was increasing. Culbert and Woodsworth held a quick summit ceremony and then started their descent. Sweeping the rocks with mittened hands, they uncovered a crack for their first rappel piton.

At the bottom of the rappel they tried to retrieve the frozen rope. It was jammed. They yanked, flipped, and cursed at it until it came down. On a lower rappel it happened again. There was more struggling and swearing. By midnight they were back at the col. Plastered with wet snow, they dug in for the night.

In the morning the two climbers were merely "two frost heaves on the ridge." All night it had snowed and now with the sun's warmth the mountain was starting to shed its heavy white mantle. Avalanches broke loose and tore down the slopes in a fury. Danger was everywhere.

Conditions became more nerve wracking as Culbert and Woodsworth renewed their descent. Protection pitons sometimes came out with a simple pull of the fingers. On reaching the glacier, visibility was reduced to zero. A complete whiteout existed; sky and land could not be differentiated. To know which way was down they rolled small snowballs. They were immensely relieved to make it to the top of the Radiant Icefall where they could discern some of its features.

There, despite twenty hours of precipitation, they found their ascent tracks still visible. The crevasses, however, were not; Woodsworth fell into one. Unharmed, he was able to pull himself out. By the time they had made their way through the treacherous maze to the Scimitar Glacier and found their snow-buried tent, they were close to their physical limit. Lucky and relieved to be safe, they fell asleep before they finished eating.

Thus ended the first ascent of Serra V near Mount Waddington, June 1964.

Richard Revis Culbert was born in Winnipeg, 24 April 1940. His father was a Mountie who had joined the RCAF when the war broke out. Graduating at the top of his class as a navigator, Fred Culbert went to war, was shot down and killed; his son and only child was about three years old at the time. Within the year, Margaret Culbert took young Dick to visit friends in Vancouver and never returned to Winnipeg.

While Dick was in junior high school in West Vancouver, he became interested in anything which generated excitement, including pyrotechnics, river running, and mountain hiking. His curiosity about pyrotechnics was prompted by thoughts of being a chemist. River running was done with several other boys, usually along Capilano Creek. They used canoes, army surplus inflatable rafts, and four-board boats (boats made essentially from four boards). It was unsophisticated, exciting, and deadly. One of the boys eventually drowned. Dick gave it up and began to spend more time in the mountains.

There was little easy access to the interior Coast Mountains in the mid-fifties, but there were peaks close to Vancouver. With no particular objective in mind, Dick roamed over Hollyburn and Grouse Mountains and into the protected watershed where foot travellers were forbidden. On Crown Mountain he was caught and reprimanded, a first transgression but not the last. His first conscious climbing objective was the Lions (1646), northwest of Vancouver. Dick and his friends climbed it without a rope, just as they climbed everything else.

"Most of the time," as Dick recalled later, "we didn't know what we were getting into, climbing with running shoes on ice and things like that." Sometimes caught in storms, the boys got soaking wet and suffered from cramps, and Dick found it increasingly difficult as time went on to coax the others to go with him. When he did, and the weather turned foul, he felt responsible.

When finally Dick's group got a rope, they climbed Siwash Rock, a sea stack and practice climb adjacent to Stanley Park. It was then Dick realized he did not know how to use a rope properly. He joined the B.C. Mountaineering Club and was taught rope and ice axe technique on Mount Shuksan, in the Cascade Range of Washington State. With this limited experience he felt ready to handle anything and rushed to make a first ascent of Devil's Tongue, a peak near Ross Lake on the International Boundary. He was annoyed to find someone had been there first.

In the late fifties, Dick, now in senior high school, met Jim Baldwin a fellow climber from Prince Rupert.[1] Baldwin had roamed a great deal in the mountains of northern British Columbia. The stories he told captured Dick's imagination. He wanted to go there, too. The two became friends and made some rock climbs. On these outings, Dick shared his recently acquired knowledge of pitons with his new companion. Dick described the pitons, which were purchased in Vancouver, as "tin foil affairs."

In 1958 Dick was invited by three other climbers to join an expedition to the Kwoiek Creek area, west of the Fraser Canyon and east of the Lillooet River. In order to find their way into the region, the party climbed a mountain, later named Tachewana Peaks (2469), and surveyed the terrain ahead. It was a first ascent for Culbert, and he made three others on this trip, all of which were later named from the

[1] Jim Baldwin was killed 19 June 1964 on the Washington Column in Yosemite National Park. It is believed he rappelled off the end of a rope in the dark and fell to his death.

local Indian dialect: Kumkan Peak (2804); Mehatl Peak (2774); and Haynon Peak (2469).

A Beaver float plane was to meet them at Chowchiwa Lake on 26 August, but the weather was stormy and unstable. The aircraft came in, circled twice and flew off. As the only other exit was the CPR line which was a couple of days away on foot, the young men set aside two day's rations, in the event of such a trip, then gathered berries, and fished. The smokers in the group resorted to cigarettes of willow leaves wrapped in Purex toilet paper.

The climbers waited a second day and on the third started to trek to the railroad. Shortly after their leaving, the Beaver returned and landed. The pilot taxied about the lake and, seeing no sign of the party, took off again. Meanwhile, on a hillside, the frantic party was anxiously trying to light a fire to attract attention. They cheered and shouted when the pilot spotted them, dipped his wings, and returned to pick them up.

Culbert graduated from high school in 1958 and spent the next year looking for jobs and roaming around the countryside. This experience changed him. He met a geologist who so interested him in this field of science that Culbert abandoned his plans to be a chemist and decided on a career in geological engineering instead. Before starting at the University of British Columbia, Culbert promised himself an expedition of his own. It was to be a hard trip.

With forty-five kilograms (100 pounds) of supplies, he hitched rides and backpacked into the Howson Range and Clore River area, located approximately equidistant from Kitimat, Smithers, and Terrace. For one month he roamed alone, overloaded and underequipped, carrying a wool sleeping robe without zipper and a piece of plastic sheet to keep him dry. Freeze-dried food was not yet available; all camping foodstuffs were heavy. The weather was consistently foul, and at one point Culbert was cut off from his pack by a rising river.

His map proved worthless. The area he was in was represented by a huge blank space. Despite this, Culbert made a few ascents, including Dog's Ear Peaks (2394). It was his most formative period and probably his most miserable. Carrying his heavy pack, going long periods without eating, and enduring cold, wet, and mosquitoes, he developed a high pain threshold. By the time he returned home he had discovered in himself an exceptional degree of self-reliance and knew he wanted to explore the mountains more than anything else.

That summer he hitchhiked to Banff to visit some girlfriends but Phyl Munday, acting as hostess at the ACC Clubhouse, thought better of telling him where they were. He was, after all, a bit alarming in appearance after so much time in the bush. Undeterred, Culbert hitched to Eisenhower Junction north of Banff and made a solo ascent of the southeast tower of Mount Eisenhower (2752). Not surprisingly, he was apprehended by the local warden and given a stern reprimand for climbing alone. That fall he entered first year geological engineering at UBC.

Culbert wrote of his experiences in the Howson Range/ Clore River country and presented the manuscript to the *Varsity Outdoor Club Journal*. It was rejected. It was "poor taste," he was told, and he was "quite irresponsible to go alone." In a period when the highlight of a teen-ager's week was taking a girlfriend to the movies and then to the White Spot for a hamburger, Culbert's strenuous and lonely activities made him distinct from his peer group. He was "an oddball," others said.

Culbert did nothing to dispel this image but, perhaps, rather enjoyed it. At UBC he was one of the first to climb buildings. Over a period of years, about a hundred routes were established. Like "cat burglars trying not to be caught," he and other students climbed at night. During his post-graduate years in the sixties, Culbert was apprehended while doing a solo on the clock tower and was told such behaviour was not acceptable from a graduate student. The number of building climbs diminished after Culbert left the university.

These forbidden activities did not mean that Culbert was

a dissident youth filled with anger and ready to revolt. He was, in fact, polite and conforming where necessary but possessed also a mildly irreverent attitude towards the established way of doing things. And beneath this exterior was a young man of considerable intellect and purpose.

No comprehensive guidebook about the Coast Mountains existed when Culbert entered UBC. Some explorations had been described in writing, the most notable being Don Munday's *The Unknown Mountain*, but, for the most part, knowledge of the area was locked in the memories of surveyors, bush pilots, hunters, trappers, and prospectors. Barely twenty years old, Culbert determined to write a guide to the Coast Mountains. With the help of others, he began his work, collecting aerial photos, archival material, and mountaineering accounts. In 1962, he went into the field for three months to compile and verify as much information as he could from first-hand observations and local sources.

To finance the operation he put to use his newly found knowledge about grubstaking, a government program which supported prospecting. Not knowing much about minerals, his friends had more trouble than he passing the required test, but they promised to do sixty days of mineral exploration and were awarded $150 each. At the end of May, Culbert, Glen Woodsworth, and Ashlyn Armour-Brown set out for the interior.

After 1950 a great deal of climbing activity had taken place south of Bella Coola in the Monarch Region, but it was done mostly by Americans. As Woodsworth put it, "We had the hope of salvaging a few first ascents for Canada and ourselves." With twenty-four day's supplies, Culbert, Woodsworth, and Armour-Brown left the tiny settlement of Atnarko on 3 June 1962 and backpacked southwards along the Atnarko River. On 11 June the three students made the third ascent of Monarch Mountain (3533).

The higher they climbed on Monarch the more difficult it became. From the corniced east ridge they crossed onto a hanging glacier covered with loose powder snow under which lay old snowcrust. It was very unstable. Culbert was leading. About a hundred and twenty metres below the summit, he reached the bergschrund and surmounted it by climbing a small overhang. He led out a full length of rope and found no adequate stance from which to protect his companions. They tied on another rope, and he led that rope out too. Still no stance. They tied all their prusik slings together, and, trailing eighty metres of mixed line behind him, Culbert finally found a rock pocket from which he was able to make an excellent belay. They were on the summit by midafternoon.

Armour-Brown suffered snow blindness from this ascent, which prevented him from climbing for a few days. One afternoon, alone in camp, he heard the sound of a porcupine outside the tent. Despite his limited vision, he killed and skinned the animal to supplement their rations. When the others returned, they roasted it and marvelled at their friend's skill at handling a porcupine while half-blind.

Culbert completed three first ascents in the Monarch region during this period, all exceeding three thousand metres: Migma Mountain, the Throne, and Mount Ratcliff. On 30 June the party gathered at Smithers and were joined by a fourth student, Arnold Shives.

After making two first ascents in the Coal Creek group, west of Smithers, the party flew to Burnie Lake, in the heart of the Howson Range. The range is heavily glaciated and very compact, with numerous peaks, some very steep and others "disgustingly rotten." None, however, posed climbing difficulties in excess of class four. All were found to have elevations lower than those posted on the map.

Together they climbed Howson Peak (2652) and, by splitting into two parties, climbed most of the remaining virgin peaks in twenty days. Usually teamed with Woodsworth, Culbert made eleven first ascents. On 2 August the party returned to Smithers and, to satisfy their boyish desires, indulged in a heavy drinking bout of milkshakes.

After a brief visit and a first ascent in the Hudson Bay

Range north of Smithers, Culbert took three days off to write exams in Prince Rupert. By mid-August he was in the Seven Sisters Range, north of Terrace. Rainy weather set in for ten days, but on 22 August it cleared. That day, Culbert and Woodsworth made three more firsts, all over twenty-six hundred metres. After the others left for home, Culbert climbed the virgin Outpost Peaks for the first time. He returned to Vancouver with a myriad of guidebook material and more than twenty first ascents to his record.

Culbert graduated from university in 1963. His next four climbing seasons were his most productive.

At that time, the Serra Peaks, a short distance east of Mount Waddington, had all been climbed, with the exception of Serra V (3597). It was a splendid, ice-covered rock tower, one of the statuesque peaks first seen by the Mundays as it rose above the Tiedemann Glacier. Serra V was the last major unclimbed summit in the Waddington Range; Culbert believed it to be the highest remaining virgin peak in provincial Canada.

In mid-June 1964 Culbert and Woodsworth landed by ski plane on the Scimitar Glacier, north of the Serra Peaks. From a camp at two thousand metres, they pursued a route from the Scimitar up the thousand metre icefall of the Radiant Glacier. Loaded with technical gear and bivouac equipment, it took tremendous effort to penetrate the tumbling terrain, ploughing upwards, weaving their way in "deep slush."

Once above the icefall, surface conditions improved, and travel was more rapid. They climbed the headwall at the head of the glacier, where Woodsworth cut steps in laminated ice. The climb of this final, steep gully brought them above the headwall to the col between Serra V and Mount Asperity. It was eleven hours since they had left camp.

As often happens in the Coast Mountains, the weather had been deteriorating appreciably since their start. Clouds were closing in. The two climbers reached the foot of the summit tower just as a storm broke.

Culbert took the lead over class four rock on the northeast face. After two rope lengths, he came to treacherous ground. Above him, snow of earlier storms had metamorphosed into ice, and verglas covered the rocks. As he climbed this section, new snow increased in depth. He kicked his crampons into the armour-plated ice. They penetrated only a little. Handholds were obscured by snow, which had to be swept away. In the cold gloom, new snow formed into slides and hissed quietly into the depths. The terrain was far more dangerous than difficult. "Hairy!" shouted Culbert as he worked way upwards.

At eight o'clock in the evening of 16 June 1964, Culbert and Woodsworth stood on the summit of Serra V. It was their most important first ascent in 1964, but it was only one of twenty-six achieved by Culbert and his friends that summer.

The following season, after three years of research and two-finger manuscript typing, a *Climber's Guide to the Coastal Ranges of British Columbia* was published. It described approximately two thirds of the Coast Mountains, from the International Boundary in the south to the Nass River in the north. Culbert, age twenty-five, became a notable figure in Canadian mountaineering almost overnight.

He spent four months that summer, 1965, working for the Geological Survey of Canada, "water skiing, climbing, and sightseeing from a helicopter." The helicopter was a definite improvement over his earlier modes of transportation, which included hitchhiking, driving unreliable cars, and riding freight. Culbert had discovered the latter method early in his career. Wandering into a freight yard, he would enquire where the cars were going and then climb onto something that "looked good." The government owned railroads, the Pacific Great Eastern and the Canadian National seemed the better choices. They gave him little trouble. The Canadian Pacific, on the other hand, "seemed to have cops who cared." When apprehended he was fined if he had any money, which he seldom did.

Culbert remembers, with amusement, once riding with Woodsworth overnight on a flatcar. It snowed heavily, and their sleeping-bagged bodies accumulated a lot of snow. A railway agent, seeing the train pass his station, was alarmed at what he saw to be two corpses on the car. He phoned down the line. The train was stopped and the "cadavers" investigated. Railway officials were more relieved than angry to find the two bodies still breathing in their snowy cocoons.

In 1966, for the first time in his career, Culbert took the winter and spring to climb outside Canada. He went to South America.

Only parties of no less than three were allowed on Aconcagua (6960), the highest peak in the Andes, but Culbert started out alone, with a heavy pack. He ran out of wind at fifty-two hundred metres and had to come down. It was his first experience with high altitude.

After completing his first solo climb, Cerro Cuerno (Horn Peak, 5639), near Aconcagua, Culbert left Argentina for Peru. He had a severe case of amoebic dysentery, a possible legacy of eating food given him by Argentinian army mule handlers. For several months he hiked and travelled on little buses through the Andes, making six climbs, including four first ascents. All were technically easy but of high elevation. The four were: Huarancante (5395), Hualca-Hualca (6096), Sabancaya (6050), and Coropuna Este (6248). He found two large sulphur pits fuming through the summit ice on Hualca-Hualca and he climbed the final sulphur slopes of Coropuna Este wearing crampons.

These mountains posed no threat, but the natives did. Indian llama herders and vicuña hunters inhabited the region, and when Culbert met them he was questioned: Where are you going? Why? Are you alone? Are you rich? Do you have a gun? Are you coming back this way? When?

Culbert never returned the same way. Instead, he played hide-and-seek, afraid of being murdered for what he was carrying on his back. After five months of roaming from Colombia to Patagonia, he returned safely home, happy to have escaped this peril.

In the summer of 1966 he worked in the northern most Cariboos for the Geological Survey of Canada, made twenty-four first ascents, and tried to avoid contact with a teeming game population. On three occasions he was charged by a grizzly; on one, he shot his attacker.

Culbert had come over the edge of a moraine into a meadow when he spotted the grizzly and her cubs. Dropping back and out of sight, he dug out his telephoto lens, which, typically, was at the bottom of his rucksack next to a revolver. He pulled out the Smith and Wesson, too.

Rising, he fired a shot into the air, hoping to make the bear stand up for a photograph, but as he scrambled up the moraine with his camera in hand he met the bear rushing towards him. Both were startled. The grizzly stood up, just as Culbert wanted, but now she was too close for the telephoto lens. Culbert fired again, and the bear and her offspring scurried off, their backsides to the photographer.

The incident was rather amusing at first, but later that day a deadly encounter with the same bears took place. Hidden in dense slide alder, the grizzly charged at very close range. With no time to divert her, Culbert drew the gun from his belt and fired point-blank. As the sound of the explosion rolled down the valley, the mother grizzly wheeled and fell into the bush, leaving blood stains about two metres from her assailant. She coughed once or twice; then her body went slack.

Culbert was stunned at the consequences of the shooting which had happened so suddenly. One of the cubs "put on a truly sobering display, trying to awaken its dead mother." Culbert sadly realized that the yearlings could not survive, but he could not bring himself to shoot them as well. Instead, he chose a peak overlooking the scene and named it Orphan Rock.

Culbert accepted his third project assignment with the GSC in 1967 and spent the summer season mapping sixty-five hundred kilometres of Pacific coastline. Afterwards he carried out a helicopter survey extending from the Monarch

Ice Cap, over the Waddington Range, to the Homathko Icefield. This work yielded ten new ascents.

In the late sixties, Culbert's career ambitions started to change. Long gone were his boyhood years of adventure, which had given way to exploration and first ascents. Now his peak-bagging days were over, too. His third phase was characterized by what mountaineers call aesthetics, climbs which yield high spiritual and intellectual satisfaction because of their purity of line and difficulty. Culbert began looking for routes which would be aesthetically rewarding.

In all his earlier ascents, Culbert had neglected the obvious Coast Mountains classic, Mount Waddington. He had been invited to join the Pigou-Owen party in 1960 but was unable to go for lack of finances. He was lucky. The party of four perished in an avalanche on the Bravo Glacier. In 1968, however, with friends Alice Purdy (his future wife), Bob Cuthbert, and Gary Kozel, he made his first climb of Waddington via its most popular route, the southeast face. Their ascent was remembered most vividly because of a rappelling accident.

Kozel was preparing to make the last rappel from the tower when an anchor sling broke. In wild flight, he tumbled down the rocks and shot off the upper lip of the bergschrund, high angle. "I thought he was a goner!" Culbert said. Miraculously, Kozel was not seriously hurt, but he had pulled all the rope down with him. It seemed the others were stuck on the tower.

Then they had their second piece of luck. The rope had snagged on a rock projection above the bergschrund. Tying their slings together, they were able to get one climber down to recover the rope.

Later, Culbert recalled that soon after this experience, Kozel became a potter and gave up mountaineering.

Culbert entered graduate studies at UBC, starting in a master's program but later abandoning it in favour of a Ph.D. in geophysics. This work kept him in Vancouver, which resulted in the pursuit of more classic routes closer to home. He climbed Mount Habrich near Squamish by two new routes and, with Alice Purdy, ascended the beautiful and rewarding southeast face of Hozomeen Mountain, just south of the U.S. border.

Culbert was writing more frequently by then, and his style, more than ever, reflected his perennially light-hearted attitude towards climbing. In commenting about his climbs of this period, one, at least, failed to meet his new standards. He wrote,

> To what extent do we climb to collect experiences? In some measure we depend on things going wrong to generate memories, although the aesthetic moments also leave their mark. Somehow this route lacked both.

And,

> Everything went smoothly. There were no crux moves and few aesthetic ones either. Cheated? — in [a thousand metres of] loose rock one expects at least something unexpected.

On 21 February 1969, Culbert, Barry Hagen, and Allen Steck from California made the first winter ascent of Mount Waddington. There were six in the party, but only these three were fit for the final climb of the tower and, even then, barely so. Sick and weak after reaching the summit, their energy levels were so low that Hagen, a doctor, believed they "would not be able to survive a bivouac." They retreated through the night, the route made easier by the fact that Waddington's famous ice feathers presented less of a problem in winter than in summer.

The ski descent with heavy loads down the glacier stuck in Culbert's memory. "I've never been a great skier, although I did do a ski ascent of Siwash Rock,"[2] he said with a laugh.

When the second edition of his climber's guide was

[2]Siwash Rock can only be reached on foot at low tide. His ski ascent, a prank, was made over bare rock. Culbert is known for other novelty climbs as well. When the reservoir of the Cleveland Dam, located on the Capilano River in North Vancouver, was emptied for repairs, he and friends pitoned their way up the face of the spillway, much to the annoyance of local authorities.

published with supplementary information in 1969, Culbert reported on the official status of climbing on this twelve-metre-high volcanic plug:

Siwash Rock

A sign has been placed on the SW face, threatening climbers with prosecution. The sign is cemented on and makes a good foothold.

The next spring Culbert made a trek in Nepal and was overcome by what he termed *Nepalassitude*. It resulted in a lot of walking, sightseeing, a few minor ascents, and some poetry, "Last March to Beni."

The Squamish Chief (652) at the head of Howe Sound dominates the town of Squamish with its imposing, vertical granite walls. Rising starkly above the adjacent highway, the Chief and its satellite faces interested progressive climbers only after the railway was constructed to the town. In the late fifties it attracted persons like Fred Beckey, Jim Baldwin, Ed Cooper, and others who saw its potential as a unique training ground for big-wall climbing.

Culbert had explored the Chief's tree-covered crown when a teen-ager and climbed its shattered north gully in nailed boots in 1958, but he never developed the depth of interest in it that others did. To him the mountain was a playground where he could go during the winter months when little else was available.

Over the years, however, he did have some memorable experiences there. Bob Cuthbert, one of his climbing partners, dropped a boot off a ledge during a bivouac one night. Another partner, Hamish Mutch, lost control of a rappel and slid off the end of the rope. By sheer chance he landed in a tree. Unhurt, it "shook him up a little bit," Culbert said, "and me, too!"

In the late sixties, Culbert climbed more actively on the Chief in order to perfect his direct aid climbing technique. He put up some new routes but concentrated mainly on repeating established big climbs such as the Grand Wall and the Western Dihedral. These two latter climbs were done in the spring of 1970, for a specific purpose: with Paul Starr and Fred Douglas, Culbert planned to climb the Devil's Thumb (2774), the big chisel-shaped granite peak located on the border of Alaska and British Columbia.

After a glacier approach, they reached the base of the mountain on its south side. "It's big," thought Culbert when he saw it at close range. They planned to ascend the east ridge, which in profile displayed two prominent steps, or knees.

They tackled the first knee shortly after dawn. The first six pitches were climbed free, because the rock was split and provided excellent climbing surfaces. Higher up, they were forced onto the south face to avoid serious overhangs.

Once above the knees, the party kept almost entirely to the narrow, exposed ridge. It was heavily iced. Ice-slush plumes affixed to gendarmes forced them occasionally onto the north face, which plummeted eighteen hundred metres to its base. Culbert had one word for it: "Wild!" Despite their experience, training, and belaying techniques, the length of the climb and its difficulties forced them to bivouac on a snow ledge before reaching the summit. Twenty hours of continuous climbing had not been enough to make the top.

The next day another twenty hours were required to gain the summit and rappel down the narrow ridge. A total of sixteen leads had been of class five difficulty.

Over the years, Culbert had developed a taste for academic life, becoming what he called "a professional student." In the fall of 1970 he accepted a postdoctoral fellowship at the University of Alberta in Edmonton. The purpose of the two-year fellowship was to develop the application of computers in the field of geochemistry. He moved to Edmonton with his wife, Alice, and their first child.

Removed as he was from the mountains, climbing continued only intermittently, but in 1972 he joined Starr and Douglas again for a return trip to Alaska. This time they wanted to make the first ascent of the spectacular spire adjacent to the Devil's Thumb, known as the Cat's Ears (2591).

The three men boarded a ferry at Seattle with twenty boxes of "hand luggage," which they stored on deck. Sleeping comfortably for two nights in deck chairs, they found the voyage enjoyable, casually ignoring frequent disapproving glances from the purser.

From Petersburg, Alaska, they made a short flight to their objective in a chartered aircraft and surveyed the mountain's astounding proportions. Almost perfectly vertical and three hundred metres high, the Cat's Ears looked more difficult than they feared.

The Beaver float plane landed them on a lake about sixteen kilometres to the west. On the following day they marched to an airdrop site on the Witches Cauldron Glacier, south of the peak. From a base camp pitched at seven hundred and fifty metres, the climbers carried supplies and climbing iron over heather and snow slopes and cached it, where it could be picked up and used the next day.

On 20 July 1972, they returned and sorted loads to about twenty kilograms each. Their equipment included bivouac gear, three day's supply of food, three ropes, forty pitons, and fifty carabiners. They followed a short glacier into a broad snow gully below the spire, where the sun soon loosened stones which began to fall about them.

In the face of this danger they traversed across a snow slope to the foot of the rock, which was overhanging and wet. Starr used direct aid to lead up. After a few pitches they discovered the Cat's Ears were separated from the Devil's Thumb by an interfacing shear zone of soft rock, all crumbling away. Four more leads over sandy slabs brought them to the base of the tower, where they excavated a platform on a sandy ledge and bivouacked.

The fine weather held the next morning. Packing all extra climbing iron, some food, and down jackets into two packs, they were able to allow the leader to climb without a load. From the notch they started up. It was tiresome work with the sun beating on their backs. At one point, Culbert led a high, class five pitch and was belaying Douglas upwards when Douglas pulled out a key handhold and pendulumed ten or fifteen metres across the face. The loss of the hold forced Douglas and Starr to jumar this section, climbing a fixed line tied by Culbert.

Eleven leads were required to the top, all class five but one. Large exfoliating slabs which formed ramps provided excellent climbing. A final lead over perfectly vertical rock brought them to the small summit by evening.

The eight double-rope rappels to the bivouac ledge were nervous affairs. At one juncture they watched several tons of rock collapse and roar past their sleeping area in a cloud of dust. The friction and crashing of the rock gave off acrid fumes. It narrowly missed their equipment.

The Cat's Ears Spire was Culbert's last big climb. In later years he looked back on it fondly as the kind which combined the better things in mountaineering life: an elegant tower of good rock in a panoramic setting and a brand new route of continuous difficulty.

Although climbing continued intermittently until 1975, a number of major changes, including the breakup of his marriage, seriously affected Culbert's mountaineering career. He went to Chile on a mining exploration assignment. A nonpolitical person, Culbert suddenly found himself at first interested in, and then sympathetic with, the resistance to Chile's police state. Upon his departure from that country at the end of 1975, he spoke Spanish fluently and brought with him his second wife, Luciana. The circumstances surrounding their departure meant Luciana would not be able to return to her homeland.

In the course of these events, Culbert's keen interest in mountaineering waned. Yet, in twenty years he had made some notable achievements. His explorations and mapping resulted in two guidebooks, his first climber's guide, and his *Alpine Guide to Southwestern British Columbia*, published in 1974. He had made about two hundred and fifty first ascents and new routes, although he says "some were not terribly important mountains." And, remarkably, he never injured himself, despite the need, on certain occasions, to climb under poor conditions. His judgement and technique never failed him.

Not yet forty, Culbert's career may not be over. Although he has interest in participating in foreign climbing expeditions, he also has been exposed to the problems facing third world countries, the kind of problems to which he could apply his intellect and adaptability with good result. He is uncertain about his future plans, but whatever he does, he will do it well.

Glossary

aid Also referred to as aid climbing or direct aid. The use of pitons, nuts, stirrups, etc. to affect direct upward or lateral movement where natural holds are insufficient and free climbing is impossible. The need for aid depends on the free climbing ability of the climber.

arête A French word, often used in English, for ridge.

belay The act of one or more climbers when using the rope to protect another climber from a fall. The belayer(s) are in fixed positions either attached to the rock or ice, or in positions where they cannot be dislodged, referred to as bomb-proof positions.

bergschrund A large marginal crevasse on a glacier where the ice separates from its rock base. Most frequently the uppermost crevasse of major proportions.

bivouac A temporary primitive camp without amenities, frequently on a ledge with a good view and little comfort.

bivouac sack A lightweight sack with a hood designed to enclose one or two persons in a sitting position. It is constructed of a material suitable to keep warmth in and moisture out.

bolts Short, small diameter, steel shafts which expand to fit tightly when driven into holes which have been drilled in rock surfaces. The end of the shaft projects from the rock and is fitted with a hanger to which a carabiner and stirrup may be attached. Bolts permit the climbing of routes over otherwise holdless rock. A very controversial technique.

bong Originally known as the bong-bong. It is a large, aluminum alloy, angle piton with several holes drilled transversely to lighten its weight. Of various sizes, they are used in cracks up to ten centimetres in width (four inches).

bulge Encountered where ice, snow, or rock projects from the face pushing the climber backwards and off balance. Less projecting than an overhang.

buttress A distinct, and usually large, dome-shaped formation which forms part of, and stands against, a mountain face. The buttress appears to hold the wall upright and in place.

cairn A small, man-made pillar of rock pieces constructed on a summit or pass to mark the location and the first ascent by climbers.

carabiner A connecting device, oval or D-shaped, made of aluminum alloy, and with a spring-loaded side gate which can be easily opened with

245

the thumb. Measuring approximately fifty by ninety centimetres, carabiners have a wide variety of uses including connecting ropes to anchors, pitons, nuts, etc.

ceiling Sometimes called a roof. A prominent overhang with a flat underside which must be passed on either side or climbed underneath and then over with the use of direct aid (see **aid**).

chimney A crack wide enough to contain the climber's body and narrow enough to be straddled.

chockstone A stone which has fallen into a crack or chimney and which has wedged firmly in place. Often used as an anchor point by passing a sling around the stone and attaching a carabiner.

cirque A large, uniform, concave face frequently found high on the mountain immediately below the summit.

classes See **grades**

col The lowest point on a ridge between two peaks. Often the pass to the opposite side of a mountain.

cornice A natural snow form which results from a build-up of wind-driven ice crystals on the lee side of mountain ridges. Over a period of time, a cornice may grow to overhang the lee face for many metres. Sometimes shaped like a violin scroll, cornices can be exceedingly treacherous when mature and decaying because they break off without warning.

couloir A wide, natural channel on a mountain face down which debris falls. It frequently contains snow and ice but poses the most danger during a rainstorm when it fills with a torrent of running water and flying rocks.

crack A separation in rock varying from a few millimetres in width to widths large enough to contain an arm or a leg.

crampons A frame of light alloy steel points fitted and strapped to boots for climbing ice and hard snow.

crest The uppermost edge of a mountain ridge.

crevasse A separation or crack in glacier ice varying in width and depth from a few centimetres to tens of metres. Distinctly different from a crevice in rock.

crux The crux pitch, or problem pitch, is the key and most difficult section of a climb.

direct aid See **aid**

double rope   Climbers may use a double rope for climbing. They may tie two rope lengths between them or double a long single rope. The double rope is used for added protection and/or use on technical climbs where one length must be tensioned to hold the leader in position such as required to climb roofs or ceilings.

exposure   When a fall would result in a vertical, or nearly vertical, descent of many tens or hundreds of metres, the climber's position is said to be exposed. The degree of exposure is a function of the length of the possible fall and the individual climber's psychological reaction to it.

face   A face is one of two planes which must intersect to form a ridge. As a geometric result, faces are steeper than the corresponding ridge which they form.

fixed ropes   Ropes tied to natural or artificial anchors for the purpose of aiding repeated ascents, either at daily intervals or over longer periods, are called fixed ropes. On big wall climbs, fixed ropes may be used for rappelling at night and for climbing the next morning with prusiks or jumars.

free climbing   Climbing over rock, snow, or ice without the use of mechanical devices for progression. Most climbing is done free.

gendarme   A rock pinnacle usually located on a ridge, which some-times blocks its entire width. Such pinnacles can pose great difficulties, especially when encountered in the latter stages of a climb.

glissade   From a French verb meaning to slide. To glissade, the climber squats and slides downhill on the soles of his boots, controlling his speed with the point of his ice axe.

grades   Various systems of grading climbs exist. In this book the words *classes* and *grades* are used interchangeably although some modern systems do not permit this liberty. To assist the general reader in his understanding of the text, the grades set out below most closely reflect Alpine standards because they are simpler than the more complex sys-tems employed in North America, where classes and grades have dif-ferent meanings and no class six is recognized.

Grades One, Two, and Three. From easy, elementary climbing to moder-ately difficult routes requiring ropes and regular belays.

Grade Four. Difficult climbing for the experienced person only. Good technique, belays, and some intermediate protection for the leader may be required on longer pitches.

Grade Five. Very difficult climbing. All belays must be anchored, inter-mediate protection essential, muscular strength and refined technique demanded. Very exacting climbing over long routes.

Grade Six. Extremely difficult climbing. The climber is often on the

247

verge of falling. Free sections frequently interspersed with aid pitches. Superior strength, balance, nerves, flexibility, technique, and courage needed. Only climbed by the exceptional and talented top echelon.

gully   A wide chimney, narrower than a couloir.

hauling line   On very high angle routes the leader climbs without the encumbrance of a climbing sack. Instead, he ties a hauling line to his waist and on reaching the next stance, hauls up the climbing sack before belaying his partner.

icefall   An icefall occurs where glacier ice must flow over steep, uneven bedrock. The ice breaks into blocks of sometimes gigantic proportions and is seen to be tumbling or tottering. It frequently collapses and endangers anyone close by. Such areas of collapsing ice are called icefalls.

jamming   A climbing technique, most usually performed on rock, in which a climber jams his body between two rock surfaces (a jam crack) and squirms his way upwards. A technique frequently used in narrow chimneys.

jumars   Mechanical devices, used in pairs, for ascending fixed ropes (jumaring). The jumar ascender fits to the rope and can be slid upwards but jams with downward pressure. Slings tied to jumars allow the climber to stand in space while attached to the rope.

knife edge   The very sharp uppermost edge of a snowridge or rock flake.

layback   A rock climbing technique in which the climber places his body in a laid back position so that his centre of gravity passes outside his feet. It is a position of body imbalance. Typically, this technique is employed to climb a right angle intersection formed by a smooth wall and a steeply sloping ledge. A hand crack must exist where the two surfaces meet.

The climber positions his hands in the crack and, with a quick step up, places his feet squarely on the ledge close to his hands. Thus doubled over, he moves along the line of the crack by alternately shifting a hand or a foot and prevents himself from overturning by pulling with his arms. This is a strenuous technique which can be tolerated only for a matter of minutes.

mantelshelf   A flat ledge above the climber's feet approximately equal to the height of a fireplace mantelshelf. To mantelshelf means to place one's hands flat on the ledge and, with a short but certain movement, to push upwards with the legs, straighten the arms vertically, and place first one foot, and then the other, on the ledge to reach a standing position. The movement is similar to getting out of a swimming pool without the use of a ladder.

massif A major rock uplift which, when viewed in its entirety, is compact and comprises more than one peak.

moraine Shattered and weathered rock, graded in size from flour to large blocks. Moraine is composed of bedrock scrapings, gathered under the force of powerful glacial movement, and the deposition of surface debris which has fallen onto the glacier from the rock cliffs surrounding the glacial channel. When the ice melts and the glacier retreats, moraines are deposited from these two sources. The relative position of the moraine to the glacier gives it a topographical identity. For example, terminal moraine is found at the nose or terminus of the glacier, lateral moraine along its borders.

nuts Also called "chocks," "stoppers," and other names. Modern climbing devices, usually made of aluminum alloy, which fit into cracks and act similarly to natural chockstones. They are fitted with either a short rope sling or small diameter steel cable and are used for both belay anchors and intermediate protection.

overhang A projection of rock which is larger than a bulge but less prominent than a ceiling or roof.

pendulum traverse On a few high angle routes, an ascent system of cracks may peter out on a blank wall with no further progress possible without the use of bolts. The system of cracks, however, may continue again to one side of the lower route, and a pendulum traverse is used to cross the blank wall between. The leader places a piton and carabiner as high as possible on the first and lower system, passes the rope through the carabiner, and descends again until sufficient rope is threaded through the carabiner for him to swing across the face. The second climber then tensions the rope, and the leader, in a giddy quick step, swings out across the wall. Several attempts to pendulum are frequently needed, each one gathering more speed, until the leader catches the parallel, but distant, upper crack system. After the leader is across, the second climber follows in a similar fashion. If the climbers are to return by the same route, the rope may be left in place. If descent is contemplated by another route, the rope is untied from one climber and drawn through the carabiner.

pitch A pitch is a section of a route between stances and is generally equal in length to the length of the rope. A route is made up of a series of pitches.

piton A short steel blade with an eye at one end. The piton is fitted into rock cracks and driven with a hammer to form an anchor point. A wide variety of piton sizes and shapes are used, made either from soft iron, spring steel, or chrome molybdenum steel. Ice pitons are longer than

249

those used for rock. Threaded tubular types, which can be screwed into ice and thus are called ice screws, are currently favoured over driven types.

protection A general term referring to anchored belays as well as running belays comprising pitons, nuts, bolts, slings, carabiners, etc., used in various combinations, and all set in place to reduce the height of drop experienced by the leader in the event of a fall.

prusik A knot which permits a small diameter rope to be affixed at any point along the length of a larger rope. When tensioned, the knot jams and holds the larger rope securely. Employed in a variety of techniques including the ascent of a fixed rope (prusiking), a method commonly used before the advent of jumar ascenders.

rappel Normally this descent technique is performed on a double rope, the centre of which is at a fixed anchor. Controlling his speed through friction on the rope, the climber slides down the rope to a lower stance, pulls one side of the double rope, and thus retrieves it from the anchor. This is a spectacular and effective method of quick descent over difficult ground. Two great dangers exist: a) the anchor may come out resulting in an instant and, most likely, fatal fall; and b) the climber may rappel off the end of the rope into space, with similar results.

roof See **ceiling**

rope Tied to frightened novices to prevent them from getting away! The earliest ropes were of quality hemp, thirteen millimetres in diameter and twenty-five metres long. After World War II, nylon came into use, about ten millimetres in diameter and thirty-five metres long. Most commonly today, perlon braided ropes are in use, eleven millimetres in diameter for rock climbing and nine millimetres for snow and ice climbing. Lengths vary from forty to fifty metres (130 to 165 feet). These modern ropes are easily handled and have elastic qualities good for absorbing shock loads.

scree Rock is weathered into many shattered pieces which fall or are washed down the mountain to form natural slopes. Such fragments are called scree and the slope formed is called a scree slope.

sea stack A vertical tower of rock eroded from a sea cliff by wave action so that it stands apart from the parent cliff. Usually approached by boat or on foot over a rock causeway at low tide.

serac An ice pinnacle or block found within an icefall.

slings Short looped sections of rope or nylon webbing used for a wide variety of purposes – anchors, rappel seats, etc.

snowbridge Snow accumulates in, and is blown across, crevasses during the winter months forming natural bridges from one edge, or lip, to the other. As thawing occurs in spring and summer, the bridges weaken and crossing them can be exceedingly treacherous. Belays are essential.

stance A position from which a climber can safely belay or rappel.

stirrups A short ladder of two, three, or four steps used for direct aid. Originally made of rope with wooden steps, and later with aluminum steps, the modern version is constructed of twenty-five millimetre solid nylon webbing tied in a series of loops. It is sometimes called an aider.

summit ridge The main ridge leading directly to the summit.

thrutch A recently developed term which represents a feeling of panic combined with desperate physical action. The climber feels he is about to fall and, faced with this imminent possibility, he attempts desperate and seemingly impossible moves in order to save himself. That part of the climb which produces this combination of fear and action is called a thrutch.

traverse A horizontal or moderately inclined section of a climb, the latter being called a diagonal traverse.

verglas When meltwater freezes on a rock surface, it produces a thin layer of hard, black ice called verglas. When several such layers exist, the ice is described as laminated. Verglas is most frequently encountered on north facing routes and is exceedingly treacherous to climb.

wall A vertical surface of rock or ice. A distinct feature in itself, a wall is most commonly found as part of a face and, in some cases, as at Yosemite, a wall may form the entire face. When a wall is encountered on a ridge, it is likely to be called a step.

whiteout A storm condition experienced on snow slopes and glaciers which is produced either by dense cloud and fog, a snowstorm, or both. To the climber, all perspectives are white, no horizon is apparent, and no shape or slope perceived; the ground melds uniformly with the sky. The climber imagines himself to be suspended in white and utterly feature-less space. Without a horizon, he quickly loses direction, depth percep-tion, and, frequently, his balance. When on skis, the climber may experi-ence a sensation of speed although he is standing still. Orientation returns only when some recognizable feature comes into view or he falls down.

wooden wedges Before the advent and common acceptance of the bong, hardwood wedges, drilled through and fitted with a rope sling, were used as pitons in wide cracks. If the crack was vertical and the wedges were skilfully placed, a rough staircase could be constructed along the line of the crack.

Selected Bibliography

Beckey, Fred. *Challenge of the North Cascades.* Seattle: The Mountaineers, 1969.

Culbert, Dick. *A Climber's Guide to the Coastal Ranges of British Columbia.* 2d ed. Banff: The Alpine Club of Canada, 1969.

_____. *Alpine Guide to Southwestern British Columbia.* Vancouver: Dick Culbert, 1974.

Ferber, Peggy, ed. *Mountaineering: The Freedom of the Hills.* 3d rev. ed. Seattle: The Mountaineers, 1974.

Jones, Chris. *Climbing in North America.* Berkeley: University of California Press, 1976.

Kain, Conrad. *Where the Clouds Can Go.* Edited by J. Munroe Thorington. 1935. Reprint. Boston: Charles T. Branford Co., 1954.

Kallen, Urs. *A Climber's Guide to Yamnuska.* 2d ed. Calgary: Urs Kallen, 1977.

Kruszyna, Robert and Putnam, William L. *Climber's Guide to the Interior Ranges of British Columbia – South.* Springfield, Mass.: The American Alpine Club and The Alpine Club of Canada, 1977.

Morse, Randy. *The Mountains of Canada.* Edmonton: Hurtig Publishers, 1978.

Munday, Don. *The Unknown Mountain.* London: Hodder & Stoughton, 1948. Reprint. Seattle: The Mountaineers, 1975.

Putnam, William L. *A Climber's Guide to the Interior Ranges of British Columbia – North.* Springfield, Mass.: The American Alpine Club and The Alpine Club of Canada, 1975.

Putnam, William L. and Boles, Glen W. *Climber's Guide to the Rocky Mountains of Canada – South.* 6th ed. Springfield, Mass.: The American Alpine Club and The Alpine Club of Canada, 1973.

Putnam William L.; Jones, Chris; and Kruszyna, Robert. *Climber's Guide to the Rocky Mountains of Canada – North.* 6th ed. Springfield, Mass.: The American Alpine Club and The Alpine Club of Canada, 1974.

Sherman, Paddy. *Cloud Walkers.* Toronto: Macmillan of Canada, 1965.

Smythe, Frank S. *Climbs in the Canadian Rockies.* New York: Norton & Co., 1951.

Taylor, William C. *The Snows of Yesteryear: J. Norman Collie, Mountaineer.* Toronto: Holt, Rinehart and Winston of Canada, 1973.

Journals
The Alpine Journal
The American Alpine Journal
Appalachia
The Canadian Alpine Journal

Index

The *n* following a page number refers to a footnote; *passim* refers to scattered references in a sequence of pages.

Victoria, Mount, 20, 38, 40, 83, 116, 117,
149; avalanche in Death Trap of,
103-104; first ascent of, 24-25; first
ascent of northeast face of, 25n.6,
46-47; first traverse of, 25n.7, 40n, 111;
first winter ascent of northeast face
of, 221; naming of, 24n
Vincent, John, 54-57, 96
Vincent, Mrs. George, 54-56

Waddington, Mount, 145-164 passim,
175n, 238; first ascent of, 160n, 168;
second ascent of, 167-171; first winter
ascent of, 239
Waputik Icefield, 25, 28, 121, 124
Washington, Al, 212n
Waterman, Frank, 58
Wates, Cyril, 47
Wedgwood, Felix 111
Weyers, William, 63-64
Wheeler, Arthur, 34, 41n, 50, 61, 89, 109,
121; disputes elevation of
Waddington, 153n.3; hires Kain,
82-83; saved by Ed Feuz, 109n.4; leads
Yellowhead Expedition of 1911, 85;
organizes search for Stone, 60
Wheeler, Oliver, 34-35, 51, 109n.4
Whitehorn Mountain, 85-87
White Pyramid, 124
Whymper, Edward, 29
Whyte, Mount, 38
Wiebrecht, Bert, 125
Wiessner, Fritz, 160n, 168
Wilson, Tom, 18-20, 23
Wiwaxy Lodge, 39-40
Woodsworth, Glen, 227-228, 232-236
passim

Yamnuska, 190-191, 192-193, 210, 215n,
215-216, 222, 222n
Yellowhead Pass Expedition of 1911, 85
Young, James, 117

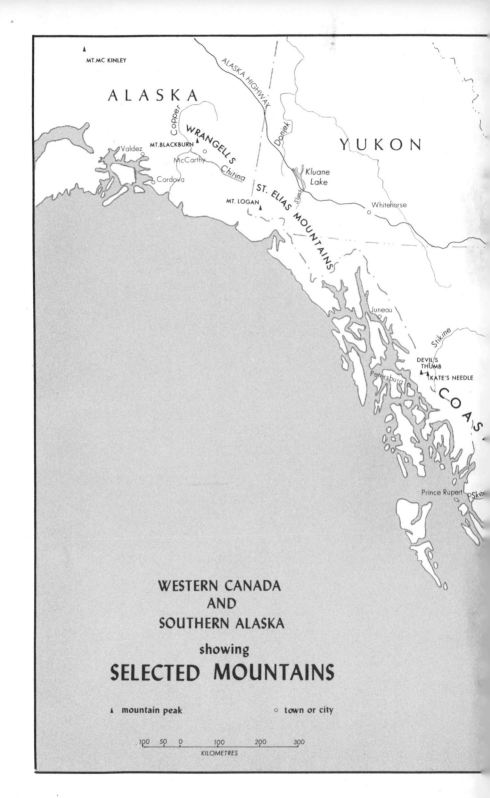

MT.MC KINLEY

ALASKA

Copper

WRANGELLS

MT.BLACKBURN

Valdez

McCarthy

Cordova

Chitina

ST. ELIAS

MT. LOGAN

MOUNTAINS

Donjek

YUKON

ALASKA HIGHWAY

Kluane
Lake

Slims

Whitehorse

Juneau

Stikine

DEVIL'S
THUMB

KATE'S NEEDLE

Petersburg

COAST

Prince Rupert

Ske

WESTERN CANADA
AND
SOUTHERN ALASKA

showing

SELECTED MOUNTAINS

▲ mountain peak   ○ town or city

100   50   0   100   200   300

KILOMETRES